Free $ For College

FOR

DUMMIES®

Free $ For College

FOR

DUMMIES®

by David Rosen and Caryn Mladen

WILEY

Wiley Publishing, Inc.

Free $ For College For Dummies®

Published by
Wiley Publishing, Inc.
909 Third Avenue
New York, NY 10022
www.wiley.com

For general information on our other products and services or to obtain technical support, please contact our Customer Care Department within the U.S. at 877-762-2974, outside the U.S. at 317-572-3993, or fax 317-572-4002.

Wiley also publishes its books in a variety of electronic formats. Some content that appears in print may not be available in electronic books.

Library of Congress Control Number: 2003101998

ISBN: 978-0-7645-5467-4

IO/RQ/QW/QT/IN

Manufactured in the United States of America

13 12 11 10

About the Authors

David Rosen and **Caryn Mladen** are business consultants, writers, and educators whose work focuses on the high-tech and financial industries. Individually, they have decades of teaching experience at the university, college, and corporate levels where they combine their years of formal training and technical experience with humor and enthusiasm.

David and Caryn served as editors-in-chief of America Online's member magazine, *Multimedia Online,* and have written or co-written hundreds of newspaper and magazine articles dealing with technology, education, law, intellectual property, and travel. Their previous books have been used as course textbooks at universities and colleges, as well as expert resource material cited in legal actions within Silicon Valley. This is their seventh book together as a writing team — and their second *For Dummies* book.

David scored his first professional writing gig back in 1977, where he was a stringer for a local community newspaper. After managing various technical and education departments within several large corporations, he turned his skills to consulting and corporate writing. Today, David is an internationally known expert in high-technology marketing and frequently consults for corporations and government agencies. He also serves as an editor for ReporterWorld, an organization that works to educate and protect reporters, correspondents, journalists and others around the world from the vocational dangers they face when keeping the world safe and informed.

In December 2001, Caryn co-founded a non-profit initiative called Privaterra, devoted to providing privacy and security technology training and support to human rights workers worldwide. As a director of this international non-governmental organization, she educates the public about privacy and security issues by speaking to the media and at conferences, universities, and special events. Caryn has appeared on television and radio news programs, and her articles and interviews have been translated into French, Spanish, Italian, Hungarian, Russian, Japanese, and other languages. Before devoting her life to consulting, education, and writing, Caryn was a lawyer specializing in technology and intellectual property.

Dedication

William Shakespeare gave good advice to every student when he wrote, "Put money in thy purse," but it was my parents, Mary and Ivor, who gave me a love of knowledge; Ron Baecker who imparted in me a love of teaching; Howard Roark, who conferred to me a love of work; and Marnie, who bestowed in me a love of life. — David

To the great teachers in my life, including Eunice Lawrence in grade school, Larry Rice and Jim Shearer in high school, Jean Smith in university, and Maureen Moloney and Andrew Petter in law school. They taught life lessons along with the required texts. And to Mark, Steve, my parents, and my pals, who teach me what's important every day of my life. — Caryn

Authors' Acknowledgments

It would have been impossible to write this book without the advice, information and insight we received from literally hundreds of educators, administrators and other professionals. We do, however, wish to single out dozens of people who went above and beyond the call of duty to help the millions of students headed off (or back) to college this year:

First and foremost, we'd like to thank the helpful editors and staff at Wiley Publishing, including Joyce Pepple, Norm Crampton, Pam Mourouzis, Tim Gallan, and Violet Gregory. Others include Dr. James Arnold, Director of Community College Articulation, Oregon University System; Brian Battle, Director of Compliance, Florida State University; Steve Bauer, Executive Director of the Federal Employee Education and Assistance Fund; Pat Bogart, Senior Director of Financial Aid, Duke University; Gavin Bradley, Assistant Director of Admissions and Financial Aid, Columbia University; Kay Brothers, Coordinator of Scholarship Services, Washington State University; Roseanne Chandler, School of Music & Theatre Arts, Washington State University; Angela Deaver Campell, Director of Scholarship Resource Center, UCLA; Sally Donahue, Director of Financial Aid, Harvard University; Harden R. Eyring, Executive Assistant to the Executive Director, Utah Higher Education Assistance Authority; Heather Gonzalez, Federal Student Aid Information Center; Steve Hill, Director of Scholarships, Brigham Young University; Gail Ishino, Assistant Director of Financial Aid Office, UCLA; Monica Lenderman, Public Relations, NCAA; Dennis Luke, Internal Revenue Service; Major Mandrick, Army ROTC, SUNY Brockport; Chris Pella, Men's Athletic Department, Brigham Young University; Patricia Restan, Department Head, City of London School for Girls; Steve Robertello, Director of Compliance,

Washington State University; Iris Rosen; Instructor, NAIT; Joe Russo, Director of Financial Aid, Notre Dame University; Michael Sondheimer, Associate Athletic Director, UCLA; Vickie Unferth, Assistant Director of Scholarships, Michigan State University; Mary Ann Welch, Director of Program Administration, Rhode Island Higher Education Assistance Authority.

In addition, the following organizations were also particularly helpful: Daughters of the American Revolution; Gates Millennium Scholars; Hispanic Scholarship Fund; Miss America Scholarship Department; NAACP Education Department; and Rotary International.

And, last but certainly not least, we wish to thank *you*, the reader. Whether you're a student heading off to college or the parent, grandparent, guardian, spouse, partner, friend, son, or daughter of someone who is, we thank you.

David and Caryn

Publisher's Acknowledgments

We're proud of this book; please send us your comments through our Dummies online registration form located at www.dummies.com/register/.

Some of the people who helped bring this book to market include the following:

Acquisitions, Editorial, and Media Development

Senior Project Editor: Tim Gallan

Acquisitions Editor: Pam Mourouzis, Norm Crampton

Copy Editor: Christina Guthrie

Acquisitions Coordinator: Holly Grimes

Technical Editor: Ellen Frishberg

Editorial Manager: Christine Meloy Beck

Editorial Assistants: Melissa Bennett, Elizabeth Rea

Cover Photos: © Garry Gay/Stock Connection/ PictureQuest

Cartoons: Rich Tennant, www.the5thwave.com

Composition Services

Project Coordinator: Kristie Rees

Layout and Graphics: Jennifer Click, Kelly Emkow, Michael Kruzil, Jackie Nicholas, Mary Gillot Virgin

Proofreaders: John Greenough, Charles Spencer, Brian Walls, Aptara

Indexer: Aptara

Special Help: E. Neil Johnson

Publishing and Editorial for Consumer Dummies

Diane Graves Steele, Vice President and Publisher, Consumer Dummies

Joyce Pepple, Acquisitions Director, Consumer Dummies

Kristin A. Cocks, Product Development Director, Consumer Dummies

Michael Spring, Vice President and Publisher, Travel

Brice Gosnell, Publishing Director, Travel

Suzanne Jannetta, Editorial Director, Travel

Publishing for Technology Dummies

Andy Cummings, Vice President and Publisher, Dummies Technology/General User

Composition Services

Gerry Fahey, Vice President of Production Services

Debbie Stailey, Director of Composition Services

Contents at a Glance

Table of Contents

Part IV: Scoping Out Free Money from Prospective Colleges

Part VI: The Part of Tens 297

Chapter 21: The Ten Best Ways to Get Free Money for College . . .299

Chapter 22: Ten Places You May Not Think to Look
for Free Money 307

Introduction

*W*hy in the world would anyone give you *free* money? Sure, if you're at the top of your class or a star athlete, you probably expect to receive some generous offers from colleges. But what if you aren't?

Relax. You can get some wonderfully lucrative offers even if you're not getting straight *A*s or catching the touchdown passes. People, companies, and organizations give away money to all kinds of different students, and chances are, a bunch of awards out there have your name written all over them.

All you have to do is get organized, research, and apply. That's it! And in this book, we show you how.

About This Book

You don't need to read this book from start to finish, taking copious notes as if you were doing your homework. You can if you want, but we've designed the book so that you can choose to go directly to whichever section interests you most.

For example, if you're not working and your parents don't work for the government, a college, or a relatively big company, you really can't ask your boss or your parents' boss to send you to school, so you may choose to just skim (or skip) Chapter 17 where we discuss this option. If you need to apply for a Federal Pell Grant in the next few hours, on the other hand, you should probably head directly to Chapter 5.

However, if you've picked up this book with plenty of time before you need to apply for scholarships, grants, and the rest of your free money options, your best bet is to read all the chapters, taking notes and using a highlighter and sticky notes to help you remember points of interest to you. We make it easier on you by emphasizing the most important items, but because literally thousands of scholarships and grants are available, you'll be better off focusing on the types that are most significant to *you*.

Conventions Used in This Book

We've used a few conventions in this book, and to make your life easier, let us explain to you what they are:

- ✔ Every time we introduce a new term or concept, we *italicize* it.
- ✔ This book is full of abbreviations and acronyms, which can get confusing. However, we try to help you out by spelling out the abbreviation upon its first mention in every chapter, and then putting the abbreviation in parentheses.
- ✔ Web sites and email addresses appear in `monofont` to help them stand out.

Foolish Assumptions

No, we're not calling you foolish. The thing is, far too many people have this ridiculous idea that they can't get scholarships and grants. Because you've picked up this book, we'd like to think that you're one of the enlightened few who understands our basic point:

EVERYONE IS ELIGIBLE FOR FREE MONEY FOR COLLEGE!

And anyone who wants to go to college can benefit from reading this book, whether you're in elementary school, high school, already in college, or a mature student just considering attending college. So can parents, grandparents, and anyone else who may have to contribute toward a college education, either financially or emotionally or both. This book is also great for you if you're one of the many people who never considered college because you always thought it was too expensive. We're here to tell you that you *can* afford it, and we show you how.

Okay, now that we've dealt with that matter, we can move on.

How This Book Is Organized

This book has six parts, with three to five chapters in each, divided into a bunch of subsections. We've tried to focus on specific topics for each chapter and each subsection, but subjects do overlap at times. When that happens, we tell you where to find more information in another part of this book.

Pretty much everyone can get a lot out of Part I and the first chapters each of Parts II, III, IV, and V. Then you can pick and choose whatever topics you like. Be warned, however, that skipping entire chapters is generally not a good idea. You may think that you have no chance to get an athletic scholarship, but Chapter 14 shows that athletic scholarships are available for non-traditional sports, such as archery, in addition to football and basketball. You may think that you could never join the military to go to college, but you may find yourself interested in the Reserves, especially after September 11. If you don't breeze through Chapter 18, you'll never know what opportunities there are to defend your country *and* get financial help for college.

Part I: The Process, the Players, and the Possibilities

This part describes the basics of scholarships, grants, and awards of all sorts, along with loans that offer money that's *free for now*. These chapters demonstrate why *every student* can apply for free money if they're applying to or attending college. This part also outlines the differences between need-based funds and merit-based funds, and it shows how they sometimes work together. Part I also explains the concept of free money — distinguishing between money that's *totally free* and money that's *free for now*. Finally, Part I helps you avoid the scams that are, unfortunately, part of the scholarship horizon.

Part II: Getting Your Due from Uncle Sam

The federal government helps more students pay for college than any other source. This part explores all the different programs available, and it shows you how to make the most of them. If you ignore the key financial aid application in this part, you'll be cutting yourself off from the largest source of free and low-cost money available to all students — not to mention most state, local, and college aid as well.

Part III: Looking Closer to Home: Free Money from Your State and Hometown

Whether in the form of state-sponsored savings plans, resident tax incentives, or outright cash giveaways, states want their native sons and daughters to go to college. This part explains the programs that states offer to help get students to school and keep them learning.

Part IV: Scoping Out Free Money from Prospective Colleges

You may be grateful just to get accepted to the college of your choice, but most students pay less than the sticker price. Don't wait for the money offer — ask for a tuition discount, or try to negotiate a better deal and while you're at it, apply for as much free scholarship money as you can get.

Part V: I Didn't Think of That! Lots More Sources of Free Money

A little research, some well-written application letters, and a few essays can save you a bundle on your college costs. You may be surprised by how many organizations and companies that you already know are offering free money — and how few students actually apply to get this money. Part V shows you where to look for all this money, and how to apply. This part also features a Resource Guide showcasing detailed contact information with special sections on major funding resources.

Part VI: The Part of Tens

What would a *For Dummies* book be without a Part of Tens? Acting as an overview and set of pointers, these lists help you focus on the most important things to do to get free money for college — and the most important things *not* to do.

Icons Used in This Book

To help you recognize when we're saying something particularly important, we use a bunch of icons to draw your attention to key ideas and pointers. That's not to say that the rest of the book can be ignored — just pay special attention when you see any of the following:

Most people think of a tip as a payment for service, but we're not handing out free money every time we use this icon. We are, however, offering up something really valuable: good advice to use in your search for free money. Grab your highlighter, make a note in the margin, or just dog-ear the page.

Sure, you should remember everything in this book. After all, we slaved over every word to make sure that you can get as much free money as possible. However, text passages with this icon beside them represent important themes or trends that tend to happen over and over in the free money search. Whenever you see this icon, take a moment to think about it and commit the point to memory. Most importantly, try to use it when you're applying for aid, filling out forms, or thinking about how to save money.

Ignore this icon at your peril. It points out something that can hurt your chances of getting free money, and that may end up costing you money, time, and hassle. Heed these warnings at all costs.

As you probably have guessed, this icon highlights information relating to all things financial. Yes, the entire book is about free money, but points illustrated with this icon relate especially to accounting, money amounts, scholarships, grants, and low-cost loans.

This icon points to reference materials, books, Web sites, and other stuff you can use as you apply for free money.

Where to Go from Here

Where to go? Why anywhere you want, of course. Just remember that this book is a guide, and reading it won't automatically win you any scholarships or grants. Instead, you need to take our advice and do the work, or at least think about what we're saying and decide if it applies to your specific financial plan for college.

This book is like a book on exercise. Knowing *how* to workout won't make you fit. You have to hit the gym and sweat a bit. Reading this book is a great first step toward getting free money for college, but after you know where and how to apply, you've got to actually do it. So get out your markers and pens, and get to work finding free money for college!

Part I

The Process, the Players, and the Possibilities

The 5th Wave   By Rich Tennant

"That reminds me – I have to figure out how to save for retirement and send these two to college."

In this part . . .

*I*f you don't have a clue where to start looking for free
money for college, start here. This part is where we
explain the basics, from who gives out free money (and
why) to who gets it. In between, we explain various terminology, such as *need-based* and *merit-based*, the kind of
money that you have to pay back versus the kind that is
totally free, how to apply for free money, and when you
need to start applying. We help you choose the options that
are best for you, and avoid the scams and time-wasters.

Chapter 1

Finding Free Money: How Can I Make It Happen?

In This Chapter

▶ Discovering the free money options

▶ Figuring out the terminology

▶ Getting yourself organized

▶ Starting on time

*O*kay, first of all, let us put to rest the myth that *billions* upon *billions* of dollars in scholarship money aren't awarded every year because no one bothers to apply for them. People *do* apply, and the money gets awarded. Sure, some awards might not get disbursed, but usually, the people in charge of the particular awards make sure that their money goes to *somebody*.

Does that mean that you might as well give up because nothing will be left for you? No way! This book helps take you through the steps to make sure you get the free money that is available to you. There's no trick to it, but the research, activities, application process, and follow-up does take some concerted effort. The good news is that anyone who is willing to put in the effort can reap the rewards.

Look at it this way: Just because other people got into college last year doesn't mean that you won't get in this year, or whenever you choose to apply. The same goes for scholarships, grants, and low-cost loans. Just because somebody else is awarded money doesn't mean that *you* can't get some money, too. The money is being offered to people just like you, but if you don't apply for it, you won't get it.

In this chapter, we explain the terminology used in the free money game, introduce the major players, and get you started assembling the tools you need to enter the competitions. Are you ready? Feeling psyched? Okay, let's hit the free money trail!

Getting Paid to Go to School

Winning free college money is rather like earning money for writing. You have to work at it, and you only get paid if you do it right. But, unlike being a professional writer, pretty much anyone can win free money for college as long as that person educates himself about the process, completes the applications properly, and follows up on a timely basis.

Perhaps you're asking yourself, "Why would *I* get free money?" That's not the question to ask. The real question to ask is, "Why *wouldn't* I get free money?" It's available, so why not try to get some of it?

What's Rule #1 in the free money process? Apply! If you don't ask, you won't get. Applying for scholarships and grants doesn't cost you anything except the price of postage and a few hours of work. So, as long as you meet the qualifications, you have no good reason not to apply for as many scholarships and grants as you can possibly manage.

Understanding the concept of free money

To get free money, you need to understand how the awards system works, who gives away the money, and what these people want in return. Then you need to get organized, focus on and prioritize the best awards for you, do a great job on as many applications as you can handle, and send them out on time. It sounds like a lot of work, but after you get the hang of it, it's really pretty easy.

First, you have to know what you're applying for exactly. Free money is generally divided into the following categories:

- ✔ **Scholarships:** If you're awarded a scholarship, a person or organization gives you money for something you've done or can do, such as getting top grades, being a basketball star, or showing exceptional leadership in the community.

- ✔ **Grants:** You can get this money for just being who you are — the African-American daughter of a firefighter from Indiana who has the marks to get into college but only half the money to pay for it, for example.

- ✔ **Low-interest or interest-free loans:** You have to pay back the loan, but you get to use the money while you're going to school, so the money is *free for now*.

- ✔ **Other stuff:** Sometimes, you don't win money; rather, you get free books, housing, or other necessities of college life. We talk more about this other stuff in Chapter 2.

The words "scholarships" and "grants" are often used interchangeably, but they do have a slightly different meaning. Scholarships are usually based on merit, and grants are usually based on need or other circumstances. In this book, we often use the generic term "award," which can mean either a scholarship or a grant. Some awards are called "prizes" and other, mostly international, awards may be called "bursaries." If an organization wants to give you money, it can pretty much call it whatever it wants.

Two other important financial aid terms are *merit-based* and *need-based.* Read on to find out what they mean.

Merit-based awards

Awards that are merit-based are given to whichever applicant is the best at the subject of the scholarship. One award may be for the highest overall grade point average (GPA) or highest marks in a particular class, such as chemistry. Another award may be based on one's ability to play softball, the flute, or do any number of things.

For a merit-based scholarship, your wealth (or your family's wealth) and income are completely irrelevant. You don't have to explain whether or not you can afford to go to college without the scholarship because you get the award for what you've done. Bill Gates' daughter can get a merit-based scholarship if she gets the grades, and so can you.

The moral of this story? Don't think that you shouldn't apply for scholarships because your family makes too much money.

Need-based awards

Awards that are need-based (primarily *grants*) are offered solely on the basis of financial need. You don't have to be the best student in the class, although you still have to get accepted at a college to qualify. Some need-based grants can require a qualifying grade level of, say 70 percent, but after you qualify, your grade is no longer taken into account. Then, the only thing that matters is your financial need.

Don't assume that you have to be living below the poverty line to qualify for a need-based grant. Many factors are taken into account, from your family income, to the number of dependents your parents are supporting, to the cost of living in the city in which your college is located. We discuss these factors in Chapters 3 and 12, but the important thing to remember is that need-based money is granted because you *need* it, not because you have the highest marks.

The moral of *this* story? Don't think that you shouldn't apply for grants because you didn't make stellar grades.

Finding out who's giving it away

Rule #2 is, "Put yourself in the shoes of the people giving out the money." After you know why they're handing out free money for college, you can shape your application so that the awarders want to give the money to *you*.

So, why do people give out scholarships and grants? Well, the government does it as part of a larger education policy. Influencing the decisions of these people is tough because they base their decisions on numbers instead of individual people. That's okay. We show you how to apply for government awards in Chapters 5 through 10, but the process is pretty cut and dried. After you send in the correct (and complete) information, you're pretty much done.

Colleges, foundations, and institutions are another story altogether. These organizations give out a lot of need-based money, but they generally have other criteria to make sure that the individuals receiving their money are also meritorious.

Colleges

Colleges give money to superior students to advance the reputation of their institutions. Colleges are more attractive to top professors and students if they have a long list of distinguished alumni, and popular wisdom dictates that distinguished alumni are most likely going to come from the top students.

Distinguished alumni are also likely to have more money to donate to the college, and the college itself is more likely to generate larger corporate donations if successful students maintain the school's high reputation. In general, college-based scholarships and other awards are intended to generate money for the college in the long term.

The best strategy, therefore, is to impress upon the college scholarship committee members that you have a brilliant future, or that you can otherwise enhance the reputation of the school in the years to come.

Foundations, institutions, and individuals

These groups also have particular motives for giving away free money. Their intentions are partially *humanitarian,* and you can't ignore that fact when you craft your application. Thus, it's in your own best interest to explicitly mention how generous these groups are to give away money for college students.

The other motive is *promotional.* These groups want to promote a particular field of study (scholarships for the top marks in economics, for example), a particular attitude (contests for the best essay about patriotism), or particular behaviors (awards for individual contributions to civil liberties). To succeed in winning awards, you need to concentrate on whatever these organizations want to promote. We're not saying that you should fake your attitudes; instead, we're saying that you should concentrate on those awards (and organizations) that mesh with your personality and beliefs.

Arguments people use to deny themselves free money

I need a lot of money, so I'll only apply for the big scholarships and grants. This argument has a lot of problems. First of all, more people apply for the bigger (and, therefore, more popular) scholarships and grants, so you'll meet big competition for your (few) applications. Second, all those smaller awards can really add up to big money, and isn't it better to have some money than none anyway? Third, winning a smaller award can have an impact on how much money you're offered by other organizations. Certainly, awarders are supposed to be completely objective, but if two people with the same grades apply and one has already won, for example, a $500 scholarship for achievement from the 4-H Club, other awarders are likely to give 4-H the benefit of the doubt and be impressed by this achievement. They may be swayed just enough to grant their scholarship to the student with an award. Beyond that, your college wants *achievers* on its campus. The college administration wants to be able to brag that a high percentage of its students arrived with a scholarship, so the college is more likely to offer you a better package just because you got that $500 award.

My family is too rich for me to qualify for an award. This problem is one that most students would love to have; however, it doesn't disqualify you from getting free money. First, you're just as eligible for merit-based awards as anyone else. Second, some need-based awards only consider annual income (as opposed to overall wealth) when determining need (we tell you more about this in Chapter 3). Don't give up on free money just because your family can afford to send you to college. Of course, if you wish to spend your family money so that someone who truly needs the assistance can get the award, what you don't get in free money you make up in Karma. But that's a topic for another book!

I'm not smart enough to win an award. If you're smart enough to get into college, you're smart enough to win an award. Remember that you don't have to get top marks for need-based awards. Besides, if you received the top marks in one course, you can apply for a scholarship recognizing achievement in that specific subject, even if your overall GPA isn't particularly impressive. Plus, many awards are offered to people who show exceptional leadership or work consistently on humanitarian causes. Don't sell yourself short!

I may have good marks this year, but my first two years of high school were terrible, and they bring down my average. That's okay, especially if you can explain what happened in those two years. Overcoming a personal or family tragedy, or simply turning yourself around can show character. Flag your poor grades and GPA in your application and explain to the awarders how you've grown (or what you've learned) since getting such low marks.

Sometimes, *hybrid awards* are offered. They're given only to individuals of a particular background (such as descendants of Confederate soldiers) or individuals associated with particular groups (children or grandchildren of members of a specific trade union). However, within this group, the competition reverts to merit. The particulars of merit may be grades, essay writing, community service, or overall achievements, but the winner is the one who shines. Whenever criteria for an award combines a particular background, need and/or merit, it is considered hybrid.

Assembling Your Materials in One Place

The best time to start working on your applications is right now, so you'd better get organized. You need to gather some background material, and you need to do some research. We don't want you to stop reading this book, but may we suggest that you use it as a workbook, too? As you do the work, file your materials neatly into your college applications folder.

Dedicate one of those big accordion folders with a bunch of pockets to this project, along with a folder on your computer, if you have access to one. Divide your folders into the following categories:

- **Personal background:** Keep your transcripts, awards, letters of recognition, letters of recommendation, and your own personal history in this folder.

- **Family background:** In this folder, keep a file on each member of your family, listing their work and education backgrounds, ethnic and religious backgrounds, affiliations, past experiences . . . the works!

- **Financial information:** Use this folder to store your tax records, bank statements, and all the other financial records you'll need to fill out your FAFSA and other forms. (More about these forms in Chapter 5.)

- **Merit-based award research:** Keep all the information you gather about your favorite merit-based awards here.

- **Need-based award research:** Do the same thing in this folder for need-based awards. Don't forget to note whether the award has a qualifying grade or GPA requirement.

- **Applications:** After you've applied for an award, keep a copy in this folder, so that you can use the information over again for other applications (as long as it's appropriate for the other award).

- **Schedules and deadlines:** This folder is crucial. Some scholarships have a specific deadline, and if you miss it, you don't get the money. Similarly, some awards are granted as applications arrive until the money runs out (similar to a rolling deadline when you're applying to college). As you can imagine, you want to be the first to apply.

Taking Action

First, you have to do your research. Delve into your background and the backgrounds of your family members and pull together a list of every possible association, union, past employer, historical affiliation (great-grandfather in the Green Berets, or who worked building the railroad), and anything else that you can discover.

Next, think about what makes *you* special, and make a list of the categories that describe you. Include what you plan to study, your top courses, and anything that you do really well. For instance, if you've been involved in Scouting for most of your life, this affiliation can be significant, even if you haven't done anything that sounds spectacular to you.

After you've done some initial research, turn your attention outward and find scholarships and grants that apply best to your particular situation. We direct you to the major awards and help you find the ones that are most applicable to you, but we can't list all awards that are available. If we did, this book would be 1000 or more pages long. Besides, that work has already been done.

 Dozens of college aid directories that list pages and pages of scholarships, grants, loans, and other awards are available to you. These directories are chock-full of raw information, such as dates and addresses, but they're scant on guidance. Most of them are divided into categories — applied sciences and ethnic backgrounds, for example. Compare your lists of personal background and achievements with the categories listed in these books. All these books are updated and republished annually, and most now come with a CD-ROM. We list a few of the most popular titles in Chapter 20.

Looking at the Documents

Some applications are a single page; others are long and convoluted. Some require an application essay or video; others do not. Some require recommendation letters from your teachers or other significant people in your life; others are satisfied with nothing more than basic information. Some require specific answers; others want you to be more creative.

As you begin your research, you'll come to recognize a few themes in the application process. For each potential award, you want to note at least the following information:

- ✔ Application deadline and whether the deadline is rolling or absolute
- ✔ Contact information

✔ Amount or type of award

✔ Whether the award is one-time or renewable

✔ Whether it's merit-based or need-based

✔ Limitations of the award (If the award is only available to those of Italian descent, for example, you may have to prove your heritage.)

✔ Requirements of the application (Check to see whether you need any of the following: application form or letter, essay, financial need analysis, recommendation letters, transcripts, SAT or ACT scores, autobiography, portfolio, photo, performance video.)

For all applications, send along a *self-addressed, stamped envelope* (SASE), so that the awards committee can return your material to you.

Applying

You can apply for awards in any order as long as you meet each of the award deadlines. This book details the different types of organizations to approach for aid. The top groups to approach are the colleges themselves; federal, state, and local government agencies; and organizations with which you have personal contact. Beyond these groups, conduct your research to figure out which ones offer the best chances of success for your particular qualities and then apply to all of them.

Here are our five magic rules for scholarship applications:

✔ **Apply for as many scholarships and grants as you can reasonably handle.** Nobody checks to find out if you've applied elsewhere, so for the price of postage you might win some cash.

✔ **When preparing the applications, put yourself in the shoes of the people giving out the money.** What would make a winning application for *them?*

✔ **Be organized.** You can reuse application essays and other materials over and over again, sometimes with only slight modifications, so keep everything where you can find it again easily.

✔ **Never lie or mislead on your application; they usually check.** Even if they don't, it's not the right thing to do.

✔ **Be on time.** You may be the most qualified applicant or demonstrate the most need, but if you apply after the deadline or after the money has run out, you're not getting the cash.

Following up

Your job isn't over after you send off your applications. You can still go a long way in influencing the decision-makers.

Making contact

Call the organization and let the folks there know you've applied for their award. Ask to confirm that your application arrived and then gush a little bit about how much this award would mean to you, and how much you appreciate being considered. Don't overdo it, but keep in mind that the fact that you called might be noted in your file and will likely reflect favorably on you.

Getting personal

Write down the name of the person who answered the phone and anyone else with whom you spoke or e-mailed. Jot down any other information you glean during your conversation. Then, anytime you have a reason to call back, you have a personal point of contact.

Getting a point of contact may sound like a minor issue, but getting personal means that someone in the office will think of you as a person instead of just another name on an application. For the subjective awards that aren't strictly based on grades, that contact might make all the difference in the world. Think about it: Would you rather give an award to an unknown student or to that person who made you smile when he remembered your name and sounded so enthused about getting an education?

Saying thank you

Whether or not you win an award, always follow up the decision by saying thank you. After all, the award committee spent time considering your application.

If you've made contact with someone in the office, ask her what made the winning application so special, and let her know that you want to try again. Saying no to applicants isn't fun, and the awarders will appreciate your kindness and dignity in thanking them for their consideration. This attitude is the sort of thing that gets you remembered the next time you apply.

Understanding Application Timelines

Governmental awards tend to have standard times for making applications, and we discuss details of the application process in Chapters 5 and 9. For other awards, the timelines are all over the calendar. Just about every month is peppered with award deadlines. So, what does that mean for you?

It means that your best bet is to prepare your applications in the summer *prior* to your final year, so that they're ready to send as soon as you go back to school in September. Now, some award programs don't want to hear from you until you've been accepted at a college, but that doesn't mean that you can't have your application, essay, transcripts, recommendation letters, and everything else ready to send as soon as you hear.

To help you apply for scholarships as early as possible, try applying for early admission at the schools of your choice. As soon as you're accepted at any college, the awarders can typically accept your application. That doesn't mean that you have to stick with that particular college if a better option comes along. Unless the award is college-specific, the awarders don't care which college you attend; they usually just want to make sure that their scholarship money is going to be used for scholarship.

We've listed the major application dates and deadlines at the end of this chapter. Customize this schedule by adding your own deadlines, and keep it current.

When you're accepted into college, the school sends you an *award letter* explaining your *financial package*. This letter explains how much you will receive from government sources and the college. After you get this offer, you can start to negotiate. But remember that the more award money you bring to the table, the more attractive you look, and the more likely the college personnel will try to ensure that you stay with them.

If you haven't prepared well in advance, make sure that you send out each scholarship application at least three weeks prior to the deadline, and call to confirm receipt. Even better, if you're concerned about missing the deadline, send your application package by overnight courier or express mail.

Application Timeline for High School Students

The following timeline gives a general overview of key college application deadlines and is by no means complete. Use it as a framework and add the specific deadlines for your particular state, college, and private awards.

Freshman Year: 9th Grade

✔ Create your College Applications folder — collect and categorize your data. Research your ethnicity and associations of your family and friends. Start a diary of important life events.

Using your awards to help get admission

Bringing along award money can also help you prior to being accepted by a college. If you've won a fantastic essay that earned a $15,000 scholarship prize, let the colleges of your choice know about it when you apply for admission. Knowing that it doesn't have to spend buckets of money so that you can attend might tip the scales in your favor when the awards committee decides what kind of a package to offer you.

This doesn't necessarily mean that a college will offer you less money if you come to it with scholarship money in tow. In some cases, it'll offer you *more*.

For example, suppose that you apply to a college with no scholarship, and your cost of attendance will be $20,000. The college might not bother to offer you a thing, recognizing that it can't afford to offer you enough to attend unless you're a top student (and let's assume that you aren't). On the other hand, if you arrive with $10,000 in awards, the college will probably take you more seriously. After all, you impressed other people enough to win the awards. The college might offer you a $10,000 award or perhaps a tuition discount combined with low-cost student loans.

✔ Take the most challenging courses you can (including all core courses) and study, study, study! Meet with your high school guidance counselor to plan your future. Keep this up throughout high school.

✔ If you want to be considered for athletic scholarships, start training now and let your coaches know about your goals. Join the high school team and the local league.

✔ Get involved in school and community service. Take a leadership role wherever possible. If your parents haven't yet started your "529 plans," now is the time to do so. (See Chapter 10 for more information on these.)

Sophomore Year: 10th Grade

✔ Athletic recruiting begins.

✔ Request college brochures and start making your comparisons. Start your college wish list.

✔ Start your serious scholarship research. Incorporate your research into your academic program.

✔ Spring: write the PSAT and the PLAN. Use books or take third-party study courses to raise your eventual SATs and ACT scores. Check out the Resource Guide in Chapter 20 for more information.

Junior Year: 11th Grade

First term

- Apply for Advanced Placement courses.

- Have your parents restructure their finances, if possible, to minimize your EFC.

- Visit schools and attend college fairs — ask about school-specific scholarships and other forms of aid.

- Conduct free scholarship searches to find the best organizations for you to apply.

- Collect scholarship applications — download them when possible or request packages.

- Start talking to prospective references about writing recommendation letters for you.

Second term

- Register for and write SATs and ACTs. If you do badly, you can rewrite them later.

- You need a Social Security Number for college. Apply online at www.ssa.gov if you need one.

- Consider earning your driver's license. It's useful to prove your in-state status for state colleges.

- Request college application packages and financial aid forms.

Summer

- Track down scholarship leads and create your checklist with application dates and materials.

- Create your scholarship application materials including your applications; bio and resume; various essays; cover letters; sample recommendation letters; documentation proving your ethnic heritage, disability or other significant factor; and compile your (and your family's) financial information. Where appropriate, prepare your portfolio, athletic video, or other entrance materials.

- Attend camps and clinics for athletes if working toward an athletic scholarship.

- Confirm your residency if you want to apply for a state college — most state colleges have legal requirements that demand at least one full year of residency to qualify as an *in-state* student.

Senior Year: 12th Grade

First term

- ✔ Take Advanced Placement courses. If necessary, rewrite SATs and ACT.

- ✔ Obtain recommendation letters for your scholarship applications. Apply for private scholarships early (some have deadlines as early as September *prior* to your freshman college year!)

- ✔ October-November: apply to colleges, requesting financial aid. Apply for departmental scholarships. Complete the PROFILE. Receive early decisions and weigh your options. Discuss financial aid options with these schools.

- ✔ College coaches will contact you if you are being offered an athletic scholarship.

- ✔ ROTC applications must be received by November 15; expect a reply by January 1.

- ✔ December: Start preparing your income taxes for FAFSA. Register for Selective Service if male 18 to 25.

Second term

- ✔ Send in your FAFSA as early as you can — you may need to estimate tax information if you have not yet received key forms such as W-2s. Some state aid deadlines can be as early as *February!*

- ✔ February: Immediately correct any errors on your Student Aid Report (SAR) and make any modifications that are necessary. Sign, date, photocopy and return the SAR. Send additional materials (such as tax forms) as necessary to college financial aid offices.

- ✔ February 15: Make sure all private scholarships are sent by this date. Many private scholarships have March 1 due dates. Call or e-mail to confirm applications arrived.

- ✔ Write Advanced Placement Exams and CLEP exams.

- ✔ Receive college acceptance letters. Wait to reply until your financial aid packages arrive. Compare the four-year costs and aid for all schools to which you've been accepted. Compile materials and letters for financial aid appeals, or requests for matching packages. Accept awards promptly and at least a week before the deadlines. Finalize your college choice and advise other colleges that you won't be accepting their offers.

- ✔ Mail thank-you notes to all individuals that helped in your scholarship search and to all organizations that awarded you prizes. Send thank-you e-mails to all organizations that did not give you awards.

Chapter 2

The Nitty-Gritty of Receiving Free Money

*W*inning scholarships and grants is fantastic, but part of your planning involves knowing exactly what you can do with your winnings. "Wait a second!" most students exclaim. "Don't I just get the check as soon as I win? Can't I use the money as I please?"

Sorry to disappoint you, but the answer to both questions is usually no. People and organizations that give away free money generally place stipulations on the money's use. They want to make sure that you really use it as a scholarship (in other words, for school, not for a new car or a trip to Europe). As well, you may get paid in stages, and usually, *you* never get paid at all. The money goes straight to your college.

In this chapter, we set you straight on the who, what, when, and how of receiving free money for college. This information can be vital if you expect to receive a chunk of cash to pay off a previous debt and then discover you don't get the money directly — and you don't even get it all at once. Read on to find out where your money goes.

Waddaya Mean I Don't Get the Money?

In this book, we often talk about *you* getting free money. However, the truth of the matter is that the money you win often doesn't go directly *to* you, it goes somewhere *for* you. When a college offers you a tuition discount or a scholarship, you never see that money. You just don't have to pay *as much* tuition. Similarly, when you get a book allowance, you generally are given a *credit* at the college bookstore. You can't use the money to party or buy pizza for your friends. Sorry about that.

However, don't dismiss the notion of getting a check altogether. Independent academic or service organizations sometimes may choose to hand you an actual check, especially when the amount is relatively small or you've won a national contest and they want a photograph of you with one of those over-sized novelty checks. Federal and state government programs may also send you or your parents a check, if that's the arrangement that's worked out with the particular college. So finding out in advance what method your chosen college uses is definitely in your best interest.

When is the money paid?

When the money is paid out is another thing. You may not receive the full amount of the award upfront. Government grants and loans are generally split into semesters or terms and may be paid either directly to you, to your college, or to your parents. (You can find out more about government grants in Chapters 5 and 6.) However, the full amount of tuition discounts and entrance scholarships are generally taken off the listed "sticker price" (the full "retail" price) of the college.

Independent institutions that award scholarships and grants generally pay you the entire amount upfront, as long as you're enrolled in an accredited university, college, or other educational institution. Sometimes, these awards are *renewable,* which means that you're eligible for additional money in subsequent years provided certain conditions are met. At other times, these awards are given on a one-time-only basis.

Is this scholarship portable?

Institutions and other independent groups may award scholarships that are portable or use-specific. When a scholarship is *portable,* it can be used at any recognized college or university, and it may be used in this year, the next year, or for the next several years. When it is *use-specific,* it may be valid only at a particular college, certain school years (such as freshman awards), or for particular programs or subjects.

How can the money be used?

Because you generally can't use the money to party, what's left? Well, plenty actually.

Putting money toward your cost of attendance

The categories listed below are used to determine the *cost of attendance* (COA) for a particular student for a particular college according to federal, state, and college guidelines. Your COA varies depending on college fees, location, course of study, and other factors. Likewise, a college doesn't have a set COA associated with it. COAs are determined by the following factors:

- ✔ **Tuition and other college fees:** Tuition obviously is the biggest factor, but related fees can quickly hike up the price even more. Other college fees include student union dues, lab fees, athletic fees, medical insurance, and other required expenditures that students must pay to attend the particular college.

- ✔ **Room and board:** The cost of housing and food is calculated either by considering on-campus housing and a meal plan or a reasonable allowance for off-campus housing and food. If you live on campus, the payment generally is made directly to the school's fees office or bursar. If not, you or your parents periodically receive a check to cover expenses for your room and board.

- ✔ **Book and supplies allowances:** The amounts for these allowances vary according to your intended course of study. Some programs and courses (drama or music, for example) have relatively small fees for books and supplies, and thus it doesn't cost the college very much money to subsidize you here). In programs such as engineering or biology, free books and supplies can really represent a large amount of cash, and so asking whether you can get your books and supplies paid for is definitely worthwhile.

Bear in mind that you'd otherwise have to buy your books at retail prices, while the college bookstore purchases its products at wholesale. The difference between retail and wholesale can be as much as 40 percent to 50 percent.

- ✔ **Living allowances:** When you're single with no dependents, then any living allowances you receive go toward local transportation, loan fees, and the basics of living. Not very much party money is involved. If, on the other hand, you have dependents, extra amounts are factored in to help you cope with your support obligations.

Getting a great deal on a shiny, new degree

When contemplating your college tuition, think about it in terms of buying a car. The sticker price for a college should always be viewed as its asking price, and the package that a college offers you with its acceptance letter can be viewed as its first discount offer. From there, getting the best possible deal you can is up to you. You can ask for a tuition discount based on your high marks, talents, or other factors that we discuss in Chapter 3. If your grades are particularly high or you're a sought-after student for other reasons, getting a better deal should be relatively easy.

✔ **Costs relating to a disability:** Not only do medical and other expenses factor into your COA, special financial aid programs are available for students with disabilities. Some colleges have been under scrutiny recently for not doing enough to make their schools accessible.

Other expenses you may be able to negotiate

Students who are in demand have more leverage to bargain with colleges. They may also target scholarships that offer some of the particular things that they need. If you're an exceptional student, consider including the following expenses in your negotiations:

✔ **Travel:** If you're an *exceptional* student and live in another state (or just far away), some colleges may fly you in for an interview or offer you a travel allowance as part of your aid package. As well, many independent foundations want you to attend an awards ceremony at which they present you with your award.

Even if you're winning a book prize of only $100, being flown to an awards ceremony (usually in a national hub such as Washington, D.C., New York City, or San Francisco) with all expenses paid will cut down your costs of conducting campus visits. If you're well organized, you can plan your interviews at the same time you'll be in town for the ceremony. Just imagine how much more impressive you'll appear when you can tell the admissions and financial aid officers that you happen to be coming to town to accept a national award!

✔ **Extra special stuff:** Okay, granted, big-ticket items such as cars rarely are used as incentives. Such awards are frowned upon by scholarly bodies, and most colleges can't afford to give them away anyway.

However, some scholarships, especially those that are sponsored by corporations, offer prizes other than money, including laptop computers and other electronic equipment, books, school supplies, and more. You'll need all these things at school, so don't ignore awards that aren't specifically financial. If it has a value and is even remotely related to studying, you can figure somebody is probably giving it away — to the right student, of course!

Working for Your Free Money

What? Work for free money? Isn't that just plain *work?* Well, it is, and it isn't. Working within the framework of college financial aid and/or tuition assistance gives you some important advantages over your friends who may simply be working at the local pizza joint to make ends meet.

You have at least five separate options to consider, and they are as follows:

- **Work-Study programs:** Federal Work-Study programs provide jobs for undergraduate and graduate students with financial need, enabling them to earn enough money to help pay many of their expenses at college. Every program is a bit different, but most encourage work specifically relating to your program of study or service work within your local community.

  You won't get rich with Federal Work-Study wages, but each program pays at least the current minimum federal wage. Some pay more, depending on your level of skills and the type of job. Federal Work-Study programs are considered financial aid awards, and thus depend on when you apply, how much financial help you need, and the funding level at your particular school. We discuss work-study programs in Chapter 12.

- **U.S. Armed Forces ROTC service:** After the events of September 11, many Americans wanted to sign up to help their country. One way for college students (or those headed toward college) to do just that and to get an education and have a job waiting for them when they graduate is through the *Reserve Officers' Training Corps* (ROTC). It's only one of the programs that enables students to attend college at reduced prices (or even free) in exchange for a few years of active service military duty after they leave college.

  Perhaps best of all, students are paid a small amount (called a *stipend*) every month while they're students discovering how to become officers. Military life isn't for everyone, and it takes a special kind of person to live within the strict rules and regulations, but significant financial advantages are available for those who can. We discuss service to Uncle Sam in Chapter 18.

- **Employee tuition discounts:** Is your father an administrator at the local college? Perhaps your mom is a senior lecturer of particle physics at the state university? Well, pack your bags for college, because you may qualify for a free ride based on your parents employment status at the school. In this case, one or both of your parents may do the work, but *you* have the employment benefit. Now, that's some fancy dancing!

Working at a college can have many benefits, not the least of which is free or low-cost tuition. Many colleges across America grant dependent children of employees (staff members) or faculty (teachers, instructors and professors) *free* or *discounted* educations. That, however, doesn't mean that the school pays for everything. In fact, tuition discounts are the main thing to look for here. Not having to pay for your courses can suddenly make your financial life much easier. And, when you live at home during your college years, you can sponge off your parents!

If you think you may qualify for a staff or faculty discount, speak with your parents immediately. They may have to check with their bosses, union representative, or school official to determine your eligibility for the program.

✔ **Tuition assistance from your workplace:** If you're currently employed and thinking about heading back to college to upgrade your educational qualifications, many companies have employee assistance programs that pay or subsidize college costs. An added benefit is that some of these employee education programs also extend benefits to dependent students. We talk more about employee programs in Chapter 17.

✔ **Retraining options and opportunities:** Many states and local governments are working hard to send under-qualified citizens back to college to update their skills. Often these programs are designed to get people back into the workforce as soon as possible, but others can extend for quite some time, teaching specific vocational skills. If this kind of program interests you, contact your state's employment agency for details.

Did You Mention a Free Lunch?

Nothing in this world is *completely* free, and free money for college is no exception. You always must give something to get your free money — or at least have something to offer.

For government programs, you must give your time and information. You must sit down and fill out the forms. Depending on how much money you're able to get in grants and scholarships, you may also have to sign a loan agreement with the government or third-party lenders, which you'll be expected to pay back after you graduate. (The good news about government-administered loans is that the interest on them is either low or nil while you're in school. We discuss loans in detail in Chapter 6.)

For colleges, you certainly must fill out forms, but you also have to show you have something special to offer. Before you even think about applying, you must spend the time needed to become a student that colleges want. (We discuss what colleges want to see in their students in Chapter 3.)

For independent institutions and organizations, you must give your information, spend some time completing forms, and often offer up your blood, sweat, and tears. You may need to write a brilliant essay or a biography that convinces the awards committee that you deserve to win the prize. Or you may need to have volunteer work under your belt, which requires hours and hours of your time doing good works in the community. (We discuss what these groups want to see in Chapters 3 and 16.)

Chapter 3

Recognizing the Realities: What Can You Truly Expect?

In This Chapter

▶ Being "attractive" to your target audience

▶ Targeting colleges, independent institutions, and government programs differently

▶ Setting your free money expectations appropriately

*Y*ou can walk around any college campus and never have a clue about who received free money and who didn't. Sure, maybe some of the sports stars will be particularly visible, but the rest?

You may be surprised to discover that some of the award recipients had only average marks, came from a normal middle-class background, and can't run a four-minute mile. They got free money, though, by focusing on their goals and doing what it takes. And you can, too!

Who Gets Free Money?

Free money gets awarded to the students who are most attractive to people awarding the money. When we say "attractive," we aren't talking about a beauty contest, so exposing yourself in a bikini is not a good idea for a video essay (despite its effect in the movie *Legally Blonde*). The most attractive students are the ones who are most likely to reflect positively on the college or the giving institution by doing well in school and becoming successful, famous, and wealthy — and, of course, giving back to the community.

Being attractive to colleges

Colleges want students who'll become distinguished alumni and give back to the college, either in reputation or with money. Attractive students are also those who'll have a positive impact during their educational years.

So who are these people? Colleges can't positively know for sure, so they make educated guesses, favoring applicants with qualities or skills that have succeeded in the past. Having any (or many) of these qualities gives you leverage in negotiating with your college for free money. Overall, whatever helps you get accepted at a college also helps you negotiate a better financial package. Take a look at some categories of students that colleges want:

- ✔ **The brilliant:** Usually, the students with the top *grade point averages* (GPAs) and class rankings receive some of the best tuition discounts and other incentives. Colleges are, after all, institutions of higher learning, and grades count for a lot.

- ✔ **The famous:** Having written a book, been featured in a major article covering your Junior Achievement project, and even appearing on the local news as a student spokesperson for an environmental group will impress the college financial aid committee. They now have reason to believe that you'll bring renown to the school. This kind of recognition can be a big help in winning scholarships from independent foundations, as well — for leadership activities, activism, or business acumen.

- ✔ **The athletic:** For colleges with a serious focus on athletic competition, football and basketball are huge moneymaking ventures. Coaches may be paid better than tenured professors, and their scouting systems rival those of the professional leagues. Not only do the colleges benefit from ticket sales and television rights, they also enjoy endorsement contracts, finder's fees, and immense increases in alumni donations if the teams do well. Naturally, these colleges want the best of the best for their teams.

In the past decade, some of the attention on sports has diversified. You can find sports scholarships offered for both men's and women's swimming, track, tennis, hockey, and a long list of other sports. You may not get the royal treatment for being a star archery champion, but you can certainly negotiate a better deal than can someone without your skills. If you specialize in a lesser-known sport, you should try to search out the schools with the best programs for your sport. We discuss athletic scholarships for all kinds of sports in Chapter 14.

- ✔ **The talented:** Fine arts scholarships are also widely available. Many colleges pride themselves on having a top-notch symphony orchestra, jazz ensemble, or literary population. If you're likely to make a name for yourself as an opera star, painter, musician, television producer, poet, or any other sort of fine artist, colleges want you. They know that the name of the college will forever be associated with your accomplishments, and they'll be able to count you as one of their distinguished alumni.

✔ **The diverse:** Look through college brochures and you can recognize the qualities they value. Scholastics, athletics, talent . . . and *diversity.* Sometimes, being from, say, North Dakota can be a benefit if you're applying to an East Coast college bereft of North Dakotans. Colleges like to be able to advertise that they have a diverse student body representing a wide variety of states, ethnicities, ages, and backgrounds. If you're underrepresented on the campus of your favorite college, let them know.

✔ **The special categories:** One college (and maybe more) offers money just for being left-handed, but the categories we are referring to here are:

- **Women:** Special grant and loan programs are available for women, especially those with dependents. However, some colleges wish to encourage women to join programs that are more heavily male-dominated, and are willing to give promising women a deal to study in a particular field, such as engineering.

- **Ethnic minorities:** Native Americans, Hispanics, African Americans, Asian Americans, and many groups can apply for special grants and scholarships.

- **Physically challenged:** Governments and many colleges have special grant and loan programs for the physically challenged, but you can also use your circumstances to leverage colleges that wish to promote their openness and diversity.

- **Mature students:** A quarter of all college students in the United States are considered "mature," that is 26 or older. Colleges with a lower percentage may want to close the gap. You can also use your greater life experience to demonstrate a wider range of interests and abilities than may be held by your younger colleagues.

Others who are likely to be able to negotiate a better deal are those students with a career direction that the college wishes to promote, such as genetics, special education, or whatever interests the school at the time. Ask around when you're applying — after all, you want to attend a college that values your field of study. Focusing on a particular field can also help you win *institutional scholarships,* usually from corporations, foundations, or individuals with the same background.

When you can combine any of these categories, your negotiating leverage rises, as does your likelihood of finding scholarships or grants that are perfect for you. For example, a judo champion may get an athletic scholarship, but a Native American judo champion with a 4.0 GPA who recently promoted her book on *Oprah* will have offers pouring in from colleges all over the country.

Being attractive to institutions

Independent giving institutions also want the students who receive their awards to reflect positively on their organization. For this reason, they often ask for some personal information, such as a personal history or bio. They're looking to do good, which usually means giving less privileged students an opportunity to go to college. Some awards offered by independent institutions are strictly merit-based, but most have a humanitarian sway.

Not surprisingly, some of the categories that are favored by colleges are also favored by independent institutions. However, the attitude toward judging them is often somewhat different. The following list gives the main categories of students that are most attractive to independent institutions:

- ✔ **The brilliant:** Grades play a big role in institutional giving, but they often aren't the only factor in any particular award. Many awards require you to fulfill at least one of the other categories as well in order to qualify. Some of the other categories include community service, leadership potential, ethnic heritage, interest in a particular major, and achievement demonstrated by an essay. Then it comes down to marks.

- ✔ **The meritorious:** Merit is a big deal because a lot of the organizations giving away money are called *service organizations*. These groups, such as the Rotary Club, the Elks, and others, get together specifically to do service in the community. They raise money for underprivileged kids, support the local eldercare facilities, and give scholarships to deserving young men and women. The kind of merit they want to see is varied — a history of public service, leadership in the community, civic-mindedness, and other high-minded ideals. Here are a few examples of what you can do: work at the local shelters, hospices, or elder-care facilities; establish a hot lunch program at your school; and other works.

Award committees are people, too

If a scholarship is offered on the basis of best essay about civic duty, why does the awarding committee want to see information about your financial need? If the award is truly given for *scholarship,* why is your financial situation an issue at all?

The award committee is human — more accurately, *several* humans. And people at foundations, individual scholarship committees, or service organizations want to see their money doing good for someone deserving. Like it or not, those who can't afford an education appear to be more deserving than those who can, all other things being equal.

✔ **The talented:** Lots of scholarships and grants are offered for those in the fine arts. The categories aren't limited to music, painting, and drama, either. You can get awards for filmmaking, fashion design, accordion playing, authorship, dance, and so on. But you must submit a portfolio, a video, or perform live for judges.

✔ **The focused:** Lots of awards are offered to students entering a particular field of study. From mortuary science to tropical ornamental horticulture, there are awards for almost anything you can study.

✔ **The ethnic:** Some awards are limited to people of a particular ethnic heritage, and others require the applicant be enrolled in courses relating to that ethnicity. For example, the Welsh National Gymanfu Ganu Association offers a scholarship to students of any ethnic background as long as they're enrolled in "courses or projects, which preserve, develop, and promote the Welsh religious and cultural heritage."

✔ **The familiar:** People like to give to their own, so you're better off looking close to home for monetary awards. Often, awards are designated for the children, grandchildren, descendants, siblings, spouses, or other close relatives of the specific group around which the award is based. The main examples are:

- **Employment:** Many trade unions and places of employment give scholarships to members and/or their relatives. Several scholarships are also available for the families of police officers, firefighters, and other emergency service workers.

- **Military:** Veterans' Affairs and the American Legion are among the larger funding organizations, supporting veterans and their families. However, more defined scholarships are available, for example, to descendants of Confederate soldiers and dependents and spouses of soldiers who are missing in action, prisoners of war, or blinded veterans.

- **Religious:** Churches, synagogues, temples, and all sorts of religious institutions routinely set up scholarships for their members. The likelihood of receiving money depends on the relative wealth of your local place of worship and your level of personal (or family) activity. However, don't forget to approach the larger organization — your local church may not have the money to offer you a scholarship but the regional, state, or federal organizations might be another story.

- **Personal contact:** Many awards are limited to members of a particular organization. Some awards further limit the applicants to those pursuing a specific field of study or to those who've achieved outstanding work in a particular field, such as insect systematics (the Thomas Say Award). Others are more open about the field of study, but may require an entrance essay.

✔ **The hybrid:** The Penelope Hanshaw Scholarship awards women studying geosciences at colleges or universities in Delaware, DC, Maryland,

> Virginia, or West Virginia. This scholarship is just one of many examples of the awards designated in very specific categories. Be encouraged — surely you'll be *perfect* for some of these awards!

Being attractive to government programs

The federal government gives out the most financial aid for education, and most of this aid is awarded based on need. However a few merit-based programs are run by the governments (federal, state, and even local), and by law these awards must treat all applicants *indiscriminately* (that is, without discrimination). That means that they look at your grades and award you merit scholarships based on those factors alone.

The people running government financial aid programs — merit-based or need-based — generally don't care about what community service you've done as long as you can get accepted to college. Sure, the awards do have some restrictions, such as never having been convicted of a drug-related crime (more on this in Chapter 6), but, for the most part, government programs lump all applicants together and compare their statistics.

The Need to Be Needy

Trying to add sparkle to your *Free Application for Federal Student Aid* (FAFSA), or beef up your PROFILE (another financial aid form used by some colleges) with tales of how you won the 5th grade spelling bee is a waste of time. The administrators are nice people, but they simply won't read about your achievements (even if you could figure out where to put this information). You become attractive to them by demonstrating the most need.

The obvious need-based applicants are those people with no money and no income. People living below the poverty line with no savings are at the top of the list for need-based funding. However, don't cut yourself off just because your family makes a decent living.

Understanding the differences between "needy" and "poor"

In Chapter 2, we explain the factors that go into determining your *cost of attendance* (COA). Your COA varies depending on the costs of your particular college, the cost of living at your particular college (or the neighboring town), and other factors. You may have a very high COA for an Ivy League school, but your COA may be only a few thousand for a state college in your hometown.

Your *expected family contribution* (EFC) is determined by your status (dependent or independent), family income, family wealth, family drain (the amount of other dependents being supported from the family pot), other financial obligations (mortgage, insurance, and legitimate loan payments — not your wish to take a trip before you start college), plus your personal income and wealth.

After these two numbers are calculated, you simply subtract the EFC from the COA to determine your financial need. In short:

Financial Need = COA – EFC

My parents make over $100,000, so how can I apply for need-based money?

Simple. You get a FAFSA, and you fill it out. The FAFSA information determines your EFC. Now, if that $100,000 figure is all the information you list, you're unlikely to get a lot of dough. However, the FAFSA asks certain financial questions to get a clearer understanding of your financial position. There are many reasons why someone in your position might get a significant amount of need-based money. For example:

✔ **Your parents are already putting their other six children through college.** Even if they're only putting one other child through college, this drain on their finances will be taken into consideration when assessing your need.

✔ **Your parents are also supporting both sets of grandparents, along with the six kids and a few orphans in Central America.** Again, the extent of their support obligations doesn't have to be quite that extreme for your EFC to diminish.

✔ **Your parents have substantial debt.** Just because your parents make a lot of money doesn't mean that they don't have a lot of obligations. The government wants to know your family's *net worth* (calculated by adding together all assets and then subtracting all of the debts). The point is, how

much money will they have left over after their financial obligations are paid, and their dependents are reasonably supported? The bottom line is that if not much is left over, you'll have a low EFC.

✔ **You aren't a dependent.** This is a big one. If you aren't a dependent and cannot reasonably expect money from your family for college, your parents' income won't be considered in determining your EFC. Then, the only income that matters is your own and, if applicable, your spouse's. Now, you can't just leave home for a week and claim to be independent, hoping to fake a low EFC. The government looks rather harshly on that. However, if you can prove that you haven't lived with your parents for a significant amount of time and don't receive financial support from them, or that you're married, or are enrolled in a masters or doctoral degree, or you have a child or other dependents who receive more than half of their support from you, or any of a number of significant factors exists, you're considered independent. You are also independent if you've served in the U.S. Armed Forces (we discuss this in Chapter 18), or if you're an orphan or ward of the court.

Let us dispel another myth: The government will *not* automatically offer you all the money to cover your financial need. There are limits to how much you can receive through each government program, as we discuss in Chapters 5 and 6. Even if you are offered all the money that you need, most of it will be in the form of loans. You don't want to graduate with a huge student loan debt, so you should apply for as many scholarships and grants as possible.

Now, winning financial awards *does* affect your financial need. In fact, it decreases your financial need because your scholarships or grants will be applied directly to the equation. However, this doesn't mean that you've won these awards for nothing. When your need is first being considered, it is being considered by the people who disburse the *grants*. If you still have financial need after you've been offered a grant, you'll then be considered for a loan.

For most students, the awards they win mean taking on less debt. Most students still have some financial need, so they still get whatever grants would've come their way even if they hadn't won any awards. There are many cases of students who are only offered loans, and not grants. However, these students generally wouldn't have qualified for need-based grants at all.

Structuring your finances

Consider the following points before you submit your FAFSA and act on them as far in advance as you can:

- ✔ The government doesn't count the value of the family home as an asset when determining EFC, so your parents might be better off paying more toward the mortgage and less toward investments. They may own a $500,000 house, but if their income is only $40,000 this year and they have few other assets, your EFC will be extremely low.

- ✔ If your mother or father works at the college of your choice, you may be able to obtain an employee *tuition discount.* Often, colleges have special rates for children of their employees. If one of your parents is switching jobs and they have the option of becoming either an administrator at a hospital or an administrator at the local college, taking the job at the college may save you (and your) parents thousands of dollars.

- ✔ The point we make earlier about taking a trip before college is important. To determine the EFC, you must submit your earnings over the last several years. You're presumed to be saving money to attend college. The fact that you decided to blow all your savings on a '67 Corvette doesn't change the fact that the EFC will calculate an amount you *should have saved* from your earnings. You won't get more need-based money just because you decided to spend your savings frivolously.

Chapter 4

Avoiding College Aid Scams

• •

In This Chapter

▶ Realizing that scams are serious threats

▶ Knowing a scam when you see one

▶ Understanding why and how people fall for scams

▶ Avoiding scams

▶ Fighting back when you've been scammed

• •

*Y*ou come home one day and start looking at the mail sitting on the book-case in the hallway. Suddenly you come across one brightly colored envelope that screams at you: YOU MAY HAVE ALREADY WON A FIFTY THOUSAND DOLLAR COLLEGE SCHOLARSHIP!

You probably already realize that your chances of actually getting that $50,000 are about the same as winning the lottery. In fact, you probably stand an even better chance of winning the lottery when you consider that U.S. lotteries are all government supervised. So, although your chances of winning the lottery jackpot are mathematically small, at least it's an honest game. Not so with scholarship scams.

We know, we know, you've probably heard some really convincing story from a friend at school who *swears* someone at a club just won a $50,000 scholarship out of the blue. Financial awards that appear from the heavens, or seem to materialize from thin air, are either fantasies or frauds.

In case you haven't guessed it already, this chapter explains how to avoid scams that guarantee free money for college, award college credit for life experiences, or require fees to release scholarship money. This chapter helps you stay focused on your goal of finding and winning legitimate grants, scholarships, and other awards. In short, it helps you keep your money where it belongs: in your own pocket!

Scam Busters of America

Scholarship scams are a *huge* problem, and every year tens of thousands of otherwise really smart kids (and sometimes their really smart parents) get taken for a ride on the Scholarship Scam Express. Every year, students send $50, $100, $200, $500, or more away to unknown organizations that claim to have access to all the scholarship money in the world or guarantee inside connections with philanthropic organizations that are just *aching* to give away their money.

The truth: The problem has gotten so bad that the United States Federal Trade Commission (FTC) and Department of Justice launched a program to catch and punish companies that commit college scholarship fraud. Dubbed, "Project $cholar$cam," these government agencies teamed up to stop the huge number of frauds that are designed to remove money from students' pockets.

You can check out the Federal Trade Commission's scholarship fraud site at www.ftc.gov/scholarshipscams. You can also see the defendants in the FTC's most recent legal actions by visiting a special site that lists each organization (and its owners) that the government has charged with scholarship fraud www.ftc.gov/bcp/conline/edcams/scholarship/cases.htm.

Illustrating the size of the problem, the government claims that the eight organizations it has charged since the project began have defrauded 175,000 students of a total of $22 million! Considering these amounts represent the actions of only *eight* organizations, you can see that the problem is massive.

Spotting Scholarship Scams

Always be extremely wary of any unsolicited scholarship offers, especially the ones that you've never heard about before. Think about it. Unless you have perfect SAT scores, you lettered in varsity track, basketball, *and* football, scored 100 percent in all your final high school courses, and were named state valedictorian, why would a scholarship foundation seek *you* out? The answer is: It wouldn't. Ah, but scam operators will. You, and thousands like you, are a potential source of revenue for scholarship scam operators!

With the exception of government-based loans and grants, few third-party scholarship funds are regulated, and that means *anyone* can send you an envelope full of promises or make a phone call full of guarantees. Students who spend hard-earned money for the chance to win a scholarship, grant, or low-cost loan are tossing their money down the proverbial drain.

One of the best ways you can tell that a scholarship offer is bogus is when it contains many promises. Legitimate organizations don't promise or guarantee anything, other than the honest, straightforward way that the award process works. Real organizations give you realistic deadlines, tell you whether or not they will respond to your application if you don't win, provide clear criteria for winning, and almost exclusively *do not* require an entry fee.

No legitimate organization will promise you that you'll win — these organizations don't even make it clear that you're *likely* to win. If an organization is giving away free money, why would it have to go to the trouble to track down someone like you who is willing to receive it? Millions of students will track *them* down. Scholarship services can't *guarantee* results, either, because it would be illegal for them to have any influence over the awards process. If an organization doesn't choose its award recipients based solely on its stated criteria (such as high marks), it's guilty of fraud and can be indicted on criminal charges and sued privately. Legitimate organizations don't want to take those kinds of risks.

Whether they contact you through mail, by telephone or via the Internet, scholarship scammers generally make one or more of these false promises:

- ✔ **"Our results are guaranteed."** In fact, no one can *guarantee* that you'll get a scholarship. Nobody. Be especially wary when a third-party, such as a scholarship service, says that it can *guarantee* the actions of another (usually real) philanthropic organization.

- ✔ **"Our offer is exclusive, and awarded to you because you're in the top five percentile (or whatever) of all students statewide."** Do some soul-searching. Despite what your proud grandparents may think, ask yourself whether you're really *so* special that you warrant the attention of people you've never heard about before? And, for that matter, how could they possibly have heard about you unless your grades or achievements are the subject of major press coverage?

- ✔ **"Our service will reduce the costs of getting scholarships."** Scholarships don't cost anything, except, of course, the thousands of hours it takes you to develop the academic, artistic, athletic, or public-speaking skills for which real scholarships are awarded. If a scholarship (or another unsolicited offer) costs you money, it's most likely a scam.

- ✔ **"We do all the work for you."** Scholarships *are* work, but most real scholarship applications consist of a form, plus some supporting material, such as an essay (writing that award-winning essay for you would be fraud by the third party), a performance video (is the third party going to play the piano or score that winning touchdown for you?), or other impressive accomplishment (that must be accomplished by *you*).

> ✔ **"We're making you this time-limited offer over the phone."** Legitimate scholarships are pretty much always offered through the mail; you may receive telephone notification that an offer is on the way, especially when you interact personally with the awards committee, but you always receive follow-up correspondence by mail. Besides, you always have a reasonable amount of time to accept an offer — sometimes months. If you're pressured in any way, hang up the phone.

When it comes to scholarships, here's a simple rule that you can follow to avoid getting burned: *If it seems too good to be true, it probably is!*

How and Why Scams Work

All scholarship frauds depend on three basic characteristics of human nature:

> ✔ **Vanity:** We all think we're very special.
>
> ✔ **Hope:** We all think we deserve to win stuff.
>
> ✔ **Greed:** We all want something for nothing.

Appealing to your personal vanity

"We're very impressed by your scholastic and extracurricular achievements after reading a recommendation about you sent by one of your teachers. We want to award you the SuperDuper Scholarship, and we think that you're just the sort of well-rounded student to represent our organization at college next year." Wow, you think, one of my teachers must really like me. Of course, the organization can't disclose to you which teacher made the recommendation because the teacher asked to remain anonymous. "Now to finalize the award, we need just a few more things from you. . . ."

Everyone thinks they're very special, so when the phone rings and the voice on the other end says you've won something, you *really* want to believe that you deserve it. Scammers know that, so they appeal to your personal vanity to overcome your natural skepticism. After you're convinced that you're special — why else would an organization offer you a scholarship? — you're primed for the next part of the scam. Scammers tell you that you'll get results if you send them a little money or perhaps your credit card information or maybe your bank transit numbers.

Another scam aimed at the vanity of students involves being offered lucrative modeling or acting contracts. It sounds something like: "If you'll pay for a few photographs for your portfolio, or an audition video, or acting lessons . . ." Students like to think of themselves as attractive — who doesn't? — and they think this is a terrific way to pay for college. Of course, the lucrative contracts never materialize after they've first paid a little money, then a lot of money, and then a lot *more* money for their portfolio.

Well-known legitimate agencies are out there that will tell you upfront (and for free) whether you have a chance in the world at modeling. Drama instructors at your high school or prospective college can give you realistic tips on breaking into the acting business. The simple rules: Don't throw away your money, speak with the acknowledged experts and focus on your studies.

Appealing to your sense of hope

"WE CAN GUARANTEE A PLACE FOR YOU AT HARVARD. . . ." screams the official-looking envelope. You open it eagerly. Perhaps Harvard has heard about how you really knuckled down last semester and raised your marks? Maybe the prestigious school is admitting you despite that 69 in chemistry (you still don't know why you didn't study harder). The letter inside confirms that you can be admitted to Harvard by sending away for this amazing book about college study habits. It's yours for only $50, plus postage and handling.

Like the scams that appeal to your vanity, scams that appeal to your sense of hope also rely on your good nature and desire for good things to happen to you. From the moment your mothers and fathers read you fairy tales to put you to sleep at night to the first time you see a Hollywood fantasy in which unknowns are plucked from relative obscurity and propelled to fame, fortune, and a great life, you are bombarded with stories that give you false hope and say that you really don't have to work for what you get.

The truth is that only Harvard can admit you to Harvard, no matter how official the envelope looks. Scams such as these (and many, many more) prey on students' hope that they've scored better than they really have. The beauty of this scam is that students can fall for the same scam more than once if different school names are used and different envelope designs are sent. After all, what student hasn't added Harvard or Yale or Princeton to their FAFSA as a long-shot, knowing full well their marks (and financial resources) will otherwise preclude them from attending?

The scam can work because many students wish they could go to Harvard but secretly know they don't qualify. When the letter arrives, blind hope replaces rational thought. Consequently, they send the money before the intelligent side has a chance to ask, *exactly why am I sending money to these people?*

Don't let this kind of scam happen to you. In the real world, you have to work for what you get, and work hard at becoming the best you can be. True scholarship winners have spent years honing their skills, and you can be one of them. This book shows how *almost any student* who wants to go to college can afford to do so. But we won't give you any false hope.

Appealing to your sense of greed

Psst, wanna buy a college education? A variety of scholarship scams make it appear as though you've won a major educational prize, but require you to pay money upfront for the funds to be released, for administrative purposes, for shipping and handling, or for any number of other semiplausible reasons.

When confronted with requests for money, please remember our simple rule: *If you have to send money to get money, it's probably a scam. Don't do it!*

Some of the college funding scams that focus on your greed include:

- ✔ **Privately-offered low interest rate scholarship loans.** Because interest rates already are so low, this scam is less prevalent these days, but it surfaces from time to time. Again, if you have to pay in advance for anything relating to saving money, don't trust it. Before signing *any* loan agreement, check with your bank manager, an accountant, or a financial advisor to ensure this deal makes financial sense.

- ✔ **Identity theft.** In this scam, you're not charged any application fee, but you are required to provide extensive personal information, including your Social Security number, a family history and even credit card numbers — just for verification, of course. Later, you start getting bills for stuff that you didn't buy. Turns out the bad guys have stolen your identity and are using your good name to run up bills — and they're in your name! There is *never* any reason to give a credit card number on a scholarship application. NEVER! If you're concerned about some offer, check it out with the Federal Trade Commission (www.ftc.gov), your state fraud agency, the local police, or your local chamber of commerce.

- ✔ **College credit for work experiences.** Many colleges entice mature students (those that are over the ripe old age of 25) by claiming that work experiences are taken into consideration for scholarships or course waivers. The scam part comes in when *high school* students are offered credit for their life experiences (which typically don't add up to a whole lot yet). Colleges that do this are probably not accredited with the regional college accreditation board and so their degrees are merely nice substitutes for wallpaper. You can easily check out whether the school in question is accredited by contacting the applicable accreditation agency in the "Nationally Recognized Accrediting Agencies" list located at the Department of Education's Web site at www.ed.gov/offices/OPE/accreditation/natlagencies.html.

Protecting Yourself from Scams

In general, a few solid rules that you can follow to reduce your chances of getting scammed by a fake scholarship companies include:

- ✔ Never, *ever* give your personal information (such as date of birth, Social Security number, address, credit-card info) until you have done *extensive* background checks on the company or organization. Just because an organization has a great looking Web site, for example, doesn't mean that it isn't operating out of a trailer somewhere.

- ✔ Always carefully check the background of the company or organization. This includes checking with the Federal Trade Commission (www.ftc.gov), local police, local chamber of commerce, the state consumer business office, and the Better Business Bureau.

- ✔ Search for the organization on the Internet using a search engine such as Google (www.google.com) or AltaVista (www.altavista.com). If others have been scammed by a particular organization, they may set up a Web site informing people about their experiences.

- ✔ Ask the organization how it found you. If the organization doesn't have a reasonable answer, stop dealing with it. Even when the answer sounds reasonable, the organization may still be lying. Double-check with the original source: Did it forward your name to the scholarship organization in question? Why?

- ✔ Never deal with an organization unless it has a physical location. Even online colleges have physical offices. The picture of that huge building on an organization's Web site may be fake.

- ✔ Never send *anyone* money in any form, even as a guarantee to hold your place, unless you've confirmed with the appropriate governing body that the organization is legitimate. Ask yourself: If this organization will give *me* money, why does it need *my* money first?

- ✔ Assume it's a scam and walk away or hang up the phone whenever the situation feels wrong or you feel pressured in any way. No legitimate scholarship organization requires you to respond immediately or risk losing out on your scholarship.

Taking Action If You Get Taken for a Ride

Okay, so you got scammed. You don't have to sit around and take it. Too many people do nothing because they become embarrassed that they were taken for a ride. But remember that many of these scams are perpetrated by professional criminals, who spent years perfecting their frauds. You're probably not their first victim. And, if you don't do anything to stop them, you can bet you won't be their last victim.

The *College Scholarship Fraud Prevention Act* was passed in 2000 to help you. Now perpetrators can go to jail for their actions, and they're subject to fines of up to $500,000. Nevertheless, reporting what happened to the Federal Trade Commission is up to you. You can call these folks at 1-800-382-4357 (1-800-FTC-HELP) or log onto www.ftc.gov. You also need to notify your college financial aid office and your local police department.

If the FTC finds that your case is truly a scam, it may launch an investigation on its own, turn the case over to the Department of Justice, or hand it over to your local police. Criminals have a tendency to start up similar operations whenever they've been successful before. Their greediness is how many of them get caught.

For more information, check out the following Web sites:

- The U.S. Department of Education (www.ed.gov) and the Federal Trade Commission (www.ftc.gov/bcp/conline/edcams/scholarship/) publish lists of known scams on their Web sites.

- FinAid (www.finaid.org) is a free public service Web site with plenty of information on scholarship scams.

- The College Board offers information about scholarship scams at www.collegeboard.com/article/0,1120,6-30-55-408,00.html?orig=sub.

- Several college Web sites include sections about scholarship scams or they post alerts regarding known scams. Purdue University, for example, outlines various scams at www.purdue.edu/DFA/sandg/scams.htm. Similarly, UCLA runs a scam alert service on its Web site at www.college.ucla.edu/UP/SRC/scam.htm.

Part II
Getting Your Due from Uncle Sam

In this part . . .

The federal government gives out more grants, low-interest loans, and other student aid than all other sources combined. Whether the money you can get from federal sources is totally free or just free for now, it's one money source every prospective student should pursue. For some students and their families who have low incomes and little credit, federal loans may be the only source of loans available.

On the downside, the forms you need to fill out can be demanding and time-consuming. On the upside, completing the forms is probably more rewarding than spending your time asking customers if they want fries with that order! Besides, we take you step by step through the major grant and loan programs, so all you have to do is fill in the blanks.

So, let's get out your financial documents and apply!

Chapter 5

Getting Help from Your Federal Friends

In This Chapter

▶ Knowing what federal grants are available

▶ Completing the FAFSA

▶ Finding out about other forms of federal aid

*T*he U.S. Department of Education will give out approximately 70 billion dollars this year to help students and their families afford the steep costs of university, college, and trade school. This whopping amount represents roughly 70 percent of *all* student aid disbursed, so it's an obvious place to start looking for free money.

In this chapter, we discuss two key federal programs that give away *grant* money, and we also tell you what you need to do to get your hands on some of it. (Chapter 6 discusses available cheap loans, which are good for supplementing grant money.) This free money is all *need-based,* and it's all courtesy of your Uncle Sam!

A Crash Course in Federal Financial Aid

Like many things in life, applying for federal student aid can appear complex. The following list outlines many of the major categories of federal student aid as well as some terms you'll probably need:

> ✔ **FAFSA:** Completing the *Free Application for Federal Student Aid* (FAFSA) is the first step in getting financial aid. Not only is the FAFSA a requirement for all federal aid, but it is also mandatory for most state and college aid as well. The amount of your *Pell Grant* (more about Pell Grants later in this chapter) is calculated by the information you provide on your FAFSA.

You typically submit an initial FAFSA at the beginning of your senior year (after January 1 and before June 30 in the year you plan to attend). Each school year thereafter, you send in a FAFSA *renewal* outlining your current financial condition. Unless you send in your renewal, you won't be eligible for federal student aid (and, possibly state aid as well) for the particular year.

The information you provide on the FAFSA is used to calculate your *expected family contribution* (EFC), which we explain in more detail later in this chapter.

In turn, your EFC determines your eligibility for numerous other need-based aid programs, including other federal programs, state-based programs, and college-based aid. You can complete the FAFSA online or use the paper version available from your high school counselor or the Department of Education. This chapter takes you through this process step by step.

✔ **SAR:** You'll receive a form called the *Student Aid Report* (SAR) a few weeks after you submit your FAFSA. The SAR gives you a chance to correct, change, or fine-tune the answers you provided in your FAFSA. The SAR also notes your EFC.

The lower your EFC, the better your chances for financial aid. Your Pell Grant amount (more about this in a few moments) is noted on your SAR. If your financial situation has materially changed since you originally applied — whether it has improved or worsened — you're required to update your information and send it back to the government so that it can generate a new EFC and possibly adjust your Pell Grant amount.

✔ **FSEOG:** If you have extreme need (a particularly low EFC), you may be eligible for a *Federal Supplemental Educational Opportunity Grant* (FSEOG). Unlike Pell Grants, which are guaranteed to be available to all eligible students by the U.S. government, FSEOG money is limited on a most-needed, first-come-first-served basis.

Also, not all colleges participate in the FSEOG program. Whether it's simply more administrative hassle for the college or the changeable nature of FSEOG funding (causing periodic crises), many schools don't offer FSEOG-based funds. Find out well ahead of aid deadlines whether each college on your wish list offers FSEOG money.

✔ **Consolidation loans:** Like Stafford and PLUS Loans, federal consolidation loans (discussed in detail in Chapter 6) are available in two different varieties: *Direct Consolidation Loans* and *FFEL Consolidation Loans*. Consolidation loans help students (and parents) streamline college loans by combining several types of loans — sometimes even if they have different repayment schedules — into one, easy-to-understand, and (hopefully) easy-to-repay loan.

- ✔ **Federal Perkins Loans:** A campus-based program, Federal Perkins Loans (see Chapter 6) are low-interest loans that are available to both under-graduate and graduate students. Undergraduates can borrow up to $4,000 for each year of undergraduate study, and graduate students can borrow up to $6,000 per year.

- ✔ **Federal Work-Study:** This campus-based program (see Chapter 12 for details) provides on-campus jobs for undergraduate and graduate students with demonstrated financial need. Ideally, your college tries to find you a job that's related to your academic program.

- ✔ **PLUS Loans:** PLUS Loans (see Chapter 6 for a complete discussion) are loans to parents, and these loans come in two varieties: *Direct PLUS Loans* and *FFEL PLUS Loans.* PLUS Loans let parents who have a good credit history borrow enough money to pay the education expenses of their dependent children.

- ✔ **Stafford Loans:** Stafford Loans (in the form of *Direct Stafford Loans* and *FFEL Stafford Loans;* see Chapter 6 for details) are a major source of finan-cial aid for students attending college. As you can probably guess from the word *loan,* Stafford Loans are supposed to be repaid — although, sometimes, repayment can be postponed or, in certain cases, the entire loan can be completely discharged or canceled.

Federal Pell Grants

By far, the most important government program of interest to students is the Federal Pell Grant program. These grants are designed for *undergraduate* stu-dents who haven't yet earned a bachelor's or professional degree — and this includes high school students heading into their first year of college. The only exception to this rule is for students who already have their undergraduate degree and are heading back to college to obtain their teacher's certification. These students can also qualify for Pell Grants.

Federal Pell Grants are especially great because they don't have to be repaid. Yes, that's right, we're taking about free money from Uncle Sam — money that you don't have to pay back! But thousands of eligible students every year miss out on getting a Pell Grant simply because they don't complete the proper paperwork, leave things to the last minute, or (gasp!) don't bother to apply at all because they wrongly think that they won't qualify or that it's too much hassle.

Some paperwork is involved with the application process — and the process can get a bit complicated at times. But before you dismiss the project just because you've heard that it'll take weeks of completing agonizing forms, know this: Anyone who can handle sixth grade math can get the paperwork done. The trick is to understand the process, leave plenty of time, get your supporting paperwork in order, and check your application form thoroughly.

Fortunately, this section spells out exactly what to expect, when to expect it, how you can increase your chances of getting a Pell Grant, and how long it will take. It also explains what to do if something goes wrong with your application (and why something might go wrong).

Understanding need

Federal Pell Grants are given to students based on *need*. The word *need* has a very special meaning within the world of colleges and universities. In short, need is defined as the difference between what you (and your parents or guardians) *can* pay and the actual cost of your education.

Notice the important distinction between *need* and *want* in this section. Although you may *want* Uncle Sam to pick up the entire tab for your education, the government doesn't likely feel that it *needs* to do so. Under the Federal Pell Grant program, the U.S. Department of Education figures out how much money you need for school (not what you want) by using a very complex formula that's based on your assets, your parents' assets, your family income, and other factors such as how many other family members your parents are putting through school.

After all your finances are taken into consideration, the government calculates a number it calls your *expected family contribution* (EFC). The EFC is the dollar amount that the government thinks your family can afford to pay toward the cost of your college education. The difference between your EFC and the actual costs of attending a particular school is defined as your *financial need*. And your financial need is how your Pell Grant is calculated.

Even if you're very needy (you have very little or no money available to spend on your education), your Pell Grant may very well max out before paying for everything you need for school. Thankfully, the government also provides additional funds through its *Federal Supplemental Educational Opportunity Grant* (FSEOG) program. We talk more about the FSEOG later in this chapter. First up, however, is the FAFSA form, the cornerstone of the federal student aid program and the basis for much state and college aid as well.

The FAFSA form

The first step in getting federal, state, and college aid is completing a form called the *Free Application for Federal Student Aid* (usually just known as the

FAFSA). The FAFSA is available from your school guidance office or from your school counselor. You can also get it online by visiting the U.S. Department of Education's Web site at www.fafsa.ed.gov. You can even complete the form online (more about this option later in this chapter).

You can complete the FAFSA in Spanish if you prefer. Either obtain a Spanish FAFSA form from your high school counselor or click on "Llenar una FAFSA en Español" on the FAFSA Web site.

The FAFSA is a four-page form that changes slightly every year to reflect new federal tax laws, the government's ever-changin' education objectives, and other factors. You must use the correct year's form; if you don't you're just wasting your time because you'll have fill out a new FAFSA all over again.

Because much of the information you'll be asked for on the FAFSA is related to your income and assets (plus, of course, the income and assets of your parents or guardians), having your parents complete their federal tax return before you complete the FAFSA is really helpful.

If you don't present the most accurate and up-to-date information on your FAFSA, you'll have to revise your application after you receive your SAR. This can mean delays in getting your student aid packages both from government sources and from prospective colleges. Some colleges may run out of financial aid money by the time you get around to providing them with your accurate information, so you might miss out on offers just because you're too late.

Now, here's where many students get fouled up. Ideally, you should complete and send in your FAFSA in January of the year you're applying for college (even though, technically speaking, the federal deadline is June 30 of the *next year*). This means that if you're planning on going to college in September 2005, you should ideally send in your complete FAFSA in January 2005.

In many cases, however, your parents won't be able to even *start* calculating their income taxes until late February (because some employers take this long to send out W-2s and other necessary forms). Thus, it's often best to *estimate* earnings and other necessary calculations to get your FAFSA done early. It's better to submit an early FAFSA (with estimated numbers) in late January, than it is to wait until you're sure of all your figures and send in your FAFSA in late April.

You can always go back and correct any errors (or bad estimates) later on. Whatever you do, don't delay sending in your FAFSA because you'll be penalized for lateness. Although you have an 18-month window in which to file your FAFSA, state aid deadlines can be as early as the *February prior to September admission*. After you miss the state deadlines, you can pretty much forget about getting state aid for that year, and likely college aid as well.

Completing the FAFSA

All income from you and your parents, as well as a complete picture of the immediate family's net worth, has to be calculated for the FAFSA.

In order to calculate your family's net worth, you need to collect a number of items before you can complete the FAFSA. Some of these items may take a bit of time to find or figure out, so you may want to get going on these even before you get your FAFSA. Many energetic students start hunting around for these things in December (or earlier). Check out this list:

- **Your Social Security number:** In order to apply for a Federal Pell Grant, you have to have your Social Security umber. If you don't already have a number, apply for one immediately by visiting your local Social Security office (check out the government pages of your telephone book for a location near you), or apply online for one at www.ssa.gov. If your Social Security number is incorrect, your FAFSA won't match up with your high school academic records, possibly delaying your financial aid applications. If you're not a U.S. citizen, you also need your *Alien Registration Card* (even through the current version is pink, this is usually known as a "Green Card").

- **Income tax return:** The information from your current federal income tax return (or a close earnings and expenses estimate) is vital to the FAFSA. In the United States, this means having your IRS Form 1040, 1040A, 1040EZ, or 1040Telefile. In other countries (and U.S. territories), it means whatever tax form is appropriate there. Even students with no income in the year previous to their application are required to enter an amount for income on their FAFSA. (If you have no income you just enter "0.")

- **Parent's tax return:** If you're a dependent student (more about the special meaning of this term later in this chapter), you also need the tax returns of each of your parents if they file separately, or just the one if they file jointly. For the purposes of the FAFSA, most students are classified as *dependent* students.

- **W-2 forms:** Not only does your W-2 itemize how much you earned over the year, it also tallies up your income tax withheld as well as other deductions, such as pension, union dues, or 401k contributions. By law, every employer for whom you've done any paid work during the last year must send out a W-2 to you. (In the United States, January 31 is the deadline.) You can also estimate the necessary amounts by adding up all the year's weekly income and deductions. Completing the FAFSA requires access to your parents' W-2 forms as well.

- **Calculation of other money earned in the last year:** If you've done any odd jobs around the neighborhood or perhaps a small consulting gig, you (or your parents) may not have had income tax deducted at source.

Nevertheless, you must calculate how much (if any) of this type of income you earned this year and include it with your overall income calculation.

✔ **Current bank statements:** These statements are needed so that any liquid assets (ones you can spend for college without much trouble) are counted in your net worth. Your net worth is important because overall financial position is considered when the government calculates your EFC (and the amount of your Federal Pell Grant). Your bank manager can probably help you if you don't have these statements at your fingertips.

✔ **Stock brokerage and other investment accounts:** Just as bank statements are helpful to find out your (and your parents') financial position, so are any stock, bond, or investment accounts. They need to be included in the FAFSA.

✔ **Current mortgage information:** If you and your parents live in a house, condo, or other dwelling on which a mortgage loan is registered, this information must be included in your FAFSA. The government wants to know how much debt your parents are already juggling before it can figure out how much additional debt they can assume for your education.

✔ **Sole-proprietorship or partnership records:** If you or your parents run a business or are in a business partnership, this information, plus the financial records of the business, is required for the FAFSA.

✔ **Your school codes:** Each college, university, or other post-secondary institution has a unique identifying *Federal School Code.* You can indicate up to six schools that will get an electronic copy of your FAFSA, and you *must* include at least one school code when applying online. Although you aren't required to add the school codes on the paper version of the form, each of your chosen schools will get your information faster if you do. And without a FAFSA on file, your prospective school may not be able to give you any financial aid because it won't know about your financial position. Keep in mind, though, that most schools require separate applications (yes, more forms) to apply for school-specific scholarships and grants.

Getting the Federal School Codes is easy. You can call the school (or visit it online), chat with your high school counselor or guidance office, or drop by your local public library. *FAFSA on the Web* (more about this option later on in this chapter) has a very cool function that lets you easily search the Federal School Code database. Check it out at www.fafsa.ed.gov/fotw0203/fslookup.htm.

When you're finished, send your FAFSA to the Federal Student Aid Programs office in the pre-addressed envelope you receive with your FAFSA materials. Oh, and one more thing: Don't send your FAFSA to each of the schools on your list. These schools will get your information from the government in a different form (and format) than you can supply.

FAFSA

JULY 1, 2003 — JUNE 30, 2004
FREE APPLICATION FOR FEDERAL STUDENT AID
We Help Put America Through School
OMB # 1845-0001

Step One: For questions 1-34, leave blank any questions that do not apply to you (the student).

1-3. Your full name (as it appears on your Social Security card)

1. LAST NAME

2. FIRST NAME

3. MIDDLE INITIAL

4-7. Your permanent mailing address

4. NUMBER AND STREET (INCLUDE APT. NUMBER)

5. CITY (AND COUNTRY IF NOT U.S.)

6. STATE

7. ZIP CODE

8. Your Social Security Number

9. Your date of birth   / / 1 9

10. Your permanent telephone number   (   )   –

11-12. Your driver's license number and state (if any)

11. LICENSE NUMBER

12. STATE

13. Are you a U.S. citizen?
Pick one. See page 2.

  a. Yes, I am a U.S. citizen. **Skip to question 15** .... ○ 1
  b. No, but I am an eligible noncitizen. **Fill in question 14.** .... ○ 2
  c. No, I am not a citizen or eligible noncitizen. .... ○ 3

14. ALIEN REGISTRATION NUMBER
A

15. What is your marital status as of today?

  I am single, divorced, or widowed .... ○ 1
  I am married/remarried .... ○ 2
  I am separated .... ○ 3

16. Month and year you were married, separated, divorced, or widowed

MONTH   YEAR   /

For each question (17 - 21), please mark whether you will be full time, 3/4 time, half time, less than half time, or not attending. **See page 2.**

17. Summer 2003	Full time/Not sure ○ 1	3/4 time ○ 2	Half time ○ 3	Less than half time ○ 4	Not attending ○ 5
18. Fall 2003	Full time/Not sure ○ 1	3/4 time ○ 2	Half time ○ 3	Less than half time ○ 4	Not attending ○ 5
19. Winter 2003-2004	Full time/Not sure ○ 1	3/4 time ○ 2	Half time ○ 3	Less than half time ○ 4	Not attending ○ 5
20. Spring 2004	Full time/Not sure ○ 1	3/4 time ○ 2	Half time ○ 3	Less than half time ○ 4	Not attending ○ 5
21. Summer 2004	Full time/Not sure ○ 1	3/4 time ○ 2	Half time ○ 3	Less than half time ○ 4	Not attending ○ 5
22. Highest school your father completed	Middle school/Jr. High ○ 1	High school ○ 2	College or beyond ○ 3	Other/unknown ○ 4	
23. Highest school your mother completed	Middle school/Jr. High ○ 1	High school ○ 2	College or beyond ○ 3	Other/unknown ○ 4	

24. What is your state of legal residence?
STATE

25. Did you become a legal resident of this state before January 1, 1998?
Yes ○ 1   No ○ 2

26. If the answer to question 25 is **"No,"** give month and year you became a legal resident.
MONTH   YEAR   /

27. Are you male? (Most male students must register with Selective Service to get federal aid.)
Yes ○ 1   No ○ 2

28. If you are male (age 18-25) and not registered, answer "Yes" and Selective Service will register you.
Yes ○ 1   No ○ 2

29. What degree or certificate will you be working on during 2003-2004? **See page 2** and enter the correct number in the box.

30. What will be your grade level when you begin the 2003-2004 school year? **See page 2** and enter the correct number in the box.

31. Will you have a high school diploma or GED before you begin the 2003-2004 school year?
Yes ○ 1   No ○ 2

32. Will you have your first bachelor's degree before July 1, 2003?
Yes ○ 1   No ○ 2

33. In addition to grants, are you interested in student loans (which you must pay back)?
Yes ○ 1   No ○ 2

34. In addition to grants, are you interested in "work-study" (which you earn through work)?
Yes ○ 1   No ○ 2

35. **Do not leave this question blank.** Have you ever been convicted of possessing or selling illegal drugs? If you have, answer "Yes," complete and submit this application, and we will send you a worksheet in the mail for you to determine if your conviction affects your eligibility for aid.
No ○ 1   Yes ○ 3

DO NOT LEAVE QUESTION 35 BLANK

For Help — 1-800-433-3243

Page 1: General information about you

Your full name. Of course, *you* know what your name is, right? Well, for the sake of accuracy and keeping things consistent, make sure that your name is spelled *exactly* the same way as your Social Security card indicates. Hopefully, this spelling is exactly the same as your school records indicate, and, if you've already started filing your own taxes, the same name under which the IRS knows you. All your records — from your report cards to your SAT scores to your FAFSA — should match exactly. If your parents remarried, or you some-how acquired a hyphenated or different last name than the name listed with Social Security or your school, *now* is the time to get these things ironed out. For things to go smoothly, everything must match up.

Your permanent mailing address. You only get one line to tell the govern-ment where you live. Try to use standardized abbreviations such as "Ave" for "avenue" or "Apt" for "apartment" if you need more space. The form's instructions also tell you which characters can be used in this field.

Highest school your father/mother completed. Currently, this information is for statistical purposes only. In subsequent revisions to the EFC formula, this information *may* be used to lower the EFCs of students whose parents did not go to college.

Selective Service questions. By law, all male U.S. Citizens must register on their 18th birthdays with Selective Service. To be eligible for *any* federal col-lege aid, you must register for Selective Service. This area of the FAFSA asks you if you're male. If you haven't already registered for Selective Service, the FAFSA process registers you automatically.

In addition to grants, are you interested in student loans (which you must pay back)? Answering this question *yes*, flags your application, so that you can receive information about Stafford and PLUS loans. (We talk more about these loans in Chapter 6.) Whether you answer *yes* or *no* does not affect your eligibility for grants.

In addition to grants, are you interested in Federal Work-Study? Like the previous question, answering *yes* to this question flags your application, so that you can receive information about Work-Study programs administered by your college. (We explain these programs in Chapter 7.)

Have you ever been convicted of possessing or selling illegal drugs? U.S. law prohibits students from receiving any federal college aid if they've been convicted of drug crimes (excluding those involving tobacco or alcohol). Keep in mind that only convictions for which the person was tried as an adult and for which no pardon has been granted should be registered. If you answer *yes* to this question, you may be still eligible to receive federal aid provided you've completed an acceptable drug rehab program.

Step Two: For questions 36-49, report your (the student's) income and assets. If you are married today, report your and your spouse's income and assets, even if you were not married in 2002. Ignore references to "spouse" if you are currently single, separated, divorced, or widowed.

36. For 2002, have you (the student) completed your IRS income tax return or another tax return listed in **question 37**?

   a. I have already completed my return.   ◯ ₁   **b.** I will file, but I have not yet   ◯ ₂   **c.** I'm not going to file. (Skip to question 42.)   ◯ ₃
                                         completed my return.

37. What income tax return did you file or will you file for 2002?

   a. IRS 1040 .... ◯ ₁   **d.** A tax return for Puerto Rico, Guam, American Samoa, the U.S. Virgin Islands, the
   b. IRS 1040A, 1040EZ, 1040Telefile .... ◯ ₂   Marshall Islands, the Federated States of Micronesia, or Palau. **See page 2**. .... ◯ ₄
   c. A foreign tax return. **See page 2**. .... ◯ ₃

38. If you have filed or will file a 1040, were you eligible to file a 1040A or 1040EZ? **See page 2**.   Yes ◯ ₁ No ◯ ₂ Don't Know ◯ ₃

For questions 39-51, if the answer is zero or the question does not apply to you, enter 0.

39. What was your (and spouse's) adjusted gross income for 2002? Adjusted gross income is on IRS Form 1040–line 35; 1040A–line 21; 1040EZ–line 4; or Telefile–line I. $ ☐☐ , ☐☐☐

40. Enter the total amount of your (and spouse's) income tax for 2002. Income tax amount is on IRS Form 1040–line 55; 1040A–line 36; 1040EZ–line 10; or Telefile–line K(2). $ ☐☐ , ☐☐☐

41. Enter your (and spouse's) exemptions for 2002. Exemptions are on IRS Form 1040–line 6d or on Form 1040A–line 6d. For Form 1040EZ or Telefile, **see page 2**.   ☐☐

42-43. How much did you (and spouse) earn from working (wages, salaries, tips, etc.) in 2002? Answer this question whether or not you filed a tax return. This information may be on your W-2 forms, or on IRS Form 1040–lines 7 + 12 + 18; 1040A–line 7; or 1040EZ–line 1. Telefilers should use their W-2 forms.   **You (42)** $ ☐☐ , ☐☐☐

                                                                               Your Spouse (43) $ ☐☐ , ☐☐☐

Student (and Spouse) Worksheets (44-46)

                                                        Worksheet A (44) $ ☐☐ , ☐☐☐

44-46. Go to page 8 and complete the columns on the left of Worksheets A, B, and C. Enter the student (and spouse) totals in questions 44, 45, and 46, respectively. Even though you may have few of the Worksheet items, check each line carefully.   **Worksheet B (45)** $ ☐☐ , ☐☐☐

                                                        Worksheet C (46) $ ☐☐ , ☐☐☐

47. As of today, what is the net worth of your (and spouse's) **investments,** including real estate (not your home)? **See page 2**. $ ☐☐ , ☐☐☐

48. As of today, what is the net worth of your (and spouse's) current **businesses and/or investment farms**? Do not include a farm that you live on and operate. **See page 2**. $ ☐☐ , ☐☐☐

49. As of today, what is your (and spouse's) total current balance of **cash, savings, and checking accounts**? Do not include student financial aid. $ ☐☐ , ☐☐☐

50-51. If you receive veterans' education benefits, for **how many months** from July 1, 2003 through June 30, 2004 will you receive these benefits, and **what amount** will you receive per month? Do not include your spouse's veterans education benefits.   **Months (50)** ☐☐

                                                        Amount (51) $ ☐ , ☐☐☐

Step Three: Answer all seven questions in this step.

52. Were you born before January 1, 1980? .... Yes ◯ ₁   No ◯ ₂

53. During the school year 2003-2004, will you be working on a master's or doctorate program (such as an MA, MBA, MD, JD, PhD, EdD, or graduate certificate, etc.)? .... Yes ◯ ₁   No ◯ ₂

54. As of today, are you married? (Answer "Yes" if you are separated but not divorced.) .... Yes ◯ ₁   No ◯ ₂

55. Do you have children who receive more than half of their support from you? .... Yes ◯ ₁   No ◯ ₂

56. Do you have dependents (other than your children or spouse) who live with you and who receive more than half of their support from you, now and through June 30, 2004? .... Yes ◯ ₁   No ◯ ₂

57. Are you an orphan, or are you or were you (until age 18) a ward/dependent of the court? .... Yes ◯ ₁   No ◯ ₂

58. Are you a veteran of the U.S. Armed Forces? **See page 2**. .... Yes ◯ ₁   No ◯ ₂

If you (the student) answer "No" to every question in Step Three, go to Step Four.

If you answer "Yes" to any question in Step Three, skip Step Four and go to Step Five on page 6.

(If you are a health profession student, your school may require you to complete Step Four even if you answered "Yes" in Step Three.)

For Help — www.ed.gov/prog_info/SFA/FAFSA

Page 2: Your income, your marital status, and your dependency status

The next few questions deal with the type of tax return you filed this year. Be sure to select the answer that's most accurate. When in doubt, ask your parents or an accountant.

What is your adjusted gross income? Haul out all the financial paperwork you gathered together (you did do your prep work, right?) and simply start copying numbers. For example, the FAFSA asks you your (and your spouse's, if you're married) adjusted gross income for the year. If you've already done your taxes, you can simply copy the numbers from your tax form directly into your FAFSA.

Worksheets A, B, and C. These worksheets are designed to estimate the exact amount of money you (and your spouse, if you're married) have earned over the past year. Each question refers to a different possible income source. In most cases, you can answer "0" because the question doesn't apply to you. That said, be sure to read every question thoroughly just in case. When in doubt, ask you parents or an accountant. You can also call the FAFSA Help Line at 1-800-433-3243 or 319-337-5665.

As of today, what is the net worth of your (and your spouse's) current investments? This question has a long list of what to include and what not to include. Read through the list of qualifying investments, add them up, and enter the total in the field provided. Do the similar calculation for the questions relating to current businesses (most students don't have any businesses, but the FAFSA asks to ensure that the government doesn't give away money unnecessarily) as well as cash, savings, and checking accounts.

The next series of questions relate to your dependency status. Whether you're dependent or independent of your parents depends on your age, if you're currently married, what degree you're going for (all things being equal, the more degrees you have, the more independent you are), and other facts such as any children you might have, if you're an orphan, or if you're a veteran of the U.S. Armed Forces. Depending on what you answer in these questions, you may be exempt from having to provide any parental information on your application.

Step Four: Complete this step if you (the student) answered "No" to all questions in Step Three. Go to page 7 to determine who is a parent for this step.

59. What is your parents' marital status as of today?

Married/Remarried .... ○ 1 Divorced/Separated .... ○ 3

Single .... ○ 2 Widowed .... ○ 4

60. Month and year they were married, separated, divorced, or widowed

MONTH | YEAR
☐ ☐ / ☐ ☐ ☐ ☐

61-64. What are the Social Security Numbers and last names of the parents reporting information on this form? If your parent does not have a Social Security Number, you must enter 000-00-0000

61. FATHER'S/STEPFATHER'S SOCIAL SECURITY NUMBER
☐☐☐ - ☐☐ - ☐☐☐☐

62. FATHER'S/STEPFATHER'S LAST NAME
☐☐☐☐☐☐☐☐☐☐☐☐

63. MOTHER'S/STEPMOTHER'S SOCIAL SECURITY NUMBER
☐☐☐ - ☐☐ - ☐☐☐☐

64. MOTHER'S/STEPMOTHER'S LAST NAME
☐☐☐☐☐☐☐☐☐☐☐☐

65. Go to page 7 to determine how many people are in your parents' household. ☐

66. Go to page 7 to determine how many in question 65 **(exclude your parents)** will be college students between July 1, 2003 and June 30, 2004. ☐

67. What is your parents' state of legal residence?

STATE ☐☐

68. Did your parents become legal residents of this state before January 1, 1998?

Yes ○ 1 No ○ 2

MONTH | YEAR
☐ ☐ / ☐ ☐ ☐ ☐

69. If the answer to question 68 is "No," give the month and year legal residency began for the parent who has lived in the state the longest.

☐ ☐

70. What is the age of your older parent?

71. For 2002, have your parents completed their IRS income tax return or another tax return listed in **question 72?**

a. My parents have already completed their return. ○ 1

b. My parents will file, but they have not yet completed their return. ○ 2

c. My parents are not going to file. **(Skip to question 77.)** ○ 3

72. What income tax return did your parents file or will they file for 2002?

a. IRS 1040 .... ○ 1

b. IRS 1040A, 1040EZ, 1040Telefile .... ○ 2

c. A foreign tax return. **See page 2.** ...... ○ 3

d. A tax return for Puerto Rico, Guam, American Samoa, the U.S. Virgin Islands, the Marshall Islands, the Federated States of Micronesia, or Palau. **See page 2.** .... ○ 4

73. If your parents have filed or will file a 1040, were they eligible to file a 1040A or 1040EZ? **See page 2.**

Yes ○ 1 No ○ 2 Don't Know ○ 3

For questions 74 - 84, if the answer is zero or the question does not apply, enter 0.

74. What was your parents' adjusted gross income for 2002? Adjusted gross income is on IRS Form 1040–line 35; 1040A–line 21; 1040EZ–line 4; or Telefile–line I. $ ☐☐☐ , ☐☐☐

75. Enter the total amount of your parents' income tax for 2002. Income tax amount is on IRS Form 1040–line 55; 1040A–line 36; 1040EZ–line 10; or Telefile–line K(2). $ ☐☐☐ , ☐☐☐

76. Enter your parents' exemptions for 2002. Exemptions are on IRS Form 1040–line 6d or on Form 1040A–line 6d. For Form 1040EZ or Telefile, **see page 2.** ☐☐

77-78. How much did your parents earn from working (wages, salaries, tips, etc.) in 2002? Answer this question whether or not your parents filed a tax return. This information may be on their W-2 forms, or on IRS Form 1040–lines 7 + 12 + 18; 1040A–line 7; or 1040EZ–line 1. Telefilers should use their W-2 forms.

Father/Stepfather (77) $ ☐☐☐ , ☐☐☐

Mother/Stepmother (78) $ ☐☐☐ , ☐☐☐

Parent Worksheets (79-81)

79-81. Go to page 8 and complete the columns on the right of Worksheets A, B, and C. Enter the parent totals in questions 79, 80, and 81, respectively. Even though your parents may have few of the worksheet items, check each line carefully.

Worksheet A (79) $ ☐☐☐ , ☐☐☐

Worksheet B (80) $ ☐☐☐ , ☐☐☐

Worksheet C (81) $ ☐☐☐ , ☐☐☐

82. As of today, what is the net worth of your parents' **investments,** including real estate (not their home)? **See page 2.** $ ☐☐☐ , ☐☐☐

83. As of today, what is the net worth of your parents' current **businesses and/or investment farms?** Do not include a farm that your parents live on and operate. **See page 2.** $ ☐☐☐ , ☐☐☐

84. As of today, what is your parents' total current balance of **cash, savings, and checking accounts?** $ ☐☐☐ , ☐☐☐

Now go to Step Six.

For Help – 1-800-433-3243

Page 3: Your parents' financial information

This page gathers information about your parents' financial position. Of course, if you are classified as an independent student, you can skip this part. The paper version of this page is colored differently from the other three pages of the FAFSA to indicate that parents — and not you, the dependent student — are supposed to complete this page. Of course, your parents can give you enough information to complete this section by letting you trot through their tax and bank records. Some parents, however, are uncomfortable with letting their kids know all their financial affairs.

If you're completing the paper version of the FAFSA, simply skip to Page 4 of the form. After you're done, you can give the form to your parents who can add their information on Page 3 and then mail the completed form. If you're completing the *FAFSA on the Web,* simply ask your parents to enter their information directly into the computer. When they're done, simply move on to the next questions.

If you're completing the FAFSA online, save your work at the end of each set of questions or each worksheet. If the power goes out, or if your Internet connection breaks off for any reason, periodic saving means you won't have to start all over again. Fortunately, the form lets you save and continue quickly by clicking on the "Save For Later" button at the bottom of the screen.

Parental information. Questions in this section start off with your parents' marital status, their Social Security numbers, and their last names. Remember that the names and other information you supply in this section of the FAFSA will be matched against the files of other federal agencies (especially the IRS and Social Security), so be sure that everything is accurate. A common mistake is to assume that your mother (or stepmother) has the same last name in the records as you and your father (or stepfather). This may not be the case if she applied for and received her Social Security Card before she got married to your father. If your mother simply uses your father's last name socially but never bothered to register the change legally, the IRS and Social Security may still have her listed under her pre-marriage name.

In general, a woman doesn't need to change her name when she gets married, but if she wants to use the new name for legal or governmental documents, she has to register the change. Your mother can check which name is "current" by telephoning Social Security at 1-800-772-1213.

Step Five: Complete this step only if you (the student) answered "Yes" to any question in Step Three.

85. **Go to page 7** to determine how many people are in your (and your spouse's) household.

86. **Go to page 7** to determine how many in question 85 will be college students, attending at least half time between July 1, 2003 and June 30, 2004.

Step Six: Please tell us which schools should receive your information.

Enter the 6-digit federal school code and your housing plans. Look for the federal school codes at **www.fafsa.ed.gov**, at your college financial aid office, at your public library, or by asking your high school guidance counselor. If you cannot get the federal school code, write in the complete name, address, city, and state of the college. For state aid, you may wish to list your preferred school first.

1ST FEDERAL SCHOOL CODE
87. OR NAME OF COLLEGE / ADDRESS AND CITY — STATE — HOUSING PLANS
88. on campus ○ 1 / off campus ○ 2 / with parent ○ 3

2ND FEDERAL SCHOOL CODE
89. OR NAME OF COLLEGE / ADDRESS AND CITY — STATE
90. on campus ○ 1 / off campus ○ 2 / with parent ○ 3

3RD FEDERAL SCHOOL CODE
91. OR NAME OF COLLEGE / ADDRESS AND CITY — STATE
92. on campus ○ 1 / off campus ○ 2 / with parent ○ 3

4TH FEDERAL SCHOOL CODE
93. OR NAME OF COLLEGE / ADDRESS AND CITY — STATE
94. on campus ○ 1 / off campus ○ 2 / with parent ○ 3

5TH FEDERAL SCHOOL CODE
95. OR NAME OF COLLEGE / ADDRESS AND CITY — STATE
96. on campus ○ 1 / off campus ○ 2 / with parent ○ 3

6TH FEDERAL SCHOOL CODE
97. OR NAME OF COLLEGE / ADDRESS AND CITY — STATE
98. on campus ○ 1 / off campus ○ 2 / with parent ○ 3

99. For contact by internet, provide e-mail address: _____ @ _____

Step Seven: Please read, sign, and date.

If you are the student, by signing this application you certify that you (1) will use federal and/or state student financial aid only to pay the cost of attending an institution of higher education, (2) are not in default on a federal student loan or have made satisfactory arrangements to repay it, (3) do not owe money back on a federal student grant or have made satisfactory arrangements to repay it, and (4) will notify your school if you default on a federal student loan.

If you are the parent or the student, by signing this application you agree, if asked, to provide information that will verify the accuracy of your completed form. This information may include your U.S. or state income tax forms. Also, you certify that you understand that **the Secretary of Education has the authority to verify information reported on this application with the Internal Revenue Service and other federal agencies.** If you purposely give false or misleading information, you may be fined $20,000, sent to prison, or both.

100. Date this form was completed.
MONTH / DAY / 2003 ○ or 2004 ○

101. Student (Sign below)

Parent (A parent from Step Four sign below)

If this form was filled out by someone other than you, your spouse, or your parent(s), that person must complete this part.

Preparer's name, firm, and address

102. Preparer's Social Security Number (or 103)

103. Employer ID number (or 102)

104. Preparer's signature and date

SCHOOL USE ONLY:
D/O ○ 1
FAA SIGNATURE

Federal School Code

MDE USE ONLY:
○ P ○ • ○ L ○ E

For Help — www.ed.gov/prog_info/SFA/FAFSA

Household information. You're asked to list any other kids your parents have (in other words, your brothers and sisters, if you have any) living in the same household or receiving support from them. In addition, you also need to indicate other family members receiving financial support from your parents (such as *their* parents or other relatives). The purpose of these questions is to estimate what your parents' current cash drain is this year, and what it's likely to be in the near future. The larger the drain, the larger your Pell Grant, all other things being equal.

Parents Worksheets A to C. All three of these worksheets are designed to get a better picture of your parents' financial situation and how they earn their money. Some of the questions in these worksheets can seem quite exotic or arcane. Have patience! Read through each worksheet question carefully. If you run into a snag, talk to your parents or an accountant or call the FAFSA Help Line at 1-800-433-3243 or 319-337-5665.

Current Investments. *Net worth* simply refers the current value of all the things your parents own minus the debt they carry. Other questions in this section include precise definitions of what qualifies to be included in each — and what doesn't. The Department of Education needs to understand what kinds (and amounts) of resources your parents can draw upon to help with your education. A common mistake is to wrongly include certain assets in the wrong categories, thus overstating your parents' net worth (and reducing your Pell Grant amount). For example, although you must include any real estate owned by your parents in the net worth calculation, you do *not* need to include the value of the family home.

Page 4: Select your schools and sign the FAFSA

Please tell us which schools should receive your information. In this section, you list the schools that you want to receive your FAFSA information. Both the paper and Web versions of the FAFSA have six spaces in which you can add your school choices. The paper version of the FAFSA lets you leave this section blank, but the Web version requires you to list at least one school at this time. (The software has been programmed to require a response in this field.) Both options let you change or add schools to your list later on after you get your *Student Aid Report* (SAR), which we cover in the next section.

Adding your schools when you submit your FAFSA speeds things along and helps you avoid any last-minute rushes later in the year. Every institution has at least one 6-digit Federal School Code number. The institutions with more than one code have different codes for different campuses, faculty, or even departments, so you have to get the correct one for you! If you're completing the Web-based FAFSA, the form prompts you for the number or automatically offers up the US Department of Education School Finder site (www.fafsa. ed.gov/fotw0203/fslookup.htm) if you need help.

If you're using the paper-based FAFSA and need the Federal School Codes, you can access the School Finder Web site directly, check out the college directories in your counselor's office, or drop by the main public library in your town. Of course, you can also contact the school itself by telephone, over the Web, or by e-mail.

Preparer's Social Security number. After you enter your school choices, the form asks for the preparer's Social Security number. This information is only necessary if someone else besides you, your spouse (if you're married), or your parents prepares your FAFSA. Even if that person didn't charge for her services, the preparer must add her Social Security number and sign the document (or add her organization's Federal Employer ID number).

Before you sign

Before you sign your FAFSA, take a few minutes to review the document. If you're using the online option, click on the "View FAFSA Summary" at the bottom of the page and review your answers. Is anything weird or amiss? Are any fields missing? A common mistake in the online form is adding a double character caused by holding down a key too long. For example, rather than reporting a combined income of $75,000, you enter $750,000 — quite a difference when the government is trying to assign Pell Grants based on need!

Sign the form

At this point, you have a number of choices about how you sign the FAFSA. If you're completing the form online, you (and your parents) can sign the report with your electronic personal identification numbers (PINs). Alternatively, you can print out the signature page, sign, and then mail it. A third option is to wait for the SAR to arrive, then review, sign, and return it. Obviously, if you're using the paper version of the FAFSA, you and your parents simply sign the form and mail it.

Strategy and paperwork

It's easy to become overwhelmed by all this paperwork and forget why you're spending time on the FAFSA. After all, completing the FAFSA requires a lot of effort. First, you have to gather all the materials to complete the form. Next, you have to carefully read the often-complex questions that pertain to profoundly personal information, such as how much you and your parents earned last year, what the value of their investments is, or if you've ever been convicted of a drug offense. Wow!

But take heart. The federal and state governments (and, eventually, each college from whom you're asking for money) are simply trying to help out the most needy, most deserving students. Certainly, completing all these forms is no picnic. However, neither is paying for the entire educational experience on your own. If you start early enough and gather all the paperwork you need, you'll have a rewarding experience.

Completing your FAFSA on the Web

If you have access to a computer, you can also complete your FAFSA online by visiting www.fafsa.ed.gov, a great site run by the U.S. Department of Education. The best reason to use the online option is speed: completing the form online is a *lot* faster. In fact, the Department of Education says that it will process your FAFSA as much as one to three weeks faster if you complete and sign your application electronically!

Your PIN

If this is the first time you've completed a FAFSA (if you're hoping to get into college as a freshman), you need an online *personal identification number* (usually shortened to PIN) to complete the *FAFSA on the Web*. Your PIN acts as an electronic signature for your online FAFSA activities. After you apply for and receive your PIN, the entire application process can be online. You request your PIN at www.pin.ed.gov.

Your parents will also have to request a PIN to electronically sign their part of the FAFSA. According to the Department of Education, only one *custodial* parent needs to sign your FAFSA (either the paper or online version). This means if your parents are divorced, the parent who has custody of you (or *either*, if they share joint custody) has to sign.

In case you were wondering, PINs are good forever; they don't need to be renewed. If you (or your parents) already have a PIN (perhaps from electronically signing another government form), you can reuse your PIN. If you're older brother or sister is already in college, your parents may already have a PIN because they've already signed a previous FAFSA online.

When your PIN submission has been successfully completed, a confirmation number will appear on the screen. If all the information you provided is correct and verified with other federal agencies, a PIN is generated and mailed to you. You can also have your PIN sent by e-mail if that's more convenient. You can get help by calling the PIN hotline at 1-800-801-0576.

Supported browsers

Although most browsers are supported by FAFSA, you may run into some surprises. Most recent versions of Microsoft's Internet Explorer and Netscape Communicator are supported on both the PC and the Mac platforms. America Online, however, is less supported, and some versions may not work well — or at all.

Fortunately, as soon as you log onto the *FAFSA on the Web* site at www.fafsa.ed.gov, the government's server tests your browser to check its compatibility. If you have an incompatible browser, you'll be told immediately so that you can upgrade your software or make arrangements to use a friend's computer. This potential snag is yet another reason to start the application process early!

Why is the online process faster?

The online submission process is faster because far fewer steps are involved, and you circumvent the sometimes-pokey U.S. Postal Service. Your paper-based FAFSA has to wait for your neighborhood postal worker to retrieve the envelope from the mailbox, toss it into a large mailbag with hundreds of other letters, and truck it to the sorting station. After a few days, your envelope is finally delivered by yet another delivery truck. After it arrives at the financial aid office, your application is opened and checked, and your information is entered (by hand) by a clerk who enters hundreds of FAFSAs every day. As you can imagine, problems in any one of these steps can delay your application.

The Next Steps after Completing the FAFSA

Whichever way you choose to complete the FAFSA, know that your information is speeding its way to the processing center. So what happens next? Well, read on and find out.

Receiving and reviewing the Student Aid Report (SAR)

As we mentioned earlier in this chapter, about a month after you submit the paper-based FAFSA (or just over one week if you use *FAFSA on the Web*), you'll receive your *Student Aid Report* (SAR).

The SAR lets you add or correct your financial information. This corrective step is necessary because almost every student who submits a FAFSA omits required fields or uses estimated (in other words, inaccurate) financial information.

The later you send in your FAFSA, the longer you'll probably have to wait for the SAR to come back to you. The reason? Many other students also wait until the last moment to send in their FAFSA, so the processing centers are deluged with applications at that time, slowing down responses. Even *FAFSA on the Web* bogs down when too many hopeful students access the site. We can't stress this point enough: Don't leave things to the last minute.

A key number in the SAR is your EFC. This number is important because it's what the government has calculated that you and your family can pay for your college education. Each college you selected on the FAFSA will use the EFC (and other information from the FAFSA) to figure out the amount and type of financial aid it will offer you. Many colleges also use their own forms or a standardized form called the PROFILE (discussed in Chapter 12).

All other things being equal, a lower EFC means that you're more likely to qualify for more financial aid.

As soon as you get your SAR, compare the printed numbers you see with the ones you entered on the copy of your FAFSA (that you stored away in a safe place, right?). Are they the same? If not, or if your financial circumstances have changed, correct the form and send it to the address provided. If you completed your FAFSA online, the Web site has an option to amend your information here, too. You'll need your PIN to access your account.

If you have any corrections to make or additional information to send in, do so and make a note of when you did it. Photocopy the form (or screenshot your screen), and store your new forms for safekeeping. Mail (or e-mail) back the SAR as soon as possible.

The earlier you send in the FAFSA, the faster you'll receive your SAR. If you don't get a SAR within a month of sending in your FAFSA (or within two weeks if you've completed the form online), phone the Federal Student Aid Information Center at 1-800-433-3243 (or 319-337-5665 outside the United States). Don't forget to ask for the clerk's name and write it down in your files (along with the date and what you discussed), and thank everybody for their time.

Contacting your schools

If you already know the schools to which you want to apply, contact them as soon as you get your SAR. By the time you get the printed SAR, the financial aid office of each school you selected likely already has your information. In some cases (especially if it's late in the school year or if you've earned impressive marks during your final high school year and written an exceptional SAT), aid offices may already be working on your file.

Speak with a financial aid officer for each school on your list. Ask if the school needs additional paperwork or applications completed — above and beyond the FAFSA — to apply for college financial aid. In many cases, you'll need to complete yet another form for each college. The first college application form may take an hour to complete and ask you many of the same questions as the FAFSA. By the time you start working on the forms for the fourth or fifth colleges, however, you'll probably be able to fill them out in your sleep — although we don't recommend that.

Changing your SAR if necessary

Remember to change your SAR information if your family circumstances change. The financial aid officer at your college can change the information that's used to calculate your EFC if you experience any significant change that will affect your ability to pay for college. If, for example, one (or both) of your parents loses a job or is injured and, therefore, unable to work, you can probably change your financial aid status.

Contact the financial aid office at your college immediately and ask for an adjustment to your file. You'll have to prove that your financial circumstances have changed significantly since the time you completed your FAFSA. This may mean supplying medical records, employment records (demonstrating the loss of employment), or whatever documentation is appropriate. We discuss this in more detail in Chapter 12.

Great expectations: Anticipating the size of your Pell Grant

The amount of your Pell Grant depends directly on three factors:

- ✔ **Your expected family contribution (EFC):** This amount is calculated by the Department of Education based on the information you supplied on your FAFSA.

- ✔ **The expected cost of attending (COA) the particular school:** The financial aid officer at each school estimates how much your degree or diploma will cost based on local factors, whether you want to live on campus in a residence hall or off campus at nearby housing, and other factors, such as the local cost of living.

- ✔ **Your enrollment status:** Your expenses will obviously be different if you plan to attend school on a full-time, part-time, or occasional basis.

The maximum Pell Grant amount changes every year. According to the Department of Education, the maximum award amount for the 2001/2002 school year was $3,750, and it was $4,050 for the 2003/2004 school year. The amount you get will vary, depending on your (and your family's) specific situation.

Getting your grant money

You can get your grant money in a few different ways. The school you select (and get accepted to) can apply your money directly to your tuition costs, thus reducing your overall debt. Alternatively, the school can give you a check. Or the school may opt for a combination of the two methods.

Although the school gets to decide how it disburses your money, by law, every school must tell you in writing how much your Pell Grant will be and how and when you'll be paid. In addition, your school must pay you at least once per term. Depending on your school's calendaring system, you get money every semester, trimester, or quarter.

The Federal Supplemental Educational Opportunity Grant (FSEOG)

No matter how desperate your financial position, the most you can expect from the Federal Pell Grant program is $4,050 per year. This means that the most needy students still have some way to go before they can afford college. Assuming that these students don't qualify for college scholarship, grants, or loans (more about college aid programs in Chapters 12 and 13), where can a student go to get more money for college tuition and expenses? The *Federal Supplemental Educational Opportunity Grant* (FSEOG) program, that's where!

According to the U.S. Department of Education, the FSEOG is a program designed for undergraduate students with "exceptional financial need." In plain English, you have to have a very low EFC, due to obvious poverty or immense financial drain on your parents (such as supporting lots of other kids in college or caring for elderly parents). The first students to get any money from the FSEOG program are Pell Grant recipients with the lowest EFCs. Like the Pell Grant, FSEOG monies don't have to be paid back.

How much you can get with the FSEOG

If you qualify, you can get between $100 and $4,000 a year, depending on when you apply, your financial need, and the funding offered at the school you're attending. Only undergraduate students who haven't earned a bachelor's or a professional degree are eligible for FSEOG awards.

Unlike the Federal Pell Grant program, which is directly administered by the U.S. Department of Education, the FSEOG is a *campus-based* program administered by the financial aid office at each participating college, university, or other qualifying school. Not all schools participate in the FSEOG program. So, if you think that you might need to supplement your Pell Grant due to excessive need, you should investigate which schools on your college wish list participate in the FSEOG program — and which ones don't.

Unless you and your parents have tons of money lying around for your college education, the financial aid package you receive from each college may very well dictate your realistic colleges choices.

Smart students investigate which colleges participate in the FSEOG long before application deadlines loom, especially if it can mean the difference between going to college and not.

One more thing to keep in mind: Just because a school participates in the FSEOG program doesn't necessarily mean that it'll have enough money to go around for all qualifying students. Campus-based programs, such as the FSEOG, get a given amount of cash every year. After the money is spent — which can happen quickly if lots of students at a given school apply for FSEOG — it's gone.

If a student applies late in the cycle for whatever reason, he or she may be out of luck. When the money allocated for a particular school is exhausted, no more awards are given that year. If you think that you may be eligible for FSEOG money, applying early is vital.

How the Pell Grant differs from the FSEOG

You may be wondering how the Federal Pell Grants are different from the Federal Supplemental Educational Opportunity Grant program. The main difference between the two programs is that the Department of Education's Pell Grant program guarantees that each school will receive enough money for each qualifying student.

No such guarantee exists with the FSEOG program. Each participating school receives a certain amount of FSEOG money each year. Whichever eligible students ask for the money first receive their awards. Those who don't ask (or wait too long to ask) have to look elsewhere for money.

Deadlines for FSEOG

Because the FSEOG is a campus-based program, deadlines vary by school — but they're just about always *earlier* than the annual FAFSA filing deadline. Early on in your final year of high school, investigate the FSEOG deadlines for each school on your wish list.

To get this information, you can contact the financial aid office in each school. Often, these deadlines are posted on the college Web site under the financial aid section, but it makes sense to double-check things with the aid office just in case the Web site hasn't been updated in a while.

Chapter 6

Getting Help from Federal Loans

- -

In This Chapter

▶ Learning what you need to know about loans

▶ Qualifying for federal loans

▶ Understanding Stafford, PLUS, Perkins, and Consolidation loans

- -

*I*n a perfect world, you wouldn't need loans to go to college. Your friendly Uncle Sam would fully realize the benefits of an educated population and would pay everybody's school expenses — even to the priciest colleges and universities in the country. Back in the real world, however, the government already spends approximately $70 *billion* to send millions of students off to college every year. Thus, the unfortunate reality: Loan money has to top off most grants.

Okay, so the thought of a loan may not sound quite as good as a grant (see Chapter 5), but the low interest rates of many federal loan programs are *effectively free* money, because you pay back much less than you do with a traditional loan. So, in this chapter, we outline how the interest (or at least part of the interest) on your student loan can be free.

Taking out college loans are usually a student's first foray into interest and debt. Helping you through this potentially nerve-racking ordeal is our goal in this chapter, which also explains the concepts behind loans, interest, credit histories, and repayment schedules. We also discuss the specifics of several federal loan programs including Stafford Loans, PLUS Loans, Federal Perkins Loans, and Consolidation Loans. Ready? Okay, let's get borrowing.

Loans and Lending 101

If you were to ask a banker to define a loan, he or she would likely tell you that a *loan* is a sum of money borrowed by a creditworthy individual (or organization) for a specific time, that must be repaid with interest.

Loans are an integral part of modern-day life. For instance, few people have the cash to buy a home outright, but they can purchase a residence through a mortgage from the bank. The bank pays the previous owner, and you pay back the *principal* (the original amount) plus a percentage of *interest* (the charge required for the use of the money) over time to the bank. We should point out that the interest percentage may be small, but it adds up so much over time that you often end up repaying more interest than principal.

Broadly speaking, loans come in two varieties: secured and unsecured. A loan is said to be *secured* when the borrower provides collateral that the lender can seize whenever the borrower is unable or unwilling to repay the loan. A house mortgage is considered a secured loan because the bank can seize (and resell) a house if the borrower can't make the mortgage payments. Secured loans are how the bank protects its large loan amount from loss.

A credit card is a good example of an *unsecured loan.* Lending institutions extend credit (loans) to many people knowing that some of these debtors will default. Rather than asking for security for the loan — as in the case with a mortgage — the banks simply jack up the interest rates to all customers to cover their losses. In effect, to make getting a credit card easy (some would say, too easy), the bank makes borrowers who repay their loans pay the same interest rates as people who walk away from the loans. Because the bank can't accurately predict who will default on their loans, it penalizes its good customers to make up for the bad ones.

In general, banks want their loans to be repaid in cash, and they don't want to seize houses to get it. Seizing houses is a big hassle for the institution, and it generates plenty of bad public relations. Banks, therefore, try to issue loans only to *creditworthy* individuals: those with good jobs, who earn good money and who haven't defaulted on a loan before. Keeping a good credit rating is important because it directly affects your ability to get loans, find a good job, get security clearance, buy a car, and purchase a house.

Interest rates are related to risk

In theory, the interest you pay helps the bank stay in business and pay its staff. Interest income from loans is a key way that lending institutions make a profit and pay their shareholders for the risks they assume in loaning out money to people who may default on their loans.

Although the U.S. Federal Reserve Bank periodically sets the nation's base (interest) rate, each lending institution is pretty much allowed to set its own lending rate to its own customers. The people with good credit histories are usually given lower interest rates.

If a bank or other lending institution thinks that *yours* is a risky loan, it can do the following:

- ✔ **Refuse your loan request.** After all, the bank is a business, not a charity. To stay in business, a bank must show a profit on all (or, at least, most) of its loans. When it doesn't, it goes out of business.

- ✔ **Jack up its interest rate for your loan.** The bank rationalizes that a higher interest rate balances the increased risk of losing out on the deal.

- ✔ **Require a guarantor.** Essentially, a *guarantor* is a person with a better credit rating than you, who's willing to guarantee your loan. When you don't pay, your *guarantor* is on the hook for your loan. Sometimes, a bank may ask your parents to guarantee your loan when you have little or no credit history. If you default on the loan, the bank demands repayment from your parents. If your parents take out a mortgage to guarantee your loan, your parents may even lose their home.

Understanding your credit history

Students rarely have good credit histories. For that matter, students rarely have *bad* credit histories. Most students have no credit history at all because they've never taken out a loan, let alone paid off (or *discharged*) a loan. In general, the more you repeat the cycle of loan/regular repayment/discharge, the better your credit history will be.

People wind up with bad credit histories by not paying back their loans on a timely basis. For example, when you fail to make your monthly credit card payments, banks grow understandably nervous because they don't see any money coming back to them. When you miss a payment or two, the bank reports these incidents to the *credit bureau* with which it deals. In some cases, even being late taking a *video* back to the rental store can be entered into your credit history, much to the dismay of people who tend to "forget" things.

When other banks or credit-granting institutions run a check to verify your creditworthiness as a prospective borrower, they can see any problems that the other institutions reported. It's all listed on the individual credit report that the credit bureau compiles in your name. Depending on the severity of the problems, a lender may ask for collateral to secure your new loan, increase the rate of interest of your loan (to compensate for its increased risk), or simply not grant you the loan.

Because we're talking about student loans in this chapter, you need to bear in mind that, although defaulting on a student loan messes up your credit rating big time, it can cause much more damage than that:

- ✔ If you default on your student loan, you won't be able to get federal jobs.

- ✔ Some states won't issue you a driver's license or renew a professional license when you're in default on your student loans.

- ✔ Perhaps worst of all, the federal government has the right to keep any tax return money you may have coming to you or even seize your wages (technically called *garnishee* but usually just referred to as *garnish* these days) until your debt is repaid.

Alas, at times, some people have repayment problems despite their best intentions. Perhaps you recently lost your job, or your spouse had large, unexpected medical expenses, or you've experienced financial loses on the stock market. Regardless of the cause, notifying the credit grantor immediately is vital whenever there may be a repayment problem.

The good news is that the bank or other institution usually works out some form of revised repayment plan with you to accommodate your new financial realities. In all but only a few cases, paying back just a few dollars a month keeps a bank happy — at least in the short term. Although still saddled with the debt, the borrower's credit rating nevertheless remains intact.

Because banks and other credit-granting institutions don't want people to default on loans, they often err on the side of being cautious — sometimes overly cautious. That means money is usually loaned only to people who can afford to repay the debt, which leads to more than one rejected loan applicant quipping, "The bank turned down my loan because I actually *needed* the money."

Qualifying for Federal Loans

Four major types of federal loans are available to students or their parents: Stafford Loans, PLUS Loans, Perkins Loans, and Consolidation Loans. Each type of loan is aimed at a different set of people, each has its own interest rate and repayment terms, and each has its own advantages and disadvantages.

Under various federal loan programs, undergraduates and graduate students are eligible for loans, and so are their parents. The maximum loan that any student can receive depends on the specific loan program (some pay out more than others) and the level of study (more money is usually available to students in higher years).

Some loans are paid to the school of your choice. Some are paid directly to you, and you must use the funds for college-related expenses.

Likewise, some loans are *subsidized,* which means that you don't pay interest on them until you graduate or otherwise leave school. In other cases, the loans are *unsubsidized,* meaning that you're charged interest from the day the loan is sent to you to the day you pay it back. If you don't keep up-to-date with the interest payments, the interest is compounded (the official government term is *capitalized*), and you end up paying interest on the interest, making your eventual repayment even more difficult.

All federal student aid (as well as state and college aid) begins with the completion of the *Free Application for Federal Student Aid* (FAFSA), which we discuss in Chapter 5. Prospective students who want a federal college loan must meet specific eligibility requirements, similar to the way they must meet eligibility requirements to receive federal grants (see Chapter 5). These requirements include the following:

- ✔ **You must have a high school diploma, a GED (a *General Education Development*) certificate, or equivalent.**

- ✔ **You must be enrolled as a regular student working toward a degree or a certificate in what the government calls an *eligible program.*** This definition changes periodically, but in general, it means that your courses must lead to a degree or certificate. You can't just take a bunch of courses in different subjects that don't lead anywhere and expect to get a loan. In addition, some loan programs have further requirements, so ask your college financial aid officer whether your program qualifies for each type of loan.

- ✔ **You must be a U.S. citizen or eligible non-citizen.** Because Uncle Sam is, in most cases, guaranteeing your student loan to the bank, he wants to know you'll stick around to repay the loan.

- ✔ **You must have a valid Social Security number.** If you don't already have one — you'll need one to complete your FAFSA — you can get one through your local Social Security office (in the government pages of your local telephone directory or online at www.ssa.gov).

- ✔ **If you're a male, between the ages of 18 and 25, you must also register with Selective Service.** If you've already completed the FAFSA, you'll probably recall that your status with the Selective Service is one of the questions on the application. You can get more information about Selective Service at www.sss.gov.

- ✔ **You must make *satisfactory academic progress* at your school and not be in default of existing student loans.** In other words, you have to pass your courses, and you can't get a further loan to pay off the first loan, unless it's a *Consolidation Loan* (which we explain later in this chapter).

The sections that follow describe each of your loan options in detail, so keep reading to find out which ones work best for you.

Footing the Bill with Stafford Loans

Stafford Loans are a huge source of financial help for many students every year. Stafford Loans come from two different sources, and each respective school chooses the way it uses money from the Stafford program. You can attend a school that either:

✔ Uses the *Direct Loan Program,* in which the U.S. government *directly* loans you the money that you need for school. Under this program, the federal government is your lender and you repay the loan to Uncle Sam (although you don't actually write "Uncle Sam" on your check).

✔ Disburses Stafford Loans in which the U.S. government *indirectly* loans you the money through its *Federal Family Education Loan* (FFEL) Program. Under this program, third-party lenders such as banks, credit unions, and other institutions are your lenders and you repay them.

The key difference between the two programs is who is lending you the money. In the first case, the federal government loans you the money; in the second case, a third-party lending institution loans you the money. In some cases, colleges may offer *both* loan programs (although this is somewhat rare). Your loan may be paid directly to you (in which case you turn around and pay your school). In other cases, the loan is simply credited to your student account. It depends on the accounting system at your college.

Subsidized and unsubsidized Staffords

Stafford Loans are classified as either subsidized or unsubsidized (see "Qualifying for Federal Loans" section earlier in this chapter). A subsidized Stafford Loan is awarded based on financial need, similar to the process involved with the Federal Pell Grants that we discuss in Chapter 5. Under this option, you won't be charged any interest until after you graduate, drop out, or leave school for other reasons. Soon after that time, interest kicks in and you have to start making periodic payments. Of course, if you can pay off the loan in full at that time, you won't have to pay any interest.

Unsubsidized loans are less advantageous than their subsidized counterparts because subsidized loans give you a free ride, without the need to service the debt (in other words, pay interest), while you're in school.

During your years in school, the federal government subsidizes your loan interest, so you can catch a break. After you graduate, Stafford Loans support a six-month grace period during which time you can hopefully get a job and start earning the money you need to repay your student loans. After the loan's six-month grace period ends, you must start paying back your loan based on one of three (if it's a FFEL Stafford Loan) or four (if it's a Direct Stafford Loan) repayment options. For more info on repayment, see the section, "Paying back your Stafford Loan," later in this chapter.

As you can probably guess, unsubsidized Stafford Loans are not subsidized by the U.S. government, meaning that interest is charged on them from the time they're disbursed until you completely pay them off.

How much can you get?

Got you thinking, huh? So now you're probably wondering why doesn't everyone just go for the subsidized Stafford Loans and forgo the unsubsidized ones? Well, there is a catch. Subsidized Staffords are awarded to students with low *expected family contribution* (EFC) amounts, based on the information they supply in their FAFSAs.

Dependent students

Right now, the *maximum* Stafford Loan for first-year *dependent* students is $2,625. It's possible to have a low enough EFC that all of your Stafford Loan for the first year will be allocated to a subsidized loan. If, however, your EFC is higher, you may have some of your Stafford Loan awarded as a subsidized loan with the remainder (up to the $2,625 maximum) awarded as an unsubsidized loan. Obviously, you don't have to sign up for the unsubsidized part of the loan, if you don't want to, because you'll have to pay interest on the unsubsidized portion as soon as it's disbursed to you.

As we say in the "Qualifying for Federal Loans" section earlier in this chapter, students receive more financial aid the further along in school they advance. During your second year at college, as a dependent student, you can get a maximum of $3,500 in Stafford Loans. And depending on your FAFSA-calculated EFC, this amount can be completely subsidized, partly subsidized, or totally unsubsidized.

In your third and fourth years, the maximum Stafford Loans available for dependent students is $5,500 for each year. As with the first and second years, the Stafford Loans awarded during the third and fourth years can either be fully subsidized, partly subsidized, or totally unsubsidized.

The maximum total debt dependent students can incur is $23,000 over four years. At first glance, this amount doesn't seem to add up. After all, when you add the maximum Stafford Loan amounts for all four years, you get a total of $17,125, far less than the $23,000 maximum. What gives?

Well, now we can tell you about another piece of the puzzle. The remaining $5,875 is an amount above and beyond the normal Stafford Loans allowance that is given only to students whose parents don't qualify for PLUS Loans, because of bad credit or other factors. We discuss PLUS Loans later in this chapter. Under these somewhat unusual circumstances, students retain their dependent status but they're also able to take on what normally would be their parents' portion of their school debt.

Independent students

If the U.S. Department of Education rules that you're an *independent student* based on your responses to the FAFSA, you can borrow more than dependent students. Unlike dependent students, for example, first-year independent students can borrow up to $6,625 in Stafford Loans, but only up to $2,625 of that amount can be subsidized.

In your second year as an independent student, you can borrow up to $7,500, with up to $3,500 of that amount being subsidized. In their final two years of college, independent students can borrow up to $10,500 each year from the Stafford Loan program, with up to $5,500 eligible to be subsidized per year.

As an independent undergraduate student you can max out your Stafford Loans at a whopping $46,000, but only $23,000 of it can be subsidized by the U.S. government.

Table 6-1 outlines the maximum Stafford Loans amounts for dependent and independent undergraduate students.

Table 6-1	Yearly Stafford Loan Maximum Amounts	
Year	Dependent Student	Independent Student
1	$2,625	$6,625 (subsidized portion is capped at $2,625)
2	$3,500	$7,500 (subsidized portion is capped at $3,500)
3	$5,500	$10,500 (subsidized portion is capped at $5,500)
4	$5,500	$10,500 (subsidized portion is capped at $5,500)
Total	$23,000	$46,000 (subsidized portion is capped at $23,000)

Graduate students

Graduate students are automatically considered independent. They're allowed to borrow up to $18,500 per year (but only up to $8,500 can be subsidized per year). In addition, the maximum amount that graduate or professional students can borrow is $138,500 during the course of their entire academic studies, including undergraduate studies, and only $65,000 of that amount can be borrowed in subsidized loans.

Interest rates for Stafford loans

By law, the interest rate on your Stafford Loan can't exceed 8.25 percent, and the actual rate is fixed once a year in late June. These days, the rate is much lower than the maximum 8.25 percent because of the low Federal Reserve interest rates. For example, interest rates for Stafford Loans during the repayment period from July 1, 2001, to June 30, 2002, were 5.99 percent. The rate for the period from July 1, 2002, to June 30, 2003, dropped all the way down to 4.06 percent.

Paying back your Stafford loan

When you leave college, you'll receive information about repaying your loan. Your repayment will depend on three factors including your total debt when you graduate, the number of years you intend to take for repayment, and the type of repayment plan you choose.

Under the *Standard Repayment Plan,* for example, students can take 10 years to repay their Stafford loans and have a fixed amount every month. Under the *Extended Repayment Plan,* students take between 12 and 30 years to repay. The advantage of the Extended Plan is that you repay a lower monthly amount (in comparison to the Standard plan). The disadvantage is that it takes years more to repay your debt (and, thus, is more expensive).

Other payment plans include the *Graduated Repayment Plan* (in which you pay lower payments at first and then higher amounts than you would otherwise under the standard plan), and the *Income Contingent Repayment Plan* (in which — you guessed it — your repayment amounts are directly linked to your ability to repay).

Postponing the inevitable — deferring (or discharging) your loan repayments

Under special circumstances, you can receive a deferment on the repayment of your Stafford Loan. When your Stafford Loan is subsidized, you won't be charged additional interest during your deferment. If, however, your Stafford Loan is unsubsidized, you still are responsible for the interest even when your loan is in deferment. In either case, you won't have to repay the loan *principal* until your deferment period ends.

In some cases, you may receive a deferment of your Stafford Loan if you're unable to find full-time employment after you graduate, or if you experience severe economic hardship. For example, many Peace Corps volunteers are eligible for Stafford Loan deferment based on economic hardship.

If deferment is of interest to you (get it, *interest?*), you need to know a couple of things. First, your loan can't be in default. If it is, you must contact the holder of the loan and get back on a satisfactory payment program. Second, you must keep making payments until you receive approval for your defer-ment. You can't simply contact the loans office, ask for the deferment, and then stop paying.

In some cases, you may be able to cancel your Stafford Loan debt. When your debt is canceled (or, to use the technical term, *discharged*), your debt is com-pletely forgiven. In case you're wondering, your loan won't be canceled just because you dropped out of college, because you didn't like the particular college, or because you couldn't find a job after you graduated. Sorry.

It can, however, be canceled if you qualify under one of the following specific circumstances:

- ✔ You become a full-time elementary or secondary teacher for five consec-utive years in an area that serves low-income families. This obligation is not to be taken lightly. Some of these areas can be pretty blighted, and it takes a special person to do the job.

- ✔ Your school closes before you can complete your program. This doesn't happen often, but it does happen.

- ✔ Your school doesn't pay out your loan amount.

- ✔ You file for bankruptcy (but only if the bankruptcy court decides that your student loan needs to be discharged — and that doesn't happen too often any more).

- ✔ You die or become permanently disabled, making work impossible.

Letting Your Parents Borrow with PLUS Loans

So your mother carried you for nine months and then struggled 42 hours in labor. So your parents worked like dogs to provide a nice home, cool clothes, and your own bedroom with high-speed Internet access. Naturally, they ferried you to and from Little League, hockey practice, gymnastics, swimming lessons, and overnight camp. How can you repay them for all this? Ask them to take out a PLUS Loan for your college education, of course!

PLUS is an acronym for *Parent Loans for Undergraduate Students*. This acronym emphasizes the fact that these *loans* are aimed at *parents* of kids who are *undergraduate students* at colleges. If you're working on your master's or professional degree, you'll have to go elsewhere for financial aid.

Like the Stafford Loan program, PLUS Loans involve financial aid for college. Unlike the Stafford Loans, which are aimed at student borrowers, PLUS Loans let *parents* who have good credit borrow to help finance their kids' college expenses. To qualify for PLUS Loans, parents must have children attending an approved educational institution who are enrolled at least half-time.

Parents who want to take advantage of the program must pass a credit check to verify that they can repay their loans. Most people pass the check, but even if they don't, they still may be able to help out if someone who's more creditworthy can guarantee the loan. Parents applying for PLUS Loans generally must pass the same general requirements as students applying for Stafford Loans. Like students, parents can't be in default of other financial aid programs to qualify.

By law, interest rates for PLUS Loans are set once a year but can never exceed 9 percent. In practice, the rate is usually well below the stated maximum, and the PLUS rate has been trending lower during the past few years. For example, the interest rate for PLUS Loans from July 1, 2001, to June 30, 2002, (the 2001/2002 school year) was 6.79 percent. Because of low overall interest rates, the PLUS Loan repayment rate dropped to 4.86 percent during the 2002/2003 school year.

Getting the money

Similar to Stafford Loans, PLUS Loans have a maximum allowable amount that can be borrowed.

Your parents can borrow up to the difference between the cost of your attendance and any other financial aid you, the student, receive (a number set by your school's financial aid office). So if the cost for you to attend college is $7,000, and you receive $4,500 in financial aid from other sources (including Pell Grants, Stafford Loans, and a Federal Supplemental Educational Opportunity Grant), your parents can borrow up to $2,500.

PLUS Loans have other similarities with Stafford Loans. For one thing, a borrower can be paid one of two ways under the PLUS Loans program: a Direct PLUS Loan or a FFEL PLUS Loan.

As you may have guessed (especially if you read the earlier section about "Footing the Bill Yourself with Stafford Loans"), you deal directly with the U.S. Department of Education when obtaining a Direct PLUS Loan. In contrast, you deal with a third-party lending institution if you take out a FFEL PLUS Loan. Whichever PLUS Loan you take, the U.S. government guarantees both Direct PLUS and FFEL PLUS versions.

Your college must adhere to a specific order when crediting your PLUS Loans to the amount you owe for your college education. First and foremost, your college must apply the money directly to college-related costs such as tuition, academic and nonacademic fees, and room and board. If any money is left over, your parents are usually issued a check by your college, and they, in turn, cash it and distribute the money to you during the school year, rather like an allowance.

The school can, in some situations, release the money directly to you (usually adding it to your student account), but they first must get your parents' permission to do so. After all, your parents are on the hook for the PLUS Loan, and it's their money. So their having some say in how the money's distributed is only fair, right?

Direct PLUS versus FFEL PLUS

The difference between Direct PLUS and FFEL PLUS Loans is small. They are both aimed at parents who have children in college, both require a regular repayment of the principal and interest, and both have the same rules concerning *forbearance* (the postponement of repaying the principal) and discharge (cancellation of the entire loan).

So what's the difference? Well, the main difference between the two programs involves exactly *who* is actually loaning the money to your parents.

With a Direct PLUS Loan, the federal government is the lender. Your repayment checks are made out to the U.S. Department of Education. A FFEL Loan, on the other hand, is made through a local bank or other participating financial institution. When your parents start paying off a PLUS Loan under the FFEL program, they make their check out to the particular bank from which the loan is drawn. Both programs:

- ✔ Provide the same type of "topping up" effect to the overall financial aid package
- ✔ Have similar repayment options
- ✔ Can be consolidated (find more about consolidation in the next section)

So why would a student (or her parent) choose one type of PLUS Loan over another? Fortunately, the choice is made for you.

As it turns out, just as it is for Stafford Loans, each college deals with either one type of PLUS Loan program or the other. Colleges are not permitted to deal with both types of PLUS Loan programs. You need to contact the individual financial aid offices of the colleges on your wish list to determine which program is used at the particular college. You can do so either by telephone or by visiting each college's Web site.

Because a college chooses whether to participate in either the Direct PLUS Loans program or the FFEL PLUS Loans program, this situation is one of the few instances that your college — and not you or your parents — decides which federal aid option you follow.

Whenever a college opts for the FFEL PLUS program, your parents must select a bank or other lending institution with which to arrange the loan paperwork and repayment schedule.

Each FFEL-based college aid program gives parents a list of participating institutions in their area. In other situations, parents are expected to find their own lending institutions. The bank where your parents already have their accounts, mortgage, and other financial dealings may be set up to provide FFEL PLUS Loans and should be the first place you look for a lending institution.

If your parents are still without a lending institution for their FFEL PLUS Loan, here's an easy way to find one. Each state has a *guaranty agency* that can provide a list of appropriate local lending institutions. A directory of these agencies also can be found at www.ed.gov/Programs/bastmp/SGA.htm.

Sorry, Pop, you gotta pay now

Unlike Stafford Loans, PLUS loans feature neither a grace period during which no payments are due nor any period during which interest does not accrue. In other words, as soon as your parents cash the PLUS Loan check (or the money from a PLUS Loan hits your account at college), the interest clock starts ticking. Thus, to maintain their credit rating, your parents must start paying off the PLUS Loans immediately and continue paying on a regular basis until the debt (and its interest) is completely repaid.

Postponing repayment of your PLUS Loan may be possible — known as *forbearance*. The same conditions that apply for you to get a postponement of your Stafford Loan also apply to your parents when they're seeking forbearance on their PLUS Loan. This means that your parents can't be in default, and they must keep making payments until they receive approval for deferment. That said, postponing your PLUS Loan repayment doesn't provide much of an advantage. Unlike Stafford Loans, PLUS Loans never are subsidized, and because interest begins accruing as soon as the loan is disbursed, parents must continue paying interest to service their loan, otherwise the government (or other lending institution) will compound the interest on the loan.

It may be possible to discharge (or cancel) your PLUS Loan. Similar to a Stafford Loan, a set of conditions is imposed on discharging a PLUS Loan. For example, it can be cancelled if the school you're attending closes before you're able to finish your degree.

Whenever you have a Direct PLUS Loan and need information about cancellations, contact the Direct Loan Servicing Center at 1-800-848-0979. If you have a FFEL PLUS Loan and need such information, contact the particular lender that holds the loan.

Finding That Last Bit in Perkins Loans

Like Stafford Loans, Federal Perkins Loans are loans guaranteed by the U.S. Department of Education and are available for undergraduates and graduate students. Unlike Stafford Loans, however, Federal Perkins Loans have a fixed rate of interest and are made by your college or other institution (the government gives the college the money, and the college distributes it). Federal Perkins Loans cannot be subsidized by the U.S. Department of Education.

Not all schools participate in the Federal Perkins Loan program, so if you expect that you'll need more money than the Stafford and PLUS Loans can provide, find out whether your college supports Perkins Loans well in advance.

When it comes time to repay your Perkins Loan, you make your checks out to your school — not to the government (as you would for a Direct Loan) or a third-party (as you would for a FFEL Loan). The amount that you can borrow under the Perkins Loans program is determined based on three factors:

✓ **When you apply.** Different colleges have different application deadlines for Federal Perkins Loans, typically *much* earlier than the June 30 FAFSA submission deadline (and very possibly earlier than your state deadline). In fact, you may not be granted your Perkins Loan if your application arrives too late for the school's particular deadline.

✓ **Your level of need.** How much of a Federal Perkins Loan you qualify for is determined by your college and is based on a number of factors including your expected family contribution (EFC) and your college's cost of attendance (COA). The maximum annual loan allowed is $4,000 for undergraduate students and $6,000 for graduate students.

The choice of how much of the maximum you borrow is entirely up to you. Even after you arrange (and are approved for) the loan, you can cancel and back away from the deal within 14 days after the date your school sends you notice that it will pay you the requested amount.

✓ **The funding level of your school.** Some schools do not participate in the Perkins Loan program; others do so but at varying amounts. Although individual schools technically can't run out of Perkins money, the level of Perkins Loans at which a particular college wants to participate can reach its limit before you're approved.

Schools generally pay out Perkins Loan payments twice a year, and they usually disburse the money by check to you or by direct deposit to your student account. Typically, you have ten years to pay back any funds disbursed under the Federal Perkins Loan program.

Putting off your Perkins payments

You automatically get a nine-month grace period with a Perkins Loan, but there may be ways to postpone repayment even longer. Under a deferment, you can temporarily stop repayment of your Perkins Loan to prevent interest from accruing. Deferment rules for Federal Perkins Loans are somewhat more relaxed than for other federal loans programs.

✔ If your course load stays above half-time student status, your Perkins Loan will be deferred. Only after you leave school and your cumulative nine-month grace period ends (or your academic course load drops below half-time) does your loan become payable.

✔ If you're a student in an approved graduate fellowship program or in an approved rehabilitation-training program for the disabled, your Perkins Loans will be deferred.

✔ If you're unable to find work on a full-time basis, deferring your Perkins Loans repayments for up to three years may be possible.

✔ If you encounter severe economic hardship, you may be able to defer your repayments for up to three years.

✔ If you become a community service worker in such professions as law enforcement, corrections, teaching in designated low-income areas, or other vocations as described in the next section, you may be able to defer your Perkins Loans *indefinitely*. You can find more information about teaching-based deferments by checking out www.ed.gov/offices/OSFAP/Students/repayment/teachers/.

As with other types of loans, you must apply for your forbearance or postponement. You can't simply satisfy one of the above conditions and stop paying. You must continue to make your payments until you receive official notification that your Perkins Loans are in forbearance or deferral. Otherwise, you may find yourself in loan default or other financial difficulties.

Canceling your debt

Out and out cancellations (or *discharges*) of your Perkins Loan debt is also possible under any of several of the following conditions:

✔ If you enlist in certain specialties in the U.S. Armed Forces, the Department of Defense may repay a portion of your Perkins Loan. Technically speaking, this payment won't necessarily *cancel* your loan, but if your loan is relatively small, it may have the same effect. Otherwise, up to 50 percent of your Perkins Loan can be forgiven provided that you serve in areas of hostilities or imminent danger.

✔ If you become a full-time teacher at a designated elementary or secondary school in a low-income area, up to 100 percent of your Perkins Loan can be forgiven.

✔ If you become a full-time special education teacher or a teacher of children with diagnosed learning disabilities at an elementary school, a secondary school, or a nonprofit institution, up to 100 percent of your Perkins Loan can be forgiven.

✔ If you perform early intervention services for the elderly on a full-time, professional basis, up to 100 percent of your Perkins Loan can be forgiven.

✔ If you become a full-time teacher of math, science, languages, bilingual education, or other fields designated by the U.S. Department of Education, up to 100 percent of your Perkins Loan can be forgiven.

✔ If you become a full-time employee of a public or nonprofit agency that provides specific services to high-risk kids or their families in poor communities, up to 100 percent of your Perkins Loan can be forgiven.

✔ If you become a full-time nurse or medical technician, up to 100 percent of your Perkins Loan can be forgiven.

✔ If you serve as a full-time law enforcement or corrections officer, up to 100 percent of your Perkins Loan can be forgiven.

✔ If you become a full-time staff member in the education division of a Head Start Program, up to 100 percent of the Perkins Loan amount can be forgiven.

✔ If you enlist in the VISTA Program or become a Peace Corps volunteer, up to 70 percent of your Perkins Loan can be forgiven.

✔ In rare cases, if you go bankrupt, up to 100 percent of your Perkins Loan can be forgiven, provided that the applicable bankruptcy court rules that repayment would cause undue financial hardship.

✔ If your school closes before you can complete the program in which you enrolled (and for which you received Perkins Loans), 100 percent of the loan amount can be forgiven.

✔ If you die or become permanently (and seriously) disabled, 100 percent of your Perkins Loan will be forgiven.

Simplifying Your Life with Consolidation Loans

A *Consolidation Loan* helps students and parents simplify the college loan repayment process. As you may guess from its name, a Consolidation Loan combines or *consolidates* various student loans that are active under your account.

All federal student loans discussed in this chapter are eligible to be combined into one consolidated loan. You can even use the Consolidation Loan program when you have only one loan.

Consolidation Loans are also useful whenever you want to extend your repayment duration from a maximum of 10 years allowable under the Standard Repayment Plan associated with the Stafford Loan to a maximum of 30 years allowable under the Consolidation Loan program. Although you can get longer repayment schedules with Stafford and PLUS Loans, Consolidation Loans have an added advantage. They enable you to roll all your (possibly varied) payments into one easy-to-handle monthly installment.

Besides extending the repayment period, a Consolidation Loan also offers potentially lower monthly payments, albeit for a longer overall repayment period. In addition, a Consolidation Loan can offer a way out when you've defaulted on your loan. Despite the default, you can find ways of rolling your existing loans into a Consolidation Loan, provided certain restructuring conditions are met.

As with the Stafford and PLUS loans, you can secure a Consolidation Loan from two sources:

- ✔ Direct Consolidation Loans are available directly from the U.S. government, specifically from the U.S. Department of Education.

- ✔ FFEL Consolidation Loans are available from a variety of participating banks, credit unions, and other lending institutions.

Blending your payments

A few years ago, Consolidation Loans had variable interest rates similar to Stafford and PLUS loans. So, if your older brother was in college then, he may have contended with Consolidation Loan payments that changed from year to year. Since February 1999, however, all Consolidation Loans have had a fixed interest rate, which makes planning future payments much easier.

Interest rates on Consolidation Loans can never exceed 8.25 percent, but rates have been much lower than that in recent years because of lower Federal Reserve rates. Consolidation Loans rely on a *weighted average* of the existing loans to be incorporated into the larger loan.

For example, say that you have two existing loans, one for $10,000 at 5 percent and another for $5,000 at 6 percent. A Consolidation Loan creates payments based on a total of $15,000 debt, at an interest rate that takes into consideration that two-thirds of the debt ($10,000 in this case) carries the interest rate of 5 percent and the other one-third ($5,000) carries a rate of 6 percent. In this example, the interest on the new Consolidation Loan should be 5.33 percent; however, interest rates for Consolidation Loans are rounded to the next highest eighth of a percent, so the new rate is 5.375 percent.

For this example, we assumed that both loans have the same remaining time left before they're properly discharged. In real life, however, you can have different loans, at different rates of interest, that extend over different periods of time, especially when you consider that you can have two, three, or four loans for each of your four years in college! As you can imagine, figuring out Consolidation Loans is quite complex!

What's nice about a Consolidation Loan is that all this magic is done behind the scenes because the folks who work out your Consolidation Loan (either the U.S. Department of Education or a third-party lending institution) simply take all your information and give you a repayment schedule. The only thing that you have to worry about is making those payments.

By law, a participating lending institution can't refuse to give you a Consolidation Loan based on the number or type of loans that you want to combine into the one loan (as long as all loans are eligible). Nor can it refuse a loan based on your school choice, school type, or the length of repayment schedule you want. Best of all, the consolidator can't refuse to offer the new loan just because the interest on other loans it holds in your account is more than you'd otherwise pay under the Consolidation Loan.

Consolidating your Stafford or PLUS Loans

If you have Direct Loans (such as Direct Stafford or Direct PLUS loans), you can get a Consolidation Loan while still attending school, during your grace period after you graduate, or once you've entered the repayment period. You can also get a Consolidation Loan when your loans are in deferment (a scheduled postponement) or forbearance (an unscheduled and temporary postponement). Most FFEL and Direct loans have six-month grace periods, whereas a Perkins Loan (which we discuss in the previous section) has a grace period of nine months.

When you have a FFEL-based loan, you have to get in touch with your FFEL lender and ask specifically whether you can roll your debt into a Consolidation Loan. If you can't get a Consolidation Loan from your lender but you're eligible for a program called the Direct Loan Income Contingent Repayment Plan, you can apply for a Direct Consolidation Loan. If you subsequently receive a Direct Consolidation Loan, the folks that you write checks to every month changes from the third-party lending institution to the U.S. Department of Education.

Repaying Consolidation Loans

Generally speaking, four repayment plans are possible for students who have taken Consolidation Loans. In some cases — notably when FFEL Loans are involved — the third-party lender may or may not offer all these payment plans. By law, however, repayment information must be disclosed when you take out your Consolidation Loan.

- ✔ **The Standard Repayment Plan:** Under the Standard Repayment Plan, your credit grantor calculates fixed monthly payments for a maximum of 10 years.

- ✔ **The Extended Repayment Plan:** Under the Extended Repayment Plan, your fixed monthly payments are guaranteed to be less than payments under the Standard Plan. The bad news is that your repayment period under this option ranges from 12 to 30 years, depending on the overall amount of your Consolidation Loan. So you'll have payments for longer, perhaps *much* longer, than with the Standard plan.

- ✔ **The Graduated Repayment Plan:** The Graduated Repayment Plan offers monthly payments that increase every two years. The advantage of this plan is that it more closely matches after-college reality when earning power usually rises with time (and job experience). This plan offers repayment periods varying from 12 to 30 years, depending on how much debt you roll into your Consolidation Loan.

- ✔ **The Income Contingent Repayment Plan (ICR):** The ICR offers monthly payments that are based on your annual income, family size, and overall debt. ICR repayments can be spread across up to 25 years.

  The ICR is not available for Direct PLUS Loan borrowers, but a plan similar to the ICR, known as the Income Sensitive Repayment Plan, is available for FFEL program borrowers.

You can get more information about Consolidation Loan options from the Loan Origination Center's Consolidation Department at 1-800-577-7392 or on the Web at www.loanconsolidation.ed.gov.

Chapter 7

Signing Up for Other Federal Benefits

*B*y some accounts, the complete set of tax acts of the United States of America, including all the supplementary manuals, forms, official notices, publications, explanations, position papers, and other assorted paperwork, stretches to more than 300,000 pages. If these estimates are true — nobody seems to know for sure — you could place all these pages end to end and make a trail more than 52 miles long!

Added to this adventure is the fact that each *state* has its own complex tax legislation, assorted forms, and interpretation bulletins, as well as other helpful publications. In short, you have a pretty complicated mass of information concerning how to keep on the right side of the folks at the tax departments. And when you factor in trying to get the best deal (and most free money) for college, the process is even more complicated. That's why we're here to simplify it for you.

This chapter outlines two important federal tax credit programs: the Hope Scholarship Credit and the Lifetime Learning Credit. Chapter 8 deals with other programs, including Coverdell Education Savings Accounts, the tax implications of student loans, tuition and fees deductions, and making early withdrawals from IRAs.

Knowing about all the federal education benefits, such as tax deductions and income shelters available to students (and their parents), can help you save money now, and it can also save you some serious money in the future. Plus, the significant tax advantages of some of these programs take years to fully develop, meaning the earlier you get started, the more money you'll save!

Uncle Sam wants YOU (to go to college)

If the only purpose of the Internal Revenue Service were to collect taxes, many accountants, tax lawyers, and financial planners (not to mention tens of thousands of bureaucrats) would be out of a job. Although the *main* focus of the IRS remains collecting taxes, it certainly has other things to do, including serving the interests of specific groups of Americans.

Many tax incentives have evolved over the years to encourage spending in certain areas of the economy. Large farming and agricultural corporations, for example, benefit from special tax treatments that the federal government has awarded them. Likewise, oil, gas, and mineral exploration firms, as well as an assortment of other organizations and sectors, benefit from specific (and often very complex) tax treatment rules that apply only to their particular industries.

However, you don't have to be a large multinational corporation to benefit from special tax treatment. Thankfully for the millions of students heading to college this year (not to mention their parents), a few of these fancy tax incentives are designed to help pay for a college education.

Although we can't outline all the ins and outs of how taxes and tax credits work for students (if we did, we wouldn't have space for anything else in this book), we can suggest that you look at IRS Publication 970, entitled *Tax Benefits for Education,* for more information on the various programs we talk about in this chapter.

You can get a copy of this helpful 58-page publication (a mere 0.0193 percent of those 300,000 pages we just talked about) by dropping in at your local IRS office. You can find the phone number for the nearest IRS office in the government pages of your telephone directory. If you just can't wait that long, you can pop over to the IRS Web site at www.irs.gov and download all the IRS publications you fancy.

All tax information (including the information in this chapter) may change at any time without notice. Students (and their parents) are advised to consult with an accountant or other qualified tax professional about their specific financial situations.

Giving Tuition Payers a Little Hope

One of the best tax incentives aimed at middle class parents of college students is the *Hope Scholarship Credit.* Under this plan, the government offers up to $1,500 per year as a tax credit to partially compensate parents (or other tuition payers) for paying their dependent student's college tuition. Independent students can also qualify for the Hope Scholarship Credit for their own education.

We want to emphasize that Hope Scholarship Credits don't refer to scholarships in the usual way that we use this term throughout the book. Instead of receiving a check to pay for school, you or your parents receive these "awards" in the form of tax *credits*. In other words, you get to deduct a certain amount of your education costs from your annual income to get a break on your taxes. In short, you get a tax credit for being or supporting a *scholar,* not for winning a *scholarship.*

The Hope Scholarship Credit can only be claimed for the first two years of college attendance. After that, you can use other programs, such as Lifetime Learning Credits (discussed later in this chapter) and Coverdell ESAs (see Chapter 8), to help with education expenses.

The amount you can claim under the Hope Scholarship Credit program is directly affected by your income. Congress has mandated that Hope Scholarship Credits be fully available below a pre-set income threshold but not available at all if your income is above another (higher) income threshold. Between these two income levels, a *phaseout calculation* gradually reduces the amount available for the credit. (We talk more about the mechanics of the phaseout calculation later in this chapter.)

In the 2002 tax year, for example, the amount of a Hope Scholarship Credit was fully available if the taxpayers' *modified adjusted gross income* (usually shortened to *MAGI*) was $41,000 or less (or $82,000 or less, if filing jointly). Between $41,000 and $51,000 (or $82,000 and $102,000 for a joint return), credits were subjected to a phaseout that gradually eliminated any Hope Scholarship Credit benefit. Above the $51,000 MAGI level ($102,000 if filing jointly), these credits were completely phased out (eliminated). Limits change all the time, so check with the IRS (www.irs.gov) to confirm this year's levels.

Who can claim the Hope Scholarship Credit?

If you "win" a Hope Scholarship Credit, you or your parents get a credit against taxes in the year paid. To receive this free money, however, you have to meet four criteria:

  ✔ **You must have paid qualified tuition and related expenses of an "eligible institution of higher education" (defined later in this section).** Claims can only be made for student tuition, and only for that portion that is not covered by other scholarships, grants, and federal loans.

- ✔ **You must pay the tuition and related expenses for an eligible student.** If your parents are footing the bills, *they* get the credit; if you pay the bills as an independent student, *you* can claim the benefit.

- ✔ **The eligible student must be yourself, your spouse, or a dependent f or which you claim an exemption on your tax return.** If you're a dependent student, you can't claim this credit. If your grandparents pay for your college tuition and you aren't their legal dependent, they can't claim the tax credit.

- ✔ **You have to complete IRS Form 8863 entitled, *Education Credits (Hope and Lifetime Learning Credits)* and attach it to IRS Form 1040 or IRS Form 1040A.** We include a copy of Form 8863 later in this chapter.

In case you were wondering, the IRS defines an *eligible institution of higher education* as "any college, university, vocational school, or other postsecondary educational institution eligible to participate in a student aid program administered by the Department of Education. It includes virtually all accredited, public, nonprofit, and proprietary (privately owned profit-making) postsecondary institutions."

Okay, what's the catch?

The IRS isn't out to get you, so you don't have to worry about obscure catches or loopholes that will prevent you from getting this credit. It really does want to help you. However, you do need to be aware of a few ways to disqualify yourself for Hope Scholarship Credit eligibility (and avoid them if you can help it):

- ✔ If your parents are married, they can't file their taxes separately if they want to claim the Hope Scholarship Credit. If you're an independent student and married, you *must* file jointly with your spouse to claim the Hope Credit. Divorced parents, on the other hand, *can* file separately.

- ✔ If you're a dependent student and listed as such on someone else's tax return, you can't file for a Hope Scholarship Credit. For this reason, *parents* file for the Hope Credit, not the dependent student.

- ✔ If your modified adjusted gross income (your MAGI) is $51,000 or more (or $102,000 or more, if you file jointly), your benefit is eliminated.

- ✔ If you (or your spouse) were classified as a nonresident alien for any part of the year for which you're filing and you did not elect to be treated as a resident for tax purposes, you can't file for a Hope Scholarship Credit. You must pay U.S. taxes to take advantage of the credit because the Hope Scholarship Credit is applied against taxes payable. If you don't file your taxes here, you can't receive credit.

> ✔ If you claim the Lifetime Learning Credit (discussed later in this chapter) for a student for a given year, you can't file for the Hope Credit for the same student.

Which college expenses aren't covered?

Some expenses aren't covered by the Hope Scholarship Credits. Although tuition and other required college fees (including lab fees, student government fees, and other fees levied by the school that must be paid to enroll) are covered by Hope Scholarship Credits (within the specified limits and limitations), some otherwise legitimate expenses aren't allowable.

For example, even though just about every college across the United States requires students to have separate health insurance coverage to attend school, these insurance expenses don't qualify under the Hope Scholarship Credit program.

Besides health insurance costs, other expenses specifically excluded from the Hope Scholarship Credits include the following:

✔ **Medical expenses (including student health fees).** The rationale behind this exclusion is that even if students weren't going to school, they would still pay for medical expenses in the normal course of life.

✔ **Room and board.** Although several federal loans programs include room and board as allowable expenses, the Hope Scholarship Credit does not.

✔ **Transportation.** Despite the fact that students might have to commute to college, Hope Scholarship Credits don't cover any travel expenses. Some students may find this exclusion particularly weird because they might have to stay home with their parents *because* college residence expenses are also not covered.

✔ **Personal or family living expenses.** These expenses are difficult to quantify and it's almost impossible to verify that students aren't "overpaying" their parents for room or board — so the government simply excludes the entire category.

How can I calculate my Hope Scholarship Credit?

You can calculate the base amount of the Hope Scholarship Credit by using this easy formula:

1. **Take 100 percent of the first $1,000 of qualified tuition and related expenses paid by you or paid by your parents *for* you.**

2. **Add 50 percent of the next $1,000 of qualified tuition and related expenses your parents paid by you or paid by your parents *for* you.**

   This number is your *maximum* allowable Hope Scholarship Credit.

The maximum amount of Hope Scholarship Credit that could be claimed in 2002 was $1,500 per student, per year. The good news is that your parents (or *you* if you're an independent student) can claim the full $1,500 for each eligible student for whom they paid at least $2,000 in qualified tuition expenses. The bad news is that the credit may be reduced based on your parents' MAGI, or yours if you're an independent student. This reduced amount is called the *allowable credit*.

The IRS uses the following formula to calculate the allowable Hope Scholarship Credit:

Allowable Hope Scholarship Credit =

Maximum Credit × (Phaseout limit – Payer's MAGI) / Phaseout Range

Here's a quick explanation:

- **Maximum Credit** is 100 percent of the first $1,000, and 50 percent of the next $1,000; tuition expenses over $2,000 are *not* recognized for this award.

- **Phaseout Limit** is the *maximum* MAGI that will qualify for the Hope Scholarship Credit. Currently, this amount is $51,000 for single parents of dependent students (the same for single independent students) and $102,000 for two-parent families (or married independent students).

- **Phaseout Range** is the dollar amount over which the Hope Scholarship Credit is phased out. For single payers, this amount is currently $10,000 (because *full* credit is given to a single payer whose MAGI is $41,000 or less, and *no* credit is given to a single payer whose MAGI is $51,000 or more). Married payers have double the MAGI allowance and thus have double the phaseout range: $20,000.

To understand how the phaseout works, we've constructed college payment scenarios for two hypothetical families.

Example #1: Payers under the phaseout limit

Mark and Mary have a combined MAGI of $75,000, and they pay $2,000 in the fall semester sending their daughter Marisa to college. The amount of $2,000 represents qualified expenses above and beyond other scholarships, loans, grants, and other sources of free (or free-for-now) money that Marisa has been awarded for college.

Because Mark and Mary file their IRS Tax Form 1040 together, and their MAGI is *under* the phaseout limit of $82,000, they're eligible to apply the entire $1,500 Hope Scholarship Credit to their tax return. (Remember that while the first $1,000 is 100 percent eligible, only 50 percent of the second $1,000 is eligible for credit.)

Example #2: Payer near the upper range of the phaseout limit

Widowed Julie, on the other hand, has a MAGI of $50,000 this year. Julie incurs an expense of $3,500 for sending one of her two sons, Jack, to college at a nice school. Alas, the Hope Scholarship Credit program only takes notice of the first $2,000, and then only the second $1,000 at 50 percent. Thus her *allowable* Hope Scholarship Credit is calculated as follows:

$$\text{Hope Scholarship Credit} = \$1,500 \times (\underline{\$51,000 - \$50,000}) / \$10,000$$

or $150

If Julie's MAGI was $1,000 more that year, her Hope Scholarship Credit would be completely zeroed out.

Lifetime Learning Credits

Another important source of free money is the *Lifetime Learning Credit* program.

Knowing how Hope and Lifetime are similar

The Hope Scholarship Credit and the Lifetime Learning Credit programs have some important similarities:

- ✔ The most obvious similarity is that the allowable credit for each program is limited by the MAGI of your parents (or you, if you're an independent student).

  Like the Hope Scholarship Credit, figuring out your Lifetime Learning Credit requires a small calculation involving the payers' MAGI. Depending on your parents' MAGI (or your MAGI, if you're an independent student), payers can get credit for up to $1,000 per year, based on a 20 percent tax credit for the first $5,000 of tuition.

- ✔ Both programs are administered by the IRS, so you have to complete Form 8863 and attach it to the traditional Form 1040 or Form 1040A tax forms in order to file for either credit. (We've added a copy of Form 8863 at the end of this chapter.)

- ✔ The credit is available for *net* tuition and fees (less grant aid and scholarships) paid for post-secondary enrollment. The credit is available on a per-family basis, and, like the Hope Scholarship Credit, requires the payer to file jointly if married.

- ✔ Like the Hope Scholarship Credit program, a phaseout limit exists for Lifetime Learning Credits. This means that although your parents may have $1,000 *maximum* credit (if they spent $5,000, and the IRS allows for 20 percent of this to be credited under the Lifetime Learning Credit program), the *allowable* credit will be phased out starting when the payer's MAGI is more than $41,000 ($82,000 if filing jointly). After $51,000 ($102,000 if filing jointly), the credits zero out, and no tax benefit is available.

  In other words, if the payer has a high MAGI, he or she won't be able to claim a credit under the Lifetime Learning Credit program.

- ✔ Like the Hope Scholarship program, Lifetime Learning Credits are claimable by the *payer* (usually the parent), not by the dependent student.

Knowing how Hope and Lifetime differ

Despite all the similarities, the two credit programs also have some important differences:

- ✔ Hope Scholarship Credits extend only two years into a student's college life. In contrast, Lifetime Learning Credits are designed for college students in their junior or senior years, as well as graduate students working on their advanced degrees. As long as you qualify, you can claim Lifetime Learning Credits any number of times throughout your lifetime.

- ✔ Lifetime Learning Credits are limited to $1,000 per return, not per eligible student. If your parents are paying for two kids in college, they can take a maximum of $1,000 per year, assuming that their MAGI doesn't phase out some (or all) of the benefit.

As we went to press, there were rumors around the IRS that the Lifetime Learning Credit would be increased for the 2003 filing year from $1,000 to $2,000. Students are urged to contact their local IRS office or check out the Web site at www.irs.gov.

For those of you who like to compare and contrast, check out Table 7-1 where we outline the differences between the Hope Scholarship Credit program and the Lifetime Learning Credit program.

Details for both programs are always subject to change. Students are urged to consult an accountant or the IRS to get up-to-the-minute information.

Table 7-1	Hope Versus Lifetime	
Category	*Hope Scholarship Credit*	*Lifetime Learning Credit*
Annual limit of credit	Up to $1,500 credit per eligible student, based on tuition paid and payer MAGI.	Up to $1,000 credit per *return*, based on total tuition paid and payer MAGI.
Who gets the benefit?	The payer, meaning the *parents* (if they are paying for a dependent student), or *you*, if you are an independent student.	The payer, meaning the *parents* (if they are paying for a dependent student), or *you*, if you are an independent student.
How long will the benefit last?	Available only until the first two years of postsecondary education are completed.	Available for all years of postsecondary education and for courses to acquire or improve job skills.
How is the benefit calculated?	Credit is calculated at 100 percent of first $1,000 paid and 50 percent of second $1,000. Tuition payments over $2,000 are not recognized.	The amount of the lifetime learning credit is calculated as 20 percent of the first $5,000 of qualified tuition and related expenses.
What are the benefit's phaseout conditions?	Allowable credit is phased out starting when payer's MAGI is more than $41,000 ($82,000 if filing jointly). After $51,000 ($102,000 if filing jointly), credits zero out, and no tax benefit is available.	Identical to Hope, allowable credit is phased out starting when payer's MAGI is more than $41,000 ($82,000 if filing jointly). After $51,000 ($102,000 if filing jointly), credits zero out, and no tax benefit is available.
What degree or program is eligible?	Student must be pursuing an undergraduate degree or other recognized education credential.	Student does *not* need to pursue a degree or other recognized education credential.
What are the restrictions on the duration of courses?	Student must be enrolled at least half-time for at least one academic period during the particular tax year.	Lifetime Learning Credits are available for one or more courses.
Do felony drug convictions limit credit awards?	Yes. Student is not eligible for Hope Scholarship Credit if he or she has a felony drug conviction.	No. Felony drug conviction is immaterial to the Lifetime Learning Credit program.

Source: Internal Revenue Service, Publication 970

Form **8863**		Education Credits (Hope and Lifetime Learning Credits) ▶ See instructions. ▶ Attach to Form 1040 or Form 1040A.	OMB No. 1545-1618 2002 Attachment Sequence No. **50**
Department of the Treasury Internal Revenue Service			
Name(s) shown on return			Your social security number

Part I Hope Credit. Caution: *The Hope credit may be claimed for no more than 2 tax years for the same student.*

1

(a) Student's name (as shown on page 1 of your tax return) First name - - - - - - - - Last name	**(b)** Student's social security number (as shown on page 1 of your tax return)	**(c)** Qualified expenses (but **do not** enter more than $2,000 for each student). See instructions	**(d)** Enter the **smaller** of the amount in column (c) or $1,000	**(e)** Subtract column (d) from column (c)	**(f)** Enter one-half of the amount in column (e)

2	Add the amounts in columns (d) and (f) . . .	**2**	
3	Tentative Hope credit. Add the amounts on line 2, columns (d) and (f). If you are claiming the lifetime learning credit, go to Part II; otherwise, go to Part III . . . . . ▶	**3**	

Part II Lifetime Learning Credit

4

Caution: *You
cannot take the
Hope credit and
the lifetime learning
credit for the same
student.*

(a) Student's name (as shown on page 1 of your tax return) First name Last name	**(b)** Student's social security number (as shown on page 1 of your tax return)	**(c)** Qualified expenses. See instructions

5	Add the amounts on line 4, column (c), and enter the total	**5**	
6	Enter the **smaller** of line 5 or $5,000	**6**	
7	Tentative lifetime learning credit. Multiply line 6 by 20% (.20) and go to Part III . ▶	**7**	

Part III Allowable Education Credits

8	Tentative education credits. Add lines 3 and 7	**8**	
9	Enter: $102,000 if married filing jointly; $51,000 if single, head of household, or qualifying widow(er)	**9**	
10	Enter the amount from Form 1040, line 36 *, or Form 1040A, line 22	**10**	
11	Subtract line 10 from line 9. If line 10 is equal to or more than line 9, **stop;** you cannot take any education credits . . .	**11**	
12	Enter: $20,000 if married filing jointly; $10,000 if single, head of household, or qualifying widow(er)	**12**	
13	If line 11 is equal to or more than line 12, enter the amount from line 8 on line 14 and go to line 15. If line 11 is less than line 12, divide line 11 by line 12. Enter the result as a decimal (rounded to at least three places)	**13**	.
14	Multiply line 8 by line 13 . . . . ▶	**14**	
15	Enter the amount from Form 1040, line 44, or Form 1040A, line 28	**15**	
16	Enter the total, if any, of your credits from Form 1040, lines 45 through 47, or Form 1040A, lines 29 and 30	**16**	
17	Subtract line 16 from line 15. If line 16 is equal to or more than line 15, **stop;** you cannot take any education credits . . . . ▶	**17**	
18	**Education credits.** Enter the **smaller** of line 14 or line 17 here and on Form 1040, line 48, or Form 1040A, line 31 . . . . ▶	**18**	

*See Pub. 970 for the amount to enter if you are filing Form 2555, 2555-EZ, or 4563 or you are excluding income from Puerto Rico.

For Paperwork Reduction Act Notice, see page 3.   Cat. No. 25379M   Form **8863** (2002)

Chapter 8

Taxing Issues: You and the IRS

*M*ost people, when asked if they would rather do their taxes or have a root canal operation, opt for the dentist. As a student, taxes can be particularly frustrating because you're trained to look for logical patterns in mathematical equations. The problem is that taxes aren't based on logic; they're based on politics. Why is tuition deductible, but not residence fees? Why does deductibility for student loan interest start to phaseout when a payer hits the magic number of $50,000 income? Because Congress says so, that's why. Your job is to work within the system and minimize the amount of taxes you (or your parents) have to pay. Think of it as a course in Chaos Theory.

Most of the things we discuss in this chapter relate to the tax implications of paying tuition, and are of primary interest to your parents (if you're a dependent student) or *you* (if you're an independent one). It doesn't mean that if you're a dependent student, you don't have to pay attention to this chapter. Be kind and share it with your parents. After all, the money they save could be put to a good use: *you*.

Just about everything we talk about in this chapter is changing all the time. Given Congress's knack for rewriting, rearranging, and reorganizing tax laws, you may feel as though you need an accounting degree just to figure out your benefits and options. Well, you don't need to go that far, but there are some key tactics that smart students (and their parents) know about paying taxes and getting free money from the federal government.

In this chapter, we outline those key tactics. We discuss the tax implications of student loans, how to account for college tuition and fee deductions, Coverdell Education Savings Accounts, making early withdrawals from an IRA, and finally, Education Savings Bond programs. Ready? Okay, sharpen your Number 2 pencil, and let's get figuring!

Tax Implications of Student Loans

In Chapter 6, we introduce you to the wonderful world of student debt by discussing federal loans, such as Staffords, PLUSes, Perkins, and Consolidations. Now, we want to tell you how to get even more out of these loans: You can often deduct the interest paid on these loans from your taxes. If you're wondering why the IRS is being so kind, read on and let us explain.

Generally speaking, the federal government lets you deduct interest on certain loans because they're considered an expense of doing business. A farmer, for example, can deduct the interest he pays on a loan for seed and other supplies to grow his crops. Likewise, a construction firm can deduct the interest paid to service the loan taken out to buy bricks and other building supplies to construct a large office building.

In both cases, the interest paid is a necessary business expense because it's required to make the finished good. In the farmer's case, the finished good is the mature crops sold to a food wholesaler that end up on our dinner table. In the construction company's case, the finished good is the completed office building that the developer will then lease out to various tenants. Interestingly, the same principle of deducting loan interest is (mostly) true for student loans. In your case, the finished product is *you* — a newly educated you who's ready to go out and be a more productive citizen.

U.S. tax legislation is a complex and ever-changing beast. You and your parents may want to consider talking with an accountant or other qualified tax professional about how your particular situation can be best handled.

Deducting loan interest is in your best interest

Up to $2,500 of student loan interest payments that your parents (or you) make, both required and voluntary, may be deductible. However, these deductions are affected by a series of phaseout limits, based on your parents' *modified adjusted gross income* (MAGI). If you're an *independent* student and the student loans are in your name, *you* can likely deduct the interest paid from your federal tax return, assuming that your MAGI isn't higher than the IRS threshold. (We introduce the term MAGI in Chapter 7, so you may want to flip back and read about it before continuing. Take your time, we'll wait. Okay, ready? Let's go.)

The amount of student loan interest deduction for the 2002 tax year was phased out (that's accountant-speak for *gradually reduced*) if the payer's MAGI was between $50,000 and $65,000 (or between $100,000 and $130,000 if the payer filed a joint return). If the payer's MAGI was *less* than the lower threshold, the full deduction was allowed. If the MAGI was *higher* than the upper threshold, no deduction was allowed. A sliding scale of deductibility lies in between these two thresholds.

The IRS is very fond of MAGI-based phaseouts, so you'll become familiar with this system if you apply for any federal tax credits.

Your parents can take the loan interest deduction if the student loans are in their name, and they're paying them back, and you were their dependent when the loan was made. Similarly, *you* can take the deduction if the loans are in your name, and you're paying them back, and if you're an independent student. In either case, if the payer's MAGI is $65,000 or more ($130,000 if filing a joint return), the tax credit will zero out.

Just what is deductible?

Generally, you can deduct almost any expense connected with the cost of attending an eligible educational institution (including, by the way, graduate school). These costs include the following:

- ✔ Tuition and fees
- ✔ Room and board
- ✔ Books, supplies, and equipment
- ✔ Other necessary expenses (such as transportation)

The IRS says that expenses for room and board must be "reasonable." This stipulation means that these expenses can't be more than the *greater* of either (1) the college's own allowance for room and board as stipulated for federal financial aid or (2) the actual amount charged if the student would have lived in housing owned or operated by the school itself.

In other words, you can't rent your Uncle Al's swank downtown penthouse and pay him $5,000 per month. Well, you *can*, but the IRS won't let you take all the interest deduction associated with it. Sorry.

Ah, yes, more deductibility rules

In Chapter 7, we outline all the deductibility rules for Hope Scholarship Credits and Lifetime Learning Credits. Well, they're back (in a somewhat different form) for loan interest deductibility. In general, you can claim the deduction if *all* the following requirements are met:

- ✔ Your filing status is anything *except* "married filing separately."
- ✔ No one else is claiming you as a dependent on his or her tax return. *Dependent* students can't claim the interest deduction.

✓ You paid interest on a loan you took out only to pay tuition and other qualified higher education expenses for yourself, your spouse, or someone who was your dependent when the loan was taken out.

✓ The education expenses were paid or incurred within a reasonable period of time before or after the loan was taken out.

✓ The person for whom the expenses were paid was an eligible student.

The Table 8-1 summarizes the tax implications of student loan interest. Like other information in this chapter, this information is subject to change.

Table 8-1	Tax Implications of Student Loan Interest
Implication	*Explanation*
Maximum tax benefit	You can decrease your taxable income up to the amount of $2,500, depending on your MAGI.
Loan qualifications	Your student loan must have been taken out solely to pay qualified education expenses and cannot be from a related person or made under a qualified employer plan.
Student qualifications	The student must be you, your spouse (if you're an independent student), or your dependent. The student must be enrolled at least half-time in a degree program to qualify for this deduction.
Time limit on deduction	Beginning with payments made in 2002, you can deduct interest paid during the remaining period of your student loan.
Phaseout limits (MAGI thresholds) for this deduction	Like other tax credits, such as the Hope Scholarship Credit and the Lifetime Learning Credit (see Chapter 7), the amount of your deduction under the Student Loan Interest Deduction depends on your MAGI. The IRS lets payers claim the full credit (up to a maximum of $2,500) if their MAGI is less than $50,000. A MAGI of more than $65,000 (or $130,000 if the payer files a joint return), zeros out any credit. In between these two thresholds, the IRS uses a formula to implement a sliding scale of deduction eligibility.

Source: IRS Publication 970

Tuition and Fees Deduction

Another source of free money is the government's deduction for tuition and fees. Beginning in 2002, students became eligible to deduct up to $3,000 in qualified tuition and related expenses paid during the year for themselves, their spouse, or a dependent.

The good news is that this deduction helps taxpayers who can't qualify for the Hope Scholarship Credits or the Lifetime Learning Credits because their MAGI is too high. The bad news is that the IRS says that the tuition and fees deduction will only be available for four years, from the 2002 tax year through 2005. By press time, Congress hadn't decided if the program would be extended.

Who qualifies for this deduction?

You can claim the tuition and fees deduction provided *all three* of the following requirements are met:

- ✔ The eligible student is you, your spouse, or a dependent for whom you claim an exemption on your tax return.

- ✔ You pay the tuition and related expenses for an eligible student.

- ✔ You pay qualified tuition and related expenses for higher education. In other words, you can't go off and buy a shiny new sports car and expect the government to give you a tax credit for it because "it's necessary for your college well-being."

Who doesn't qualify for this deduction?

Now that you know who qualifies for the deduction, it's only fair that we talk about who *can't* qualify. According to the IRS, you can't take the tuition and fees deduction if *any* of following situations applies to you:

- ✔ Your filing status is "married filing separately." This stipulation is consistent with the other federal tax credit programs we discuss in this chapter and in Chapter 7.

- ✔ Another person is entitled to claim an exemption for you as a dependent on his or her tax return. You can't take the deduction even if the other person doesn't actually claim that exemption.

- ✔ Your MAGI is more than $65,000 ($130,000 if you're filing a joint return). This amount will increase as time goes on. Chat with the folks at the IRS to get the most up-to-date MAGI thresholds.

- ✔ You were a nonresident alien for any part of the year and did not elect to be treated as a resident alien for tax purposes. Again, this is because the deduction is a *credit* against your U.S. taxes. Obviously, if you don't file U.S. taxes, you can't get the credit!

✔ You or anyone else claims a Hope Scholarship Credit or Lifetime Learning Credit (see Chapter 7) in the same year with respect to expenses of the student for whom the tuition and related expenses were paid. You get credit only once for the same set of expenses.

The IRS looks at your whole enchilada

No, we're not talking about cooking here (or cooking the books, either). Rather, we want to emphasize that the IRS looks at your entire financial situation when deciding how much of a deduction for higher education expenses they'll allow you to take. As we mention in the previous section, for example, you're not allowed to deduct tuition expenses for any tax-free educational assistance you received from other sources.

This means that any tuition tax credit you receive has to be applied *after* any scholarships, Pell grants, employer-provided educational assistance (if your employer pays for you to go to college to upgrade your skills), or any veterans' educational assistance you receive are applied to your eligible tuition and fees. Only after all these other sources reduce your eligible tuition and fee expenses are you able to claim a tax credit for the remaining (if any) amount.

Considering the complexity of this deduction, you may want to consult with an accountant or other qualified tax professional about how to structure your financial affairs to maximize your allowable deductions under various federal tax credits.

Table 8-2 lists common questions related to the tax implications of student tuition and fees and then gives the answers. Like other material in this chapter, this information is subject to change.

Table 8-2	Student Tuition and Fees Q and A
Question	*Answer*
What is the maximum credit under the tuition and fees deduction?	You can decrease your taxable income by up to $3,000.
Where is the deduction taken?	Payers take this deduction as a reduction to income on IRS Form 1040 or Form 1040A.
What are the student qualifications?	According to the IRS, you, your spouse or your dependent must be enrolled in an eligible educational institution. Dependent students cannot claim this tax credit on their own returns.

Question	Answer
What tuition and fees are deductible?	Tuition and fees required for enrollment or attendance at an eligible postsecondary educational institution are included. Personal, living or family expenses, including room and board, are not.

Source: IRS Publication 970

The Lowdown on Coverdell ESAs

Technically speaking, a *Coverdell ESA* (short for "Education Savings Account") is a trust or custodial account created solely for the purpose of paying the qualified education expenses of the designated beneficiary of the account. Whew! That's a mouthful, huh?

If the term *Coverdell ESA* is unfamiliar to you, it may be because these savings plans were, until July 26, 2001, known as *Education IRAs* (known as "individual retirement arrangements" by tax experts or as "individual retirement accounts" by those in education circles). Some people (as well as some older books and Web sites) may still refer to the Coverdells using these older terms. That's okay. Although we use the new name in this book, all three names refer to the same government program: registered savings plans used expressly for tuition payments.

According to current law, a Coverdell ESA must be established before the 18th birthday of the designated student beneficiary. In some cases, a Coverdell ESA can also be established for people over the age of 18, notably dependent students classified by the IRS as "special needs beneficiaries."

Congress has constructed Coverdell legislation to allow for as many family members (or even friends) to contribute to your future schooling as you can convince to do so. Accordingly, the IRS has ruled that there's no limit on the number of separate Coverdell ESAs that can be established for a designated beneficiary. That said, the *total* dollar amount of contributions for a given beneficiary can't exceed $2,000 in any calendar year.

MAGI-based phaseout for Coverdells

Although the payer's MAGI limits Coverdell contributions, these thresholds are substantially higher compared to other federal tax credit programs.

If, for example, your parents were married and filed a joint return for the 2002 tax year, their Coverdell contribution limit remained intact, provided their modified adjusted gross income was $190,000 or less. Contribution limits were gradually phased out if your parents' MAGI was more than $190,000 but less than $220,000. If your parents' MAGI was $220,000 or more, their contribution to your Coverdell ESA was zeroed out. Congress apparently thinks that people who make this kind of money don't need the tax break that the Coverdell brings.

Of course, just because your *parents* can't contribute to your Coverdell, doesn't mean your grandparents, cousins, and friends can't contribute — up to the annual limit of $2,000! See the section on Coverdell contribution limits later in this chapter for more details.

Although contributions to Coverdell ESAs are *not* tax deductible, amounts deposited in them can appreciate tax free inside the account until they're withdrawn. Plus, any withdrawals from a Coverdell account aren't taxed provided they don't exceed the designated beneficiary's qualified education expenses at an eligible educational institution for that particular year. That means there are no tax implications if you use the money in your Coverdell account for tuition, school fees, and other education expenses.

Coverdell contribution limits

Parents (or you, if you're an independent student) have to be aware of two yearly limits in order to keep the IRS happy with your Coverdell ESA. Here they are:

- ✔ If a student has only one Coverdell ESA account, payers can contribute up to that year's limit (for the 2002 tax year, this amount was $2,000). Of course, the contribution allowances are subject to the MAGI-based Coverdell phaseout limits outlined earlier in this section.

- ✔ If a student has multiple Coverdell ESA accounts set up for him or her (for example, one set up by parents, a second by grandparents, and a third by the extended family), the sum of *all* contributions cannot exceed the single $2,000 yearly limit. As an example, if your parents are divorced and each has a separate Coverdell ESA for you, they need to communicate with each other to make sure that their combined contributions don't exceed the $2,000 limit.

Your parents (or other potential Coverdell contributors) should be especially careful about the $2,000 maximum. The IRS penalizes overcontribution by putting a 6 percent excise tax on "excess" money that's in the Coverdell ESA at the end of the year. For more information about contribution options and penalties, check out IRS Publication 970, available from the IRS Web site at www.irs.gov.

Coverdells cover all education levels

Of all the federal credit programs we outline in this chapter, the Coverdell ESA is perhaps the most versatile. Not only can Coverdell ESAs pay for qualified expenses for college students, they can also do the same thing for eligible *elementary* and *secondary* school students.

This information is perhaps surprising considering all the press that Coverdell ESAs get for the college-bound student. Nicely, though, Coverdell-eligible schools also include any public, private or religious school that provides elementary or secondary education (kindergarten through grade 12). The only stipulation the IRS puts on these schools is that the appropriate state educational department must approve them.

Like other federal tax credit programs, a Coverdell ESA can pay for eligible expenses, such as tuition and fees, as well as all necessary books, supplies, and equipment needed for school. Unlike other programs, however, Coverdell ESAs can also foot the bill for certain types of academic tutoring! In addition, Coverdell ESAs also cover certain special-needs services for special-needs beneficiaries.

Coverdell ESAs can also be used to pay for room and board, any school uniforms students may need, transportation to and from school, and even a computer and related equipment, such as printers, software, and other accessories.

Now, before you run out to the local video store to pick up some computer games, you should know that the IRS won't let you expense software designed for "sports, games, or hobbies unless the software is predominantly educational in nature." Sorry about that.

Early Withdrawals from IRAs

Another option for parents trying to afford to send their dependent kids to college, or independent students trying to scrape together enough money for school, is to withdraw some money from their Investment Retirement Account (IRA).

According to the IRS, anyone making a withdrawal from their IRA before they reach age 59½ is *not* liable to pay the usual 10 percent tax penalty provided they use the money to pay qualified higher education expenses for themselves, their spouse, their kids, or their grandchildren. Put another way, the proceeds from the IRA withdrawal must still be included as income for that year, but there's no early withdraw penalty if the proceeds are used for eligible education.

Is early withdrawal a good idea?

Obviously, withdrawing money from a retirement account to pay for college tuition is a decision not to be taken lightly. Like other tax-related financial options we discuss in this chapter, students and their parents are encouraged to seek advice from an accountant or other qualified tax professional before rushing into uncharted territory.

That said, many parents of dependent students (as well as independent students themselves) take advantage of this option every year. After all, if the only choice to finance a college education is either to withdraw some money from an IRA or go into debt using a PLUS Loan, many parents choose the former option.

How much can I withdraw without penalty?

Provided that you (and, hopefully, an accountant) have done the math and have determined that IRA withdrawal is a good idea, you now need to find out how much you can take out without paying the 10 percent penalty.

The IRS says that you must determine something called your *adjusted qualified higher education expenses*. Don't worry. Despite this scary term, the calculation is relatively straightforward. Simply add together any tax-free withdrawals from any Coverdell ESAs, any tax-free scholarships received, any tax-free employer-provided educational assistance given, and any other tax-free payments obtained.

After you've figured out this amount, simply subtract it from the year's education expenses (including tuition, fees, books, supplies, and equipment). Anything left over is the amount that's *not* subject to the 10 percent withdrawal penalty.

About Education Savings Bond Programs

Generally speaking, anyone who owns savings bonds must pay tax on the interest earned, either every year or when the bonds are cashed in. However, you can purchase certain types of savings bonds under a formal education savings bond program whose interest isn't subject to federal tax.

According to the IRS, a *qualified* U.S. savings bond is a series EE bond issued after 1989 or a series I bond. The bond must be issued either in your name (as the sole owner) or in the name of both you and your spouse (as co-owners). The owner must be at least 24 years old before the bond's issue date.

As usual, the IRS has put qualifications upon how (and on what) you can spend the bonds' proceeds. Although required tuition and fees are allowed under the bond program, expenses for room and board are *not*. Nor are courses involving sports, games, or hobbies unless they're part of a degree or certificate program.

If you've already figured out your adjusted qualified higher education expenses to determine your IRA early withdraw possibilities, you've already done most of the work involved with figuring out the tax-free portion of your education savings bonds (usually referred to by the IRS as your *interest exclusion*).

Finally, as with other programs described in this chapter, the interest exclusion of the Education Savings Bond program is subject to a MAGI-based phaseout amount. If your taxable income is below $57,600 ($86,400 if you're filing jointly), all your eligible interest exclusion is allowed by the IRS. Above the threshold of $72,600 (or $116,400 if you're filing jointly), any interest exclusion is zeroed out. In between these thresholds, a sliding scale amount, determined by IRS Form 8815, is yours for the filing.

Part III

Looking Closer to Home: Free Money From Your State and Hometown

The 5th Wave   By Rich Tennant

ORIGINAL VAN-GOGH-OF-THE-MONTH CLUB

"I just don't know where the money's going."

In this part . . .

Although the federal government gives away billions of dollars annually to hundreds of thousands of students across the country, your state has a greater incentive to focus on *you*. Every state offers great financial programs for state residents, from outright grants to low-cost state colleges.

In addition, states and local governments also use some less obvious methods to ensure that their own native sons and daughters get an education. Whether in the form of tax incentives, lottery-based scholarships, tuition savings plans, loan forgiveness, or local scholarship programs, your state government and local interests have many important sources of college cash. Why not turn to the folks who are close to home and who want to see one of their own go to college?!

Chapter 9

Getting Free $ from Your State

In This Chapter
▶ Finding out about state residency requirements
▶ Determining your eligibility for state-based financial aid
▶ Figuring out deadlines
▶ Getting the state secrets. A state-by-state directory of financial aid contacts

*W*hen singer-songwriter Billy Joel croons *I'm in a New York State of Mind,* he's probably not thinking about colleges and the great benefits that individual *states* bring to the student financial aid table. Nevertheless, considering that states play such an important role in making college affordable for millions of Americans each year, Joel could've just as easily written that he was in Kansas, South Carolina, California, Massachusetts, New Jersey . . . well, you get the idea.

This chapter outlines how every state in the Union actively encourages students and their parents to get free money for college through various state-sponsored scholarship programs, grants, prepaid tuition plans, and other aid. We show you how to find the information relevant to your state and integrate it into your overall plan for free money.

Understanding State Residency

Did you know that part of the taxes that you (if you're working) and your parents pay out of every paycheck goes to running your state colleges? Now, if you never go on to a postsecondary school, every dollar spent in this way is pretty much lost to you. Sorry about that. If, however, you have your sights set on earning a college degree (and not paying an arm and a leg for the privilege), finding out how your *state* provides financial aid can really shave some serious money off your college tuition.

Your state can save you money in two specific ways:

✔ It can provide lower-cost tuition to certain state-run colleges and universities.

✔ It can provide impressive financial aid awards to in-state students who study at state colleges.

State-based financial aid first goes to residents of that particular state because they (and their parents) are the ones who've been paying the taxes that go to the state-funded colleges and universities. With a few exceptions, state residents can get free money (in the form of reduced college tuition and awards) just for living in the state. Cool, huh?

We should emphasize that states provide an *automatic* college fee reduction to state residents. Just about every state college sets its tuition fees (and sometimes its on-campus housing fees, as well) higher for out-of-state students.

Often, this difference can be quite substantial. The University of Florida, for example, charged its undergraduate students $2,630 during the 2002/2003 school year, provided they were classified as *in-state resident* students. Out-of-state students, on the other hand, were charged a whopping $12,096 for the exact same program — almost five times as much! At the same school, in-state graduate students had to pay $4,470 per year; in contrast, out-of-state students forked over $16,165!

In other jurisdictions, the difference between in-state and out-of-state tuition can be less dramatic. Nevertheless, residency is an important discount factor in many state colleges (and some non-state schools as well). Essentially, in-state students get some free money that out-of-state students don't.

We can't stress enough the need to plan ahead to investigate all the options open to you. Start investigating scholarships, grants, loans, bursaries, and other financial aid well before your final year of high school, preferably *much* earlier. In order to fully understand the complex financial opportunities open to you, it certainly helps to be organized, methodical, and to take your time.

How does a state figure out your residency status?

Individual states have different eligibility requirements to determine whether prospective college students are state residents for the purposes of state financial aid. Generally speaking, a prospective student is eligible for state aid if he or she has been physically located and residing in the state for a given time (usually a year, but this rule varies by state). The prospective student must also carry on his or her life in the new state, attending high school, opening and using a bank account, getting a driver's license in the new state, and, if old enough, registering to vote there and paying taxes (if working).

Depending on your situation, relocating may not be worth the trouble, and some states have more stringent residency requirements than others. For example, not only does New Mexico require students to live within its borders for a period of at least a year before they can apply to be classified as residents, it also requires that *parents* of dependent students also live in the state. And the residency requirements don't stop there.

New Mexico also requires a written declaration to relinquish residence in any other state and establish residency in New Mexico, along with various overt acts of residency, such as employment, paying income taxes, having a driver's license and vehicle registration, and having registered to vote in New Mexico. If all these overt acts aren't fulfilled, the prospective student must submit documentation explaining why he or she is not capable of doing so. We're telling you, they're serious about residency in New Mexico!

Of course, what's necessary in New Mexico may not be necessary in New Hampshire or Wyoming. Every state is different, and residency requirements also change from time to time, usually (but not always) getting more rigid. If you think that your residency may be in question, check it out well ahead of your expected arrival at college — at least a year ahead. Doing so *is* worth the effort. The financial aid program you receive from your state or college could very well depend on your residency status.

In effect, paying taxes in your state partly funds your college tuition. Determining your state of residency is key in getting college aid because it determines which state will give you preferential aid treatment. We include a directory of state financial aid offices later in this chapter.

How does a state know I want to attend college there?

Ah, the government knows *all* about you. It's been watching you for years.

Feeling nice and paranoid now? Well, actually, the truth is that state financial aid offices get their information from you. When you complete the *Free Application for Federal Student Aid* (FAFSA), your information also goes to the states in which your colleges of choice are physically located. (We discuss school selection using the FAFSA in Chapter 5).

The question of residency is very important; it determines the following:

✔ Whether you're eligible for state-based scholarships and grants

✔ Whether you qualify for any special state-originated loans or guarantees

✔ Whether you qualify as an in-state student for purposes of college-based awards and discounts

Reciprocity agreements for residency status

If you live in one state and the college of your dreams is in another, you may still qualify for lower-priced college education if both states have reciprocity agreements.

Reciprocity agreements are agreements in which one state will consider out-of-state students on an equal (or near-equal) footing to its own in-state applicants for the purposes of student aid and discounted state college tuition fees. Generally, the *other* state reciprocates, which is why these agreements are referred to as reciprocity agreements. However, in some cases, one state will offer in-state status to students from a particular state even though the other state does not reciprocate. For example, Rhode Island offers reciprocity to students from every state, but it receives reciprocity from only five.

We let you know which states have reciprocity agreements in the directory of state financial aid offices later in this chapter. However, remember that specifics of these agreements can be complex and are subject to change at any time. When in doubt, ask!

Residency advantages: An example

To understand the advantages of residency, take a look at one example.

Suppose that you were born, raised, and live in Buffalo, New York. You're thus a resident of New York State for the purposes of state-based financial aid. One of the nice things about living in New York is that this state offers a high degree of resident-oriented financial aid and has lots of programs of interest to those looking for free money.

The New York State Tuition Assistance Program (TAP), for example, helps eligible New York residents attending in-state colleges (and other postsecondary institutions) pay for tuition. Depending on the academic year in which you begin your studies, the annual TAP award can be as high as $5,000 per year.

Best of all, New York's TAP is a *grant,* meaning that you don't have to pay any money back! (Check out the sidebar, "One state's eligibility requirements," for the eligibility requirements for the TAP.) The state has other resident-only programs as well, such as the New York State Scholarships for Academic Excellence, Robert C. Byrd Honors Scholarship, and Persian Gulf Veterans Tuition Awards.

Relocation (Go west, young man or woman)

Every state in the Union offers plenty of scholarship and loan opportunities. The common themes running through all these programs is that they give preference to *state* residents, and depending on the particular program, each can provide some serious free money if you qualify.

Some students, hearts set on a particular out-of-state college, have been known to relocate to another state to gain residency status. Depending on your particular financial situation, and perhaps whether you're willing to work for a year in another state and pay taxes, relocation may be an option for you to consider.

Relocation, however, may also cost mom or dad a whole lot more than they realize if they're transferred from one state to another for work. If you suddenly change states in your senior year of high school, you may find yourself ineligible for certain types of state-based financial aid. Considering that you may be treated as an out-of-state student by your new state *and* by your college, your parent's transfer may end up costing the family a huge amount of cash.

Is relocation worth the trouble? After all, depending on the state, you may have to be a legal resident (pay taxes, get a new driver's license, get on the voter's registration list, and so on) for at least one year.

When in doubt, contact the financial aid office of your prospective state to see if it has a reciprocity agreement with your old state. As well, don't forget to chat with the financial aid office of your college to determine the ramifications of your new status. Last, but certainly not least, get everything in writing whenever possible, and get the names of people with whom you speak. You may have to prove that you were acting on official advice when you try to establish your residency.

Becoming Eligible for State-Based Aid

Eligibility varies from state to state, and the guidelines always seem to be changing. A particular state's eligibility requirements may be straightforward or complex, or somewhere in between. To further complicate matters, each award program is slightly different from the next, with a different set of forms, qualifications, and, possibly, skill requirements.

You may have already done the work!

You've probably heard the old expression, "The journey of 10,000 miles starts with a single step." Well, the vast majority of most state-based financial aid starts in one place — the FAFSA. That's right, the Department of Education's Free Application for Federal Student Aid is where many states derive their information about your financial need.

After your FAFSA information is entered by hand and checked by the Applications Center (or just *checked,* if you've used *FAFSA on the Web*), the Department of Education forwards your information automatically to the state financial aid offices in the states where the colleges you indicated on your FAFSA are physically located. For instance, if you complete the FAFSA and name, say, the University of Miami as one of your six colleges, the state of Florida will get your financial information. You get the idea.

Those wacky state deadlines

Now, you probably remember that the FAFSA deadline of June 30. If the individual *states* get their information from the FAFSA, their deadline should be *after* the FAFSA deadline, right?

Truth is, it depends. In a few cases, deadlines for state-based financial aid are, indeed, after the June 30 FAFSA deadline. Other states share the June 30 date with the feds. Most state deadlines, however, are *earlier* than the June 30 federal deadline! You should know that while the feds let you retroactively file for aid (actually letting you file your FAFSA during an 18-month window), the states don't!

Even if your state shares the June 30 federal deadline, don't wait until the last moment. If you submit your FAFSA on June 27, for example, Arizona or South Carolina (two states with June 30 deadlines) probably won't receive your application in time. There is a slight delay getting information from one level of the government to the other.

Other states have deadlines that are significantly earlier than June 30, so you must submit your FAFSA well before the federal deadline. For example, high school seniors in Michigan must apply to their state by February 21, Rhode Island's application deadline is March 1, and students applying for North Carolina state aid must do so by March 15. Missouri's deadline is April 1 (April

Fool's Day — is this state trying to tell us something?), and the deadline in Oklahoma is April 30. It turns out that state financial aid deadlines (like the states themselves) are all over the map.

Perhaps even trickier is the fact that deadlines tend to change from time to time. Just because your older sister could wait until mid-May to apply for state aid, doesn't necessarily mean that *you* can do so this year. Your state financial aid office may have changed its deadline, or your sister may have been applying to a state with a later deadline than yours. It really pays to know your deadline and set aside enough time to get your application in well beforehand. Plus, if you have schools on your wish list that are located in different states, you have to deal with those other deadlines as well.

Most states get their information from the FAFSA. If you haven't submitted your application by the particular state's deadline, you probably won't qualify for state-based student aid that year. You must research all relevant state deadlines and keep in mind that they may be before — in some cases, *well before* — the FAFSA deadline of June 30.

A few states have their own general financial aid application forms, and still others have supplemental forms that ask *additional* questions. (After finishing the FAFSA, you probably thought that they'd run out of questions, didn't you?)

The point here is that state-run scholarship and grant programs can be quite rewarding and broad based, but you have to be alert to receive awards from them. There's no trick to the application process; you simply have to be eligible and apply to the program before the deadline.

What those state deadlines really mean

Some of the state deadlines we mention in the previous section are *drop-dead* deadlines, meaning that if you fail to apply by the date specified, you won't receive aid for that year. Other deadlines represent *priority consideration dates,* meaning that the state will give those students who apply by this specified time (or earlier) a better chance at financial aid. The state may have financial aid left after a priority consideration deadline — but it also may not, in which case, you're out of luck.

Deadlines usually represent the *date your application must be received,* meaning that you have to make sure that your application gets to the state financial aid office by the date indicated. If you've left things to the last minute, consider taking on the extra expense of a courier rather than trusting the U.S. Postal Service. Deadlines for other states are considered *postmarked-by dates:* If your aid application is postmarked by the U.S. Postal Service by the date specified, the aid office will accept it, regardless of when it arrives.

One state's eligibility requirements

New York State's TAP (Tuition Assistance Program) has several eligibility requirements, but they paint a picture of an average New York state student. Remember that the definition of eligibility varies from state to state and even from award to award, so always check for details as far in advance as possible. To be eligible for New York State's TAP, you must:

✔ Be a U.S. citizen or eligible non-citizen. Remember from your FAFSA, an eligible non-citizen is a student here on a legal visa, on a visa waiver, or otherwise permitted to study here and be a resident by the U.S. *Immigration Naturalization Service* (INS).

✔ Be a legal resident of New York State. Most states grant you residency status after living in the particular state for a period of at least one year, but this rule can vary.

✔ Study full time (in New York's credit semester system, "full time" means at least 12 credits per semester). This study must be at an *approved* New York State postsecondary institution. Just about every college and most other schools qualify. When in doubt, check with the particular school and verify this information with the state financial aid office.

✔ Have graduated from high school, or have a GED, or have passed a federally approved exam demonstrating that you can benefit from the education offered.

✔ Be matriculated in an approved program of study and be in good academic standing.

✔ Have at least a cumulative "C" average after receipt of two annual payments. You must keep your college grades up in order to continue to receive the TAP award.

✔ Be charged at least $200 tuition per year. Any college, as well as most trade schools and institutes of higher learning, is certainly qualified under this provision.

✔ Not be in default on a student loan guaranteed by the New York State Higher Education Services Corporation (HESC) and not be in default on any repayment of state awards.

✔ Meet income eligibility limitations.

Source: New York State Higher Education Services Corporation

In some cases, the type of financial aid or classification of award dictates when your deadlines will be set. New Jersey, for example, has a system in which its *Tuition Aid Grant* recipients must apply by June 1, but students looking for other types of aid have until October 1, (all dates assume that students are starting in the usual fall term). Pennsylvania has a similar system: *All State* grant (that's the name of the award, not everybody in the state, by the way) hopefuls must apply by May 1, but students looking for other awards can wait until August 1.

Many students are surprised (and disappointed) every year by differences between the FAFSA deadline and the state ones. Our advice? Do the research (we've assembled all the contact information you need on a state-by-state basis later in this chapter) and enter your deadlines on the calendar we provide in Chapter 1 and on a large wall calendar that you'll use solely for tracking financial aid and other deadlines. This way, every deadline will be easy to remember — and easy to meet.

State-by-State Contacts

This section offers a list of higher education offices throughout the country, so you can investigate the most up-to-date information about state-based financial aid programs. The list includes the name of the particular organization, its mailing address, telephone number, toll-free telephone number and fax number (when available), and Web address. Please note that the toll-free numbers are often restricted to callers from *within* that particular state.

This contact information is particularly subject to change, so use the included Web addresses to confirm all information, including each state's reciprocity information, which, in the words of one state financial aid officer who spoke with us, "changes so frequently *we* can't keep up with the list."

Alabama
Alabama Commission on Higher Education
100 North Union Street
P.O. Box 302000
Montgomery, AL 36130-2000
Tel: (334) 242-1998
Tel: (800) 843-8534 (toll free for
 AL residents only)
Fax: (334) 242-0268
Internet: www.ache.state.al.us/
Reciprocity: No

Alaska
Alaska Commission on Postsecondary Education
3030 Vintage Boulevard
Juneau, AK 99801-7100
Tel: (907) 465-2962
Tel: (800) 441-2962 (toll free)
TTY: (907) 465-3143
Fax: (907) 465-5316
Internet: www.state.ak.us/acpe/
Reciprocity: No

Arizona
Arizona Commission for Postsecondary Education

2020 North Central Avenue, Suite 550
Phoenix, AZ 85004-4503
Tel: (602) 258-2435
Fax: (602) 258-2483
Internet: www.azhighered.org
Reciprocity: Yes, AK, CA, CO, HI, ID, MT, NV, NM, ND, OR, SD, UT, WA, WY
Note: This small (but helpful) office administers only two financial aid programs: LEAP and PFAP (see the Web site for information on these programs). Students should call the office only if they have questions about material found on the Web site. Most inquiries and applications can be handled electronically.

Arkansas
Arkansas Department of Higher Education
114 East Capitol
Little Rock, AR 72201-3818
Tel: (501) 371-2000
Fax: (501) 371-2003
Internet: www.arkansashighered.com/
Reciprocity: Yes, varies by college or other educational institution.

California
California Student Aid Commission
P.O. Box 419027
Rancho Cordova, CA 95741-9027
Tel: (916) 526-7590
Tel: (888) 224-7268 (toll free)
Fax: (916) 526-8004
Internet: www.csac.ca.gov/
Reciprocity: No

Colorado
Colorado Commission on Higher
Education
1380 Lawrence Street, Suite 1200
Denver, CO 80204
Tel: (303) 866-2723
Fax: (303) 866-4266
Internet: www.state.co.us/
cche_dir/hecche.html
Reciprocity: Yes, NM

Connecticut
Connecticut Department of Higher
Education
61 Woodland Street
Hartford, CT 06105-2326
Tel: (860) 947-1855
Tel: (800) 842-0229 (toll free)
Fax: (860) 947-1310
Internet: www.ctdhe.org/
Reciprocity: Yes, DC, DE, ME, MA,
NH, PA, RI, VT

Delaware
Delaware Higher Education
Commission
Carvel State Office Building
820 North French Street, Fifth Floor
Wilmington, DE 19801
Tel: (302) 577-3240
Tel: (800) 292-7935 (toll free)
Fax: (302) 577-6765
Internet: www.doe.state.de.us/
high-ed/
Reciprocity: Yes, PA

District of Columbia (Washington, DC)
District of Columbia Department of
Human Services
Office of Postsecondary Education,
Research, and Assistance
2100 Martin Luther King, Jr. Avenue,
SE, Suite 401
Washington, DC 20020
Tel: (202) 698-2400
Fax: (202) 727-2739
Internet: dc.gov/citizen/
education.shtm
Reciprocity: No

Florida
Florida Department of Education
Office of Student Financial
Assistance
Turlington Building
325 West Gaines Street
Tallahassee, FL 32399-0400
Tel: (850) 487-0049
Internet: www.myfloridaeducation.
com/doehome.htm
Reciprocity: No

Georgia
Georgia Student Finance Authority
State Loans Division
2082 East Exchange Place, Suite 230
Tucker, GA 30084
Tel: (770) 724-9000
Tel: (800) 776-6878 (toll free)
Fax: (770) 724-9263
Internet: www.gsfc.org/Main/
main.cfm
Reciprocity: No

Hawaii
Hawaii Department of Education
P.O. Box 2360
Honolulu, Hawaii 96804
Tel: (808) 586-3230
Fax: (808) 586-3234
Internet: doe.k12.hi.us/
Reciprocity: Yes, some Pacific Islands
administered by the U.S.

Idaho
Idaho State Board of Education
P.O. Box 83720
Boise, ID 83720-0037
Tel: (208) 334-2270
Fax: (208) 334-2632
Internet: www.idahoboardofed.org/
Reciprocity: Yes, WA (specifically identified participating schools on both sides of the border), and Idaho State University and Utah State University also have a reciprocal agreement.

Illinois
Illinois Student Assistance Commission
1755 Lake Cook Road
Deerfield, IL 60015-5209
Tel: (847) 948-8500
Tel: (800) 899-4722 (toll free)
TTY: (847) 831-8326
Fax: (847) 831-8549
Internet: www.isac1.org
Reciprocity: No

Indiana
State Student Assistance Commission of Indiana
150 West Market Street, Suite 500
Indianapolis, IN 46204-2811
Tel: (317) 232-2350
Tel: (888) 528-4719
Fax: (317) 232-3260
Internet: www.in.gov/ssaci/
Reciprocity: No

Iowa
Iowa College Student Aid Commission
200 10th Street, Fourth Floor
Des Moines, IA 50309
Tel: (515) 242-3344
Tel: (800) 383-4222 (toll free)
Fax: (515) 242-3388
Internet: www.iowacollegeaid.org
Reciprocity: No

Kansas
Kansas Board of Regents
Curtis State Office Building
1000 SW Jackson Street, Suite 520
Topeka, KS 66612-1368
Tel: (785) 296-3421
Fax: (785) 296-0983
Internet: www.kansasregents.org/
Reciprocity: Yes, MO, depending on the college, also member of the Midwest Student Exchange Program giving reciprocity to KS, MI, MN, MS, NE, and ND students.

Kentucky
Kentucky Higher Education Assistance Authority
1050 U.S. Highway 127 South
Frankfort, KY 40601-4323
Tel: (502) 696-7200
Tel: (800) 928-8926 (toll free)
TTY: (800) 855-2880
FAX: (502) 696-7496
Internet: www.kheaa.com/
Reciprocity: Contact organization for information on your specific situation.

Louisiana
Louisiana Office of Student Financial Assistance
P.O. Box 91202
Baton Rouge, LA 70821-9202
Tel: (225) 922-1012
Tel: (800) 259-5626 (toll free)
Fax: (225) 922-0790
Internet: www.osfa.state.la.us/
Reciprocity: No

Maine
Maine Education Assistance Division
Finance Authority of Maine (FAME)
P.O. Box 949
5 Community Drive
Augusta, ME 04332-0949
Tel: (207) 623-3263
Tel: (800) 228-3734 (toll free)

TTY: (207) 626-2717
Fax: (207) 632-0095
Internet: www.famemaine.com/
Reciprocity: Yes, AK, CT, DC, DE, MA, MD, NH, PA, RI, VT

Maryland
Maryland Higher Education Commission
Office of Student Financial Assistance
839 Bestgate Road, Suite 400
Annapolis, MD 21403
Tel: (410) 260-4500
Tel: (800) 974-1024 (toll free for MD residents only)
TTY: (800) 735-2258
Fax: (410) 260-3200
Internet: www.mhec.state.md.us/
Reciprocity: Yes, contact schools to see if member of Academic Common Market.

Massachusetts
Massachusetts Board of Higher Education
Office of Student Financial Assistance
454 Broadway, Suite 200
Revere, MA 02151
Tel: (617) 727.9420
Fax (617) 727.0667
Internet: www.mass.edu/
Reciprocity: Yes, DC and New England States

Michigan
Michigan Higher Education Assistance Authority
Office of Scholarships and Grants
P.O. Box 30462
Lansing, MI 48909-7962
Tel: (517) 373-3394
Tel: (888) 447-2687 (toll free)
Fax: (517) 335-5984
Internet: www.michigan.gov/mistudentaid/
Reciprocity: No

Minnesota
Minnesota Higher Education Services Office
1450 Energy Park Drive, Suite 350
Saint Paul, MN 55108-5227
Tel: (651) 642-0567
Tel: (800) 657-3866 (toll free)
Fax: (651) 642-0675
Internet: www.mheso.state.mn.us/
Reciprocity: Yes, IO, ND, SD, MN, WI, and the Midwest Student Exchange

Mississippi
Mississippi Office of Student Financial Aid
3825 Ridgewood Road
Jackson, MS 39211-6453
Tel: (601) 432-6997
Tel: (800) 327-2980 (toll free for MS residents only)
Fax: (601) 432-6527
Internet: www.ihl.state.ms.us/
Reciprocity: Yes, some schools and programs in neighboring states, such as AL, AR, FL, GA, KY, MD, SC, TN, TX, VA, WV.

Missouri
Missouri Department of Higher Education
3515 Amazonas Drive
Jefferson City, MO 65109-5717
Tel: (573) 751-2361
Tel: (800) 473-6757 (toll free)
TTY: (800) 735-2966
Fax: (573) 751-6635
Internet: www.cbhe.state.mo.us/
Reciprocity: Yes, member of the Midwest Student Exchange Program giving reciprocity to KS, MI, MN, MS, NE, and ND students.

Montana
Montana University System
2500 Broadway
P.O. Box 203101
Helena, MT 59620-3103
Tel: (406) 444-6570

Fax: (406) 444-1469
Internet: www.montana.edu/
wwwoche/
Reciprocity: No

Nebraska
In this state, students must apply for financial aid at their chosen institution in Nebraska to receive any state need-based financial aid. The institution determines which students qualify and allocates state dollars to those individuals.
Reciprocity: Yes, the state is also a member of the Midwest Student Exchange Program, giving reciprocity to KS, MI, MN, MS, NE, and ND students.

Nevada
Although this state has various college savings programs, financial scholarship assistance is provided through each individual college.
Internet: www.nevada.edu/
Reciprocity: Yes, Nevada participates in some reciprocity programs; eligibility is assessed through individual colleges.

New Hampshire
New Hampshire Postsecondary Education Commission
3 Barrell Court, Suite 300
Concord, NH 03301-8543
Tel: (603) 271-2555
TTY: (800) 735-2964
Fax: (603) 271-2696
Internet: www.state.nh.us/post secondary/
Reciprocity: Yes, New England states if student can't find program in New Hampshire.

New Jersey
Higher Education Student Assistance Authority (New Jersey)
P.O. Box 540, Building 4
Quakerbridge Plaza
Trenton, NJ 08625-0540
Tel: (609) 588-3226
Tel: (800) 792-8670 (toll free)
TTY: (609) 588-2526
Fax: (609) 588-7389
Internet: www.hesaa.org/
Reciprocity: No

New Mexico
New Mexico Commission on Higher Education
1068 Cerrillos Road
Santa Fe, NM 87505
Tel: (505) 476-6500
Tel: (800) 279-9777 (toll free)
TTY: (800) 659-8331
Fax: (505) 476-6511
Internet: www.nmche.org/
Reciprocity: Yes, AZ, CO

New York
New York State Higher Education Services Corporation (HESC)
99 Washington Avenue
Albany, NY 12255
Tel: (518) 473-1574
Tel: 1-888-NYSHESC [1-888-697-4372] (toll free)
TTY: (800) 445-5234
Fax: (518) 474-2839
Internet: www.hesc.com/
Reciprocity: No

North Carolina
North Carolina State Education Assistance Authority
P.O. Box 13663
Research Triangle Park, NC 27709-3663
Tel: (919) 549-8614
Tel: (800) 700-1775 (toll-free number for NC residents only)
Fax: (919) 549-8481
Internet: www.ncseaa.edu/
Reciprocity: No

North Dakota
North Dakota University System
North Dakota Student Financial
Assistance Program
10th Floor, State Capitol
600 East Boulevard Avenue,
Department 215
Bismarck, ND 58505-0230
Tel: (701) 328-2960
Fax: (701) 328-2961
Internet: www.ndus.edu/
Reciprocity: Yes, member of the
Midwest Student Exchange Program,
giving reciprocity to KS, MI, MN, MS,
NE, and ND students. Also, North
Dakota is a member of the Regional
Graduate Program for graduate stu-
dents.

Ohio
Ohio Board of Regents
State Grants and Scholarships
Department
P.O. Box 182452
Columbus, OH 43218-2452
Tel: (614) 466-7420
Tel: (888) 833-1133 (toll free)
Fax: (614) 752-5903
Internet: www.regents.state.oh.
us/sgs/
Reciprocity: Yes, PA

Oklahoma
Oklahoma State Regents for Higher
Education (OSRHE)
655 Research Parkway, Suite 200
Oklahoma City, OK 73104
Tel: (405) 225-9239
Tel: (800) 858-1840 (toll-free)
Fax: (405) 225-9230
Internet: www.okhighered.org/
student-center
Reciprocity: Yes, contact OSRHE
office for reciprocity details on a
state-by-state, program-by-program
basis.

Oregon
Oregon Student Assistance
Commission
1500 Valley River Drive, Suite 100
Eugene, OR 97401
Tel: (541) 687-7400
Tel: (800) 452-8807 (toll free)
Fax: (541) 687-7419
Internet: www.osac.state.or.us/
Reciprocity: No

Pennsylvania
Office of Postsecondary and Higher
Education (Pennsylvania)
Department of Education
333 Market Street
Harrisburg, PA 17126-0333
Tel: (717) 787-6788
Internet: www.pdehighered.state.
pa.us/higher/site/default.asp
Reciprocity: Yes, some neighboring
states, but not NY, NJ, and MD.

Rhode Island
Rhode Island Higher Education
Assistance Authority
560 Jefferson Boulevard
Warwick, RI 02886
Tel: (401) 736-1100
Tel: (800) 922-9855 (toll free)
TTY: (401) 734-9481
Fax: (401) 732-3541
Internet: www.riheaa.org/
Reciprocity: All U.S. states, Canadian
provinces, and Mexico

South Carolina
South Carolina Commission on
Higher Education
1333 Main Street, Suite 200
Columbia, SC 29201
Tel: (803) 737-2260
Tel: (877) 349-7183 (toll free)
Fax: (803) 737-2297
Internet: www.che400.state.
sc.us/
Reciprocity: No

South Dakota
South Dakota Board of Regents
306 East Capitol Avenue, Suite 200
Pierre, SD 57501
Tel: (605) 773-3455
Fax: (605) 773-5320
Internet: www.sdbor.edu/
Reciprocity: Yes, MN

Tennessee
Tennessee Higher Education
Commission
404 James Robertson Parkway
Parkway Towers, Suite 1900
Nashville, TN 37243-0830
Tel: (615) 741-3605
Fax: (615) 741-6230
Internet: www.state.tn.us/thec/
Reciprocity: Yes, within 30 miles of
Austin Peay State University.

Texas
Texas Higher Education Coordinating
Board
P.O. Box 12788
Austin, TX 78711-2788
Tel: (512) 427-6340
Tel: (800) 242-3062 (toll free)
Fax: (512) 427-6127
Internet: www.collegefort
exans.com
Reciprocity: Yes, states immediately
adjacent to TX.
Please note, in most cases, the
appropriate contact for financial aid
for students in Texas is the financial
aid office at the college or university.

Utah
Utah Higher Education Assistance
Authority
Board of Regents Building, The
Gateway
60 South 400 West
Salt Lake City, Utah 84101-1284
Tel: (801) 321-7200
Fax: (801) 321-7299

Internet: www.uheaa.org and
www.utahmentor.org
Reciprocity: Yes, some graduate
programs. Contact Utah Higher
Education Assistance Authority for
details.

Vermont
Vermont Student Assistance
Corporation
Champlain Mill
1 Main Street, Third Floor
P.O. Box 2000
Winooski, VT 05404-2601
Tel: (802) 655-9602
Tel: (800) 642-3177 (toll free)
TTY: (802) 654-3766
TTY: (800) 281-3341 (toll free)
Fax: (802) 654-3765
Internet: www.vsac.org/
Reciprocity: Yes, certain majors
through the New England Regional
Student Program.

Virginia
State Council of Higher Education for
Virginia
James Monroe Building
101 North 14th Street, Ninth Floor
Richmond, VA 23219
Tel: (804) 225-2600
TTY: (804) 371-8017
Fax: (804) 225-2604
Internet: www.schev.edu/
Reciprocity: Yes, AL, AR, FL, GA, KY,
LA, MD, MS, SC, TN, TX, WV, and
other members of the Southern
Regional Education Board (SREB).
Updates at www.sreb.org

Washington
Washington State Higher Education
Coordinating Board
P.O. Box 43430
917 Lakeridge Way
Olympia, WA 98504-3430
Tel: (360) 753-7800

TTY: (360) 753-7809
Fax: (360) 753-7808
Internet: www.hecb.wa.gov/
Reciprocity: Yes, states and
provinces adjacent, including BC
(Canada), ID, and OR.

West Virginia
West Virginia Higher Education
Policy Commission
1018 Kanawha Boulevard East
Charleston, WV 25301
Tel: (304) 558-2101
Fax: (304) 558-0259
Internet: www.hepc.wvnet.edu/
Reciprocity: Yes, PA

Wisconsin
Wisconsin Higher Educational Aids
Board
131 West Wilson Street, Room 902
Madison, WI 53707-7885
Tel: (608) 267-2206
Fax: (608) 267-2808
Internet: heab.state.wi.us/
Reciprocity: Yes, MN

Wyoming
Wyoming Community College
Commission
2020 Carey Avenue, Eighth Floor
Cheyenne, WY 82002
Tel: (307) 777-7763
Fax: (307) 777-6567
Internet: commission.wcc.edu/
Reciprocity: Yes, AK, AZ, CA, CO, HI,
ID, MT, ND, NE, NM, NV, OR, SD, UT,
WA

Chapter 10

Trying Harder with Your State

In This Chapter

▶ Understanding the differences between state and federal student aid

▶ Keeping track of state deadlines

▶ Contacting your state financial aid office

Chapters 5, 6, and 7 deal with federal-based student aid and how you can get your fair share of this free (or almost free) money. Chapter 9 covers how state residency can cut your college tuition costs. We discuss state-based aid in this chapter, too, but from a different perspective. This chapter outlines the subtle, but important, differences concerning how the federal and state governments calculate your eligibility for student financial aid. Being denied federal-based financial aid doesn't necessarily mean that you won't get money from your state. And if you *are* getting federal aid, your state will probably help you out, too!

We also discuss how state-sponsored tuition plans work and how you can gain valuable free money by using these financial strategies. These plans let you and your parents stash away some cash for your college education, and they also allow for significant tax advantages for both parents and kids.

Finally, we cover how to get free money from your state's lottery-based financial aid scholarships. No, we're not urging you to run out and buy a big wad of lottery tickets, just in case you win big. Rather, some states now offer additional need and merit-based scholarships funded by lottery revenues. It may not be as good as winning the jackpot, but some students *can* get lucky!

Going for State Aid Even If the Feds Have Turned You Down

Even if the federal government says no to your grant or scholarship requests, your particular state still may say yes. This interesting difference of fiscal opinion can come to pass due to the different ways that state and federal governments figure out financial aid eligibility.

The federal government (through your old friend, the *Free Application for Federal Student Aid,* or FAFSA) assesses your financial need based on your income (and, of course, your parents' income if you're a dependent student). Beyond income, the complex FAFSA calculations also take into consideration your assets (and your parents' assets). This is the reason behind many of the financial questions on the FAFSA, especially the seemingly arcane ones on the worksheets dealing with your parents' assets. (For more on the FAFSA and how the feds determine your financial aid eligibility, see Chapter 5.)

On the other hand, many states only care about how much money you and your parents *earn.* This distinction is an important one for middle-class students whose parents may have nice homes but modest incomes.

Despite the fact that states usually get their information about you solely from your FAFSA, they usually don't take assets into consideration when awarding financial aid. Even in states that do take notice of assets, only a small percentage of your assets are typically considered. This distinction is a clear advantage for most middle-class students and their families. Consequently, applying for state-based financial aid is a good idea whenever possible.

Reducing income without going broke

Chapter 6 shows you some perfectly legal ways to appear more needy for federal aid. Parents can, for example, cash in their various liquid investments and pay down their home mortgage with proceeds. The federal government doesn't include your parents' principal residence in its assets calculation (but *does* include liquid assets, such as stocks and bonds), so cashing in these investments may make sense.

Similarly, you and your parents would be wise to consult with an accountant to find out whether you can structure your finances to appear more needy for state-based aid. Does Mom want to leave work to start a small business? Maybe Dad has always wanted to write the Great American Novel and has accumulated enough in his pension plan that he can take a leave of absence. Or, one of your parents may have to leave work suddenly due to health reasons or to take care of their parents' failing health.

By reducing their income, your parents qualify you for more state-based student aid. Naturally, we're not suggesting that your parents quit their jobs and go on welfare just so that you can get more student aid. Not only would that be a crazy idea, but tempting fate in this way would also be bad karma. That said, lots Americans have been laid-off in the last few years, clearly affecting their ability to pay for tuition and other college expenses.

While we're on the topic of income, if one or both of your parents have been *recently* laid-off, this change may not immediately show up in the income calculations that many states use for student financial aid. If income levels are derived from, say, your parent's W-2 forms (showing *last year's income*), the application won't necessarily pick up the fact that mom or dad hasn't worked in 6 months — and the family's been dipping into savings to cope.

In this case, talking with the financial aid office and explaining these (and other) extenuating circumstances is a good idea. Aid officers may often be able to take into consideration recent changes in your family's income level that aren't yet reflected in your annual tax returns. Talk with an aid officer as early as possible and see what can be done to help. As one of our mothers used to say, "If you don't ask, you won't get." 'Nuff said.

Meeting those pesky state deadlines

As we mention in Chapter 9, although states take much of the financial information they need from your FAFSA, they frequently have *earlier* deadlines to receive this information than the traditional June 30 federal deadline. These earlier deadlines are very important for students who wouldn't be able to attend college without state-based student aid.

Every year, unprepared freshman students (not ones who read *this* book, of course) hear about the FAFSA deadline and wrongly assume that their state financial aid deadline falls on the same date. The predictable result is a financial shortfall and, in extreme cases, a missed school year.

Every state is different, and savvy students find out the applicable state deadlines well in advance, preferably months in advance so that things aren't done at the last moment. Keep in mind that state deadlines can vary substantially, so just because *your* state deadline happens to fall on May 1 doesn't necessarily mean that the state next to yours also has the same May 1 deadline. It just doesn't work that way.

You have to be aware of state deadlines for all the colleges on your wish list, not just for your own home state. If you're thinking about attending UCLA, the University of Chicago, and Columbia University, you have to contact the financial aid offices of all three states (California, Illinois, and New York, respectively). Ask their officials about deadlines for first-year students and then mark the *earliest* one on your calendar and make that deadline.

Chapter 9 contains a handy state financial aid directory that you can use to confirm deadlines and ask questions.

Also know that state deadlines can change from year to year. Perhaps your older brother had to contend with an April 15 deadline when he was a freshman three years ago. This year, the state may have moved up (or moved back) the date. Imagine your surprise if you thought that your application deadline was April 15, and it was actually April 1. Of course, asking the right people (in this case, the state financial aid office personnel) the right questions is vital to qualifying for your free money.

First-year college students may have *earlier* financial aid application deadlines than other students already in the system. Sophomores, juniors, and seniors commonly have later financial aid deadlines because most of their paperwork is already done, so make sure that you know of earlier deadlines for freshmen. Otherwise, you'll be out of luck.

Financial aid renewals typically take less time because these *in-system* students are already in the aid database and have been previously approved. The same, however, can't be said about freshman college students. Many first-year students can't (or don't) figure out what to do on time, omit vital pieces of info from their applications, and generally make more of a mess of things — at least the first time around — because they're unfamiliar with the process.

Getting the paperwork in order

Although most states take the financial information they need from your FAFSA, some states require a separate form to apply for financial aid. In most cases, a short supplemental form is all that's required. Interestingly, most states that require supplementary forms have deadlines well *before* the June 30 FAFSA deadline.

Thus, students who are planning to attend college in these early-deadline states have two additional things to worry about: supplemental, *state-specific* student aid applications coupled with an early deadline to submit the forms.

These supplemental forms are available from the state financial organization that's charged with offering student loans and grants, usually the state-based Treasury or Finance Department. You can use the list in Chapter 9 to contact the appropriate office. Alternatively, your prospective college may have links to the correct forms to use. Finally, high school counselors may have a small supply of these forms, just in case.

As with the FAFSA, students and their parents are encouraged to seek the advice of an accountant or other qualified financial planner before signing on the dotted line. Because deadlines for state aid applications are often earlier than the FAFSA deadline, the window in which these supplemental forms must be completed is much narrower, sometimes as short as eight weeks!

Some state aid programs are merit-based (or a combination of merit- and need-based), so you may have to meet additional requirements besides being financially needy. Your marks in the form of GPA or ACT/SAT scores (or both!) may be required. In some cases, the state financial aid office may also require recommendation letters from teachers. Ask, and ye shall know.

The Cal Grant program

Here's an example of a state-based financial aid application:

New applicants applying for the Cal Grant programs are required to complete and file a FAFSA after January 1, but no later than March 2, of the year immediately preceding the fall term in which they hope to receive a Cal Grant.

Cal Grant applicants must also submit a Commission Grade Point Average (GPA) Verification form, including a GPA verified by a school official. The Commission GPA Verification form may be obtained from high school counselors or college financial aid offices throughout California. Cal Grant applicants who wish to receive written confirmation of their award status must file a FAFSA and the Commission GPA Verification form by the March 2 deadline.

Applicants must obtain a $.75 U.S. Postal Service Certificate of Mailing in order to prove that the filing deadline was met and that each form was mailed to the appropriate mailing address.

Source: California Student Aid Commission

State-Sponsored Tuition Plans: Money for Those with Foresight

Pssst. Wanna get a cheap college education? How about getting your parents to stash away a few bucks every week, or maybe $100 a month. Keep this scheme going for a few years. By the time *you* need the money for college, you'll have a huge amount of cash to reduce your tuition, pay for books, or live on campus and even pay for food. Better yet, the entire lot is tax-free!

Is this some crazy dream? Nope, it's an accurate scenario of what you (or, actually, your parents) can do to sock away money for your college education. The money that your parents put into this fund will accumulate tax-free until it's withdrawn. And, if it's used for your education, all the money put into the plan plus the accumulated interest is tax-free! It's a really cool plan — especially if your parents can do their bit on a regular basis.

State-based college savings plans typically come in two flavors:

- Prepaid tuition programs
- Savings plans

As you may guess, the first option gives parents the opportunity to prepay future college tuition based on today's costs. Most importantly, these prepaid tuition programs guarantee that they'll keep pace with tuition inflation. This means that a half-year of tuition paid today will be worth a half-year of tuition by the time you get to college — no matter when you get there.

The second type of state-based savings plans involves dedicated savings accounts that provide families a variable rate of return. Rather than buying a specific period (such as a half-year) or one full-time course or a set number of course hours, this savings plan simply tries to accumulate enough money so that when college time comes, your parents will have sufficient funds to pay your college education.

Plan 529 from outer space

You may come across the terms *529 Plan, Section 529 Plan,* or *Plan 529 compliant* in your research about state-sponsored college savings plans. Being the inquisitive young adult headed for college that you are (and naturally terrified about missing *any* important bit of information that could affect your eligibility), you're probably wondering what the heck does the *529* mean?

Relax. It turns out that 529 refers to the fact that both prepaid college tuition plans and college savings plans are *qualified state tuition programs* under the Internal Revenue Code Section 529 (26 U.S.C. 529). These types of plans are recognized by the IRS and outlined in Section 529 of its tax code.

Your accountant or other qualified financial planner will know all about Section 529 plans and how they should be accounted for on your (and your parents') tax returns. All you have to remember is that Section 529 plans are merely the technical name for IRS-recognized college savings plans.

Each state plan is different, but similar

The United States doesn't have a standard, generic college savings plan for all the states. Rather, all plans are built on a hypothetical standard model. Depending on where you live, your state-sponsored tuition will include some (or many) of the following points:

- ✔ Typically, parents can open a savings account with an initial deposit of $250, although the initial amount may be higher in some jurisdictions.

- ✔ All state-run or state-sanctioned savings plans have significant tax benefits, both at the federal and state levels. These benefits typically allow people who donate money to your plan to get a deduction from their federal or state tax payable. When the plan is collapsed, all money inside (both principal and accumulated interest) can be removed tax free, as long as all funds are used for tuition. In some states, the proceeds from college savings funds can also be used to pay for books, room and board, and other college-related expenses.

- ✔ Most plans have a variety of deposit options and minimum donation amounts, often as low as $50 per month. Some states require postdated checks; others can set you up on an automatic withdrawal plan from a bank account. This way, every time your parents get paid (every week, two weeks, twice a month, or every month), the savings plan automatically withdraws some money from the account at a pre-determined interval.

✔ A few states now let donators use their credit cards to make contributions to your savings plan. And, if credit card purchases earn customer reward points for the donator, paying for your tuition can effectively generate more free money!

✔ Some plans are open only to parents or custodial guardians; others let anyone deposit money into your account, including you, your grandparents, and even your friends. Imagine if all your relatives didn't give you toys one year for your birthday, but instead donated $25 each into your college fund. Sure, this gesture might not fill your heart with warmth at the time, but when all these small monetary gifts accumulate over time, they can effectively provide some serious tuition cash by the time you get to college.

✔ Some states allow estates to gift large sums of money to college savings plans without tax penalties. This means your dear old aunt, grandfather, or other relative can help out with your college tuition by remembering you in the will. Another good reason to be nice to your elders!

✔ Most states run their own college savings plan, but a few use third-party financial service providers, such as Fidelity Investments or an organization called CollegeInvest. The federal government insures some plans, while the respective state governments back some others. Still others are backed only by the organization that offers them. Insurance is valuable to protect your future college tuition (and your parents' investment).

✔ Some plans can be started when you're only an infant; others require a minimum age. Starting early (where possible) is best because regular contributions accumulate over time to become a healthy college nest egg.

✔ Some plans can be transferred to other siblings or rolled into other tax-deferred shelters, in case you decide that college isn't for you.

✔ Some plans have a wide variety of educational options to which their funds can be directed; others stipulate that the beneficiaries (the students) only use the funds for college. Depending on your career aspirations, this restriction may or may not be important.

College savings plan list by state

The following list outlines each state's college savings plan, its associated Web site, and, of course, the phone number of the aid office specifically concerned with these plans. Although this list was thoroughly checked before publication, this information is subject to change.

Alabama
Prepaid Affordable College Tuition
(PACT)
Tel: 1-800-252-7228
Internet: www.treasury.state.
al.us/

Alaska
University of Alaska College Savings
Plan
Tel: 1-866-277-1005
Internet: www.uacollegesavings.
com/

Arizona
Arizona Family College Savings
Program
Tel: 1-602-258-2435
Internet: www.acpe.asu.edu/

California
California Golden State Scholarshare
Trust
Tel: 1-877-728-4338
Internet: www.scholarshare.com/

Colorado
(This state uses CollegeInvest to run
its plan)
Colorado CollegeInvest
Tel: 1-800-478-5651
Internet: www.collegeinvest.org/

Connecticut
Connecticut College Savings Program
Tel: 1-888-799-2438
Internet: www.aboutchet.com/

Delaware
(This state uses Fidelity Investments
to run its plan)
Delaware College Investment Plan
Tel: 1-800-292-7935
Internet:
personal321int.fidelity.com/
planning/college/content/
delaware.html

**District of Columbia (Washington,
DC)**
DC College Savings Plan
Tel: 1-800-987-4859
Internet: www.dccollegesavings.
com/

Florida
Florida Prepaid College Program &
College Savings Program
Tel: 1-800-552-4723
Internet: www.florida529plans.
com/

Georgia
Georgia Higher Education Savings
Plan
Tel: 1-877-424-4377
Internet: www.gacollegesavings.
com/

Hawaii
TuitionEDGE - A Hawaii 529 College
Investment Program
Tel: In Hawaii: 643-4529 Outside:
1-866-529-3343
Internet: www.tuitionedge.com

Idaho
IDeal Idaho College Savings Program
Tel: 1-208-334-3200
Internet: www.sde.state.id.us/
Dept/

Illinois
College Illinois!
Tel: 1-877-877-3724
Internet: www.collegeillinois.
com/

Indiana
Indiana College Choice 529
Investment Plan
Tel: 1-866-400-7526
Internet: www.collegechoiceplan.
com

Iowa
College Savings Iowa
Tel: 1-888-672-9116
Internet: www.treasurer.state.
ia.us/

Kansas
Kansas Learning Quest Education
Savings Program
Tel: 1- 800-579-2203
Internet: www.learningquest
savings.com/

Kentucky
Kentucky Education Savings Plan
Trust
Tel: 1-877-598-7878
Internet: www.kentuckytrust.org/
Kentucky's Affordable Prepaid
Tuition
Tel: 1-888-919-5278
Internet: www.getkapt.com/

Louisiana
Louisiana Student Tuition Assistance
and Revenue Trust (START)
Tel: 1-800-259-5626 ext.1012
Internet: www.osfa.state.la.us/

Maine
NextGen College Investing Plan
Tel: 1-800-228-3734
Internet: www.nextgenplan.com/
Finance Authority of Maine (FAME)
Tel: 1-800-228-3734
Internet: www.famemaine.com/
html/education/index.html

Maryland
College Savings Plans of Maryland
Tel: 1-888-463-4723
Internet: www.collegesavingsmd.
org/

Massachusetts
Massachusetts U.Plan and U.Fund
Tel: 1-800-449-6332
Internet: www.mefa.org/index.php

Michigan
Michigan Education Trust (MET)
Tel: 1-800-638-4543
Internet: www.michigan.gov/
treasury
Michigan Education Savings Program
(MESP)
Tel: 1-877-861-6377
Internet: www.misaves.com/

Minnesota
Minnesota College Savings Plan
Tel: 1-877-338-4646
Internet: www.mnsaves.org/

Mississippi
Mississippi Prepaid Affordable
College Tuition Program (MPACT)
Tel: 1-800-987-4450
Internet: www.treasury.state.ms.
us/mpact.htm

Mississippi Affordable College
Savings (MACS) Program
Tel: 1-800-987-4450
Internet: www.collegesavingsMS.
org/home.html

Missouri
Missouri Saving for Tuition Program
(M$ST)
Tel: 1-888-414-6678
Internet: www.missourimost.org/

Montana
Montana Family Education Savings
Program
Tel: 1-800-888-2723
Internet: montana.college
savings.com

Nebraska
College Savings Plan of Nebraska
Tel: 1-888-993-3746
Internet: www.planforcollegenow.
com/

Nevada
America's College Savings Plan
Tel: 1-877-529-5295
Internet: www.nevadatreasurer.
com/College/

New Hampshire
New Hampshire Unique College
Investing Plan
Tel: 1-800-544-1722
Internet: www.state.nh.us/
treasury/

New Jersey
New Jersey Better Educational
Savings Trust
Tel: 1-877-465-2378
Internet: www.hesaa.org/intro.
asp

New Mexico
Education Plan of New Mexico
Tel: 1-800-499-7581
Internet: www.tepnm.com/
education/splash.jsp

New York
New York's College Savings Program
Tel: 1-877-697-2837
Internet: www.nysaves.org/

North Carolina
North Carolina National College
Savings Plan
Tel: 1-800-600-3453
Internet:
www.cfnc.org/savings/cv0021.
jsp

North Dakota
North Dakota College SAVE
Tel: 1-800-472-2166
Internet: www.mystudentloan
online.com/index.jsp

Ohio
Ohio CollegeAdvantage
Tel: 1-800-233-6734
Internet: www.collegeadvantage.
com/

Oklahoma
Oklahoma College Savings Plan
Tel: 1-877-654-7284
Internet: www.ok4saving.org/

Oregon
Oregon College Savings Plan
Tel: 1-866-772-8464
Internet: www.estrong.com/strong
web/strong/jsp/oregon/index.
jsp

Pennsylvania
Pennsylvania Tuition Account
Program
Tel: 1-800-440-4000
Internet: www.patap.org/

Rhode Island
Rhode Island CollegeBound*fund*
Tel: 1-888-324-5057
Internet: www.collegeboundfund.
com

South Carolina
South Carolina Tuition Prepayment
Program
Tel: 1-888-772-4723
Internet: www.scgrad.org/
SC Future Scholar 529 Program
Tel: 1-800-765-2668
Internet: www.futurescholar.com/

South Dakota
South Dakota College Access 529
Tel: 1-866-529-7462

Tennessee
Tennessee Baccalaureate Education
System Trust Savings Plan and
Tuition Plan
Tel: 1-888-486-2378
Internet: www.tnbest.org/

Texas
Texas Guaranteed Tuition Plan and
Tomorrow's College Investment Plan
Tel: 1-800-445-4723
Internet: www.texastomorrowfunds.
org/

Utah
Utah Educational Savings Plan Trust
Tel: 1-800-418-2551
Internet: www.uesp.org/

Vermont
Vermont Higher Education
Investment Plan
Tel: 1-800-637-5860
Internet: www.vsac.org/invest
ment_plan/main.htm

Virginia
Virginia Prepaid Education Plan and
Virginia Education Savings Trust
Tel: 1-888-567-0540
Internet: www.virginia529.com/

Washington
Washington State's Guaranteed
Education Tuition Program
Tel: 1-877-438-8848
Internet: www.get.wa.gov/

West Virginia
West Virginia SMART529
Tel: 1-866-574-3542
Internet: www.SMART529.com/

Wisconsin
Wisconsin EdVest
Tel: 1-888-338-3789
Internet: www.estrong.com/strong
web/strong/jsp/edvest/index.
jsp

Wyoming
Wyoming College Achievement Plan
Tel: 1-307-777-7408
Internet:
treasurer.state.wy.us/college
plan.asp

Chapter 11

Going Local

In This Chapter

▶ Talking to everyone

▶ Making the little prizes into a big payoff

▶ Changing the way you search

*F*inding the big scholarships is easy. Get one of those huge scholarship directories and turn to the first page. Search the Web and the big scholarships are the first ones on the list. These research methods lead you to the same scholarships that *everyone* else can find and that *everyone* else applies for. Because they receive an enormous number of applications, those who award the big scholarships can't give your application any more time than a quick glance. You fit the criterion, or you don't. If you do, they usually rank you according to grades, SAT/ACT scores, or other quantitative measurements.

Finding those scholarships where you can really distinguish yourself, where the scholarship committee will take the time to read every word of your application and get to know you is much harder. Finding the people who'll take an active interest in your welfare is harder because finding them takes more than a Google search. But, after you find them, the rewards can be well worth the effort. The best place to start looking is your own hometown.

Starting with the Basics

We don't want to discourage you from applying for the national or statewide scholarships, but we do want to encourage you not to ignore the "smaller" awards offered on a local level. Now, when we say smaller, we don't necessarily mean that you'll only be able to win $20 or so. Although many of these scholarships offer prizes of only $100 to $500, some are larger, around $1,000 to $5,000. The thing is, even the smallest scholarships can add up to serious money.

Local scholarships also tend to offer money to fewer students than their state or federal counterparts — often only one student per year. But since fewer students *apply* for these scholarships, you may have better chances of winning these awards than the so-called "big money" national scholarships.

What do we mean by "local"?

If you live in a small town where everybody knows everybody else, the definition of "local" may seem pretty obvious. But what is "local" to someone who lives in New York City or Los Angeles?

Local means the area that you're comfortable calling your own. It means an area with some sort of government administrator responsible for it. New York City may be vast and more populous than several countries, but it's divided into five boroughs, and each of these is divided into council blocks. There are scholarships that focus on students from Brooklyn, for example, that aren't available to residents of Manhattan.

To get more local, target the city councilor responsible for your neighborhood and the businesses in your area. Our advice is to start with what you know and move outward, encompassing a wider area — without sacrificing quality in your applications. Those living in a small town may want to expand their meaning of *local* to include their overall region or county. For example, no grants may be targeted to someone living in Meat Camp, North Carolina, but several are available to students from the Appalachians.

Local government programs

When it comes to government programs, we have good news and bad news. The bad news is that it can be hard slogging trying to find out what sort of scholarships are offered, where to apply, and what you need to send. Searching the Web often elicits nothing more than contact information hidden in a badly organized Web site. You have to do the legwork by contacting these folks and discovering the details for application.

The good news is that the tougher it is to find this information, the fewer applications the scholarship committee receives. Some programs operate virtually by word of mouth, so go talk with your local government representatives. Drop in on the office, explain that you're looking for locally based scholarships, and ask for the appropriate person. If the people in the office don't know where to send you, go up the ladder and chat with a city councilor, alderman, or even the mayor.

Depending on the size of your town, any scholarship you receive can get you local press coverage. Your local government representative would undoubtedly love that sort of exposure, standing beside you in the photo, described as the dedicated public servant who made it happen.

Don't forget your high school . . . or your friend's high school

The first person to talk to about getting free money (other than your parents) is your high school counselor. Part of his or her job is to keep up on grants, scholarships, and loans that may be available for students from your school. Of course, some counselors are better at their job than others, and some may just be too busy with more pressing matters to have the time to investigate beyond the basics. Don't be shy about pooling your resources (meaning your free money research) with pals who attend other high schools. The more people you talk with, the more information you're likely to get.

Your counselor isn't the only one who knows about free money for college. Talk to your teachers about the colleges they attended and ask them for scholarship help. Even if your teacher has no specific information, he'll probably make a good reference if you decide to apply to his alma mater.

Contact your local Parent Teacher Association (PTA) for information about scholarships and grants. Some PTAs administer scholarship programs, and most have information about them. If the person you talk with at the PTA isn't helpful, ask to be given access to the national association of PTAs. The national association is very busy but is an excellent source of contacts if you have time and patience.

Expanding the Search

Don't stop now. You have many more opportunities available beyond your local government and schools. Here are a few ideas.

Local businesses and local heroes

Other than the government, who's most likely to give out free money for college? Why, those who have the money to give, of course. Within your town or area, look toward local businesses, service organizations, and individuals who hold an important role in local activities.

Your local Chamber of Commerce should be able to help you identify the top businesses in town. Once in a while, you'll find that a Chamber of Commerce offers a scholarship of its own, but this is rare. Look around and discover which companies are sponsoring the little league teams — companies that like to see their names on the backs of young athletes may also enjoy the prestige that comes with a scholarship presentation ceremony.

Don't be surprised if scholarships come from a notable family in your area. Many wealthy individuals choose to create or endow charitable foundations in their wills as a legacy. These scholarships are often administered by family members with the assistance of their financial experts.

Another excellent source of information is the local banking community. Scholarships are held in endowments, and someone has to administer these endowments. Talk to the manager of your bank and any other banks in the area to find out about any grants or scholarships they administer.

We discuss getting free money from organizations in Chapter 16, and in Chapter 20, we list some of the top service organizations that have chapters throughout the country. These groups are the first ones to approach, but be sure to continue to search for other groups specific to your area. Also, service organizations often interact with each other, so ask people you meet in one organization to introduce you to all the other organizations they know.

Make sure that you read the fine print before applying for any so-called scholarship. When dealing with locally based grants, we've discovered an inordinate number of prizes that limit use of the funds awarded to an event having nothing to do with attending college. These awards may be "scholarships" to attend a particular conference, or to cover the costs of an entrance exam for a course that you may not wish to take. Always check the details before you spend your time applying for something that may be worthless to you.

That being said, don't avoid applying for prizes just because they don't offer enough money. Even those awards that offer book prizes can be valuable in other ways. If you haven't won an award in the past, this small prize allows you to call yourself an "award-winning scholar" on your applications for other scholarships. Awards offered by local chapters of major organizations, such as the Rotary Club, sometimes get administered in stages — you win a small local prize and are automatically entered into the national competition.

Finally, don't forget to approach your local church, synagogue, mosque, temple or other religious institution. Sometimes, you don't have to be a practicing member of the congregation, but it usually helps if you are. Like service organizations, religious institutions are parts of regional, national, and international organizations. Awards may be available from any level. Ask!

College grants tied to your town or region

Individuals or organizations may endow scholarships in many different ways. There may be a general call for applications, but most of them have qualifying criteria. Frequently, you'll find free money available to be won only by a student who plans to attend a specific college. To find these scholarships, talk to the financial counselor at the college in question.

Interestingly, several such scholarships target students who are from outside the home state of a particular college. Naturally, when you're planning which colleges you may wish to attend, cost is a factor. If you can get a town-based scholarship by going to College A that isn't available if you go to College B, College A might deserve some special attention.

The problem is that with thousands of colleges in the United States, how do you find out which colleges offer scholarships to people from your town or region? The answer is close to home — check out the local newspaper. Every day, get into the habit of scanning the news for scholarship announcements, and keep a clippings file. When it comes time to apply to colleges, contact each scholarship committee mentioned in your clippings file and get the application details for the particular programs.

If possible, try to chat with the individual who endowed the scholarship in the first place. Because he or she probably has at least something in common with you — being born in your area and attending the targeted college — you may be able to get a prized recommendation out of this meeting, and help increase your chances of achieving your goal.

Local Search Tools

Searching for money locally is different from searching for federal, state, or college-based money. And you use the tools of the trade differently, too. When researching federal grant programs, you can find pretty much all you need on the Internet, and you'll probably never meet face-to-face those who give out the money. The situation is reversed for local scholarship programs.

The Internet

The Internet is a fantastic tool for bringing the world to your hometown. Unfortunately, it's not a lot of help when trying to bring your hometown to you. Search engines show you lists of pages about local government scholarship programs in Australia, Japan, and Nigeria. Perhaps surprisingly, Main Street America can often be less available on the Web.

The Yellow Pages

Instead, open your local phone book. Start with city or town government resources. After you've dealt with them, move on to the section called

Organizations, or Service Clubs, or any combination or variation on the theme. Then, try the biggest companies in town. For example, if Coca-Cola operates a bottling plant in your town that employs half the citizens, you better believe that the company has a local scholarship program.

Locals

Another excellent local resource is the other people in your town. Get to know the town's head librarian, civic leaders, and activists. Let them tell you all the wisdom and information they've collected over the years about scholarships. These people are likely to be involved in administering local awards, and they may choose to nominate you for a scholarship! Being nominated by a person respected by the scholarship committee (or even *on* the scholarship committee) can sure influence the decision makers!

The telephone

After you've identified the most likely candidates, give them a call and ask for details. You can try to find them on the Web — it's easier after you've identified them — and send an e-mail. But a phone call is more personal and more likely to elicit better results.

Your shoes

Walk to the mayor's office, the Legion Hall, or the bottling plant and talk to the people in the offices. People might ignore an e-mail, but ignoring the request of a fresh-faced kid standing right in front of them is much harder to do. Be polite and patient, but be persistent and get the information you need.

Part IV

Scoping Out Free Money from Prospective Colleges

The 5th Wave   By Rich Tennant

"OH GREAT! THE ONE PART OF THE INTERVIEW PROCESS I DIDN'T PRACTICE FOR!"

In this part . . .

You may feel a bit skittish about asking a prospective college for money. After all, you're grateful that you even got accepted in the first place. You don't want the kind folks at the admissions office to withdraw their offer, do you?

Ignore that feeling and ask for the money. Trust us. Colleges won't withdraw their offer just because you apply for scholarships or ask for tuition discounts. They rarely offer much more than a token entrance scholarship upfront unless you specifically ask for more. So they expect students to ask; that's why they have an entire office devoted to financial aid. The people in the financial aid office are the experts about the free money available at their college. Befriend them, play up your strengths, and ask them for help. After all, you've worked hard, and you deserve it!

Chapter 12

Getting a Better Deal on Tuition

. . . .

In This Chapter

▶ Figuring out how much your college education will really cost
▶ Paying for the Ivy League
▶ Appealing for more money

. . . .

*A*fter government sources, the next best place to look for free money is at your college. Depending on the institution, colleges may give tuition discounts or waivers, college-based grants and scholarships, departmental grants and scholarships, athletic and arts grants and scholarships, merit-based funding, and need-based funding. And they may administer loans, Work-Study programs, external grants and scholarships, as well as federal and state funding. Whatever you do, *do not* forget to approach your college about free money.

Considering how much funding the college administers, you may think that the process would be centralized, allowing you to approach a single office, fill out a single form, and get all the free money to which you're entitled. If so, please let us set you on the right path!

Most colleges have a financial aid office that administers need-based funding. This office may — or may not — administer college-based grants and scholarships, if they exist at the particular school.

The college may also have a scholarships office that deals with college-based and/or external scholarships, such as money from donors who want their gift associated specifically with the college. This office may be able to help you with other institutional and organization-based funding — or you may be completely on your own.

As well, the departmental, athletic, and arts scholarships tend to be administered by each individual department, so it's rare that any one office in a college knows about *all* the money that may be available to you.

Confused yet? Don't worry. In this chapter (and in Chapters 13 and 14), we outline all the different forms of free money you can get through your college.

We also explain who gets offered aid, for what reasons, and the steps you can take to (hopefully) increase the package you're offered.

Getting Accepted Is Just the Beginning

When you apply for college, you're advised to submit several financial aid documents at the same time. You have no reason not to submit these documents and every reason to do so. You can win need-based money even if your family makes $150,000 a year or more, depending on your circumstances.

The worst that can happen is that you'll be denied any need-based aid. In other words, they say *no*. If that happens, you're no worse off than if you hadn't applied. If, on the other hand, you do receive some need-based aid, you win! If the only need-based financial aid you're offered is a loan and you can obtain the money from other sources, you can always decline the offer. We've never heard of financial aid being forced down anyone's throat!

The financial aid documents that you can submit include the following:

- **The FAFSA:** We discuss the *Free Application for Federal Student Aid* in Chapter 5. This application is the cornerstone of most student financial aid.

- **The PROFILE:** More than 300 colleges and other educational institutions use this supplementary financial aid application form to help them award nonfederal student aid. Administered by the College Board's *College Scholarship Service* (CSS), the PROFILE should be completed by every student looking for financial aid from any of the colleges that use the CSS/Financial Aid PROFILE service. Students must first register for the PROFILE, pay a small fee, and then complete the form. The questions asked are similar to those in the FAFSA, but they're not exactly the same. Your information goes directly to the schools you list, so make sure that each school you're applying to is included.

   The bottom line is that completing the PROFILE may make you eligible for more financial aid. Check it out at `profileonline.collegeboard.com` (note that this URL has no "www" prefix).

- **College-specific financial aid documents:** Some colleges have their own forms for you to fill out to determine if you're eligible for their need-based funding. Be sure to look through *all* the documentation you receive from your target schools to figure out if you need to send in additional information, and give the financial aid offices a call just in case.

- **Supplementary materials:** Tax returns are an obvious example of the extra documentation you may be asked to have on hand. Savvy students are prepared to submit documentation to prove anything that they declare in the various aid applications.

Beyond filling out the paperwork, you can do a lot to decrease the amount you have to pay. But first, allow us to dispel a myth in the next section.

Will applying for financial aid hurt your chances for admission?

A popular myth going around these days is that applying for financial aid when you apply for admissions adversely affects your chances of being offered a spot at the college. *This myth is absolutely untrue!* In fact, most admissions offices and financial aid offices are kept separate to avoid even the appearance of bias when assessing a student's worthiness for admission.

However, accepting *early admission* may hurt your chances of getting entrance scholarships. Most financial aid packages — including tuition discounts, waivers, entrance scholarships, and other scholarships — are offered in the late spring along with general admissions. Early admissions merely tell you that the college is offering you a spot and you'll hear the financial news later. Unfortunately, the college wants to know immediately if you'll accept its offer. You can defer the offer, but then, who knows, it may not be available later. And, after you've accepted, the college has little reason to offer you a financial incentive because you've already committed yourself.

In this situation, talk with both the admissions officer and financial aid officer at the college as soon as possible. Explain that you want to attend the college, but you can't commit until you know that you can afford it. Do your best to convince them to offer you your college-based financial incentive now. If the financial aid officer knows that he or she can justify it, making the offer may be worthwhile to cut back on paperwork later.

Deciphering the financial aid package

Okay, back to pursuing more money. Along with your acceptance letter, you'll also receive your financial aid package. This package tells the following:

- **The full sticker price of the first year of your college education.** The college sets the sticker price independent of anything to do with you, and this price is rarely the final amount you have to pay anyway. In fact, at most colleges, the majority of students pay less than the full sticker price.

- **How much money the federal and state government programs have decided to offer you, and in what form — grants, loans, or Work-Study — along with your** *expected family contribution* **(EFC) according to the federal government.** This amount takes into consideration your educational savings, your personal savings, and the amount your parents are expected to chip in. It also considers the amount of any external scholarships not administered by the college that you've won and reported.

We discuss the federal and state programs, along with EFCs in Parts II and III of this book.

✔ **The amount, if any, of tuition discounts or waivers your college offers you.** Tuition discounts are explained in detail later in this chapter. The main thing to realize is that these awards are offered because you qualify for them automatically or because the college administration wants to add an incentive to make you choose their college. The second type of tuition discounts may also be called *entrance awards,* and many are nonrenewable, meaning that you only get them in your first year.

✔ **Any other college-based scholarships you've been awarded, if you applied for them with your application to college.** These can be college-wide, departmental, or external awards administered by the college. We discuss these awards in more detail in Chapter 13.

✔ **The amount, if any, of the other financial aid your college has chosen to offer you, and in what form — grants, loans, or Work-Study.**

✔ **The gap, or the remaining amount that you have to pay somehow.** Colleges that commit to "meeting the entire need of all students we admit" will have no gap. However, you might find that the amount apportioned to *loan-based* financial aid is fairly significant.

One-time awards versus recurring awards

Certain colleges offer *entrance awards* on a one-time, non-recurring basis. These awards can either be offered automatically to anyone with high enough marks, or as part of your specific aid package because the college wishes to entice you to join its ranks. Though these awards are frequently tools of colleges that need to take extra steps in order to fill their first-year classes, entrance awards are also offered by some prestigious colleges to recognize merit.

Recurring awards, on the other hand, are those that you continue to receive every year. You often have to maintain a minimum GPA in order to continue receiving the funds, but you don't need to compete with other students to receive them again.

Renewable awards are similar to recurring awards, but you must reapply for them each year. Most renewable awards are written to allow for automatic renewal as long as you submit your application on time and maintain a predetermined GPA. Some require you to maintain a particular standing, such as being in the top 25 percent (sometimes referred to as *top quartile*) of your class. You always want to read the fine print of any award.

To make the process just that much more difficult, you'll quickly realize that your financial aid package may not use the words *entrance, recurring,* or *renewable* to define your awards. These terms tend to be the words used in studies of trends in financial aid. Your prospective colleges may tell you that you won the George Washington Award, and you may receive the particulars about it, but it's up to you to determine what kind of an award it is and what you have to do to accept the award and ensure that you get all the money due to you.

Maintaining your GPA or ranking is a significant undertaking. Just because you did well in high school doesn't mean that you'll breeze through college. Many top students get swept up in the party atmosphere of college, fail to make a sufficient effort when they don't have parents or teachers pestering them to study, or simply underestimate the competition or the workload.

Applying for scholarships after the first year

The scholarship application process doesn't end after you enter college. Several scholarships are available only to sophomores, juniors, seniors, or even graduate students. The principles we advise for finding first-year scholarships apply just as well to finding scholarships for later years. The point is to continue your search and keep up with those application deadlines.

Tuition Discounts: Cha-Ching!

Another confusion in terminology comes when we discuss the forms of financial aid known as *tuition discounts* and *waivers.* Some consider these to be strictly the financial aid offered based on eligibility, which we discuss later in this section. Others define tuition discounts as including anything offered by the college that reduces the amount a student is required to pay for tuition. In this section, we discuss both eligibility-based discounts and other forms of tuition reductions.

When you're offered a tuition discount, the college quotes you its full sticker price and then offers to reduce the amount for you. The reduction may be a specific dollar amount of money or a percentage of the total.

You never get to see or hold the money when you receive a tuition discount. Your college bill is simply *reduced* by the discount amount so that you only have to pay the net amount.

Tuition discounts, by definition, only cover tuition. Some colleges may extend the discount to other required fees, such as lab fees, but this is rare and must be confirmed in advance.

For instance, if you've budgeted $30,000 per year to attend a particular college, including tuition, residence, meal plan, books, and other costs, and you get a "30 percent tuition discount," don't expect to get $9,000 off the top. If $15,000 of the total cost is for tuition, a 30 percent tuition discount reduces your cost by $4,500. You'll still have to cover the remaining $10,500 in tuition plus the *entire* $15,000 for other expenses each year.

You may be wondering why colleges would even offer you a discount. Well, here are the two main reasons:

- You're eligible due to family, employment, religious, or other association, and everyone who's eligible gets offered a tuition discount.

- The college admissions officers want to give *you* a specific incentive to attend their college because they consider you to be special, valuable, and worth spending a little more money to win over.

The money the college offers you may be called a tuition discount, an entrance award, or a specific college-based grant, but the effect is the same: The amount you have to pay is less than the quoted sticker price.

We haven't found an instance of state colleges offering the second type of tuition discount because tuition is kept relatively low for students residing in that state. State taxes subsidize state colleges, so prices are much lower for those living there, and state colleges rarely need to beef up enrollment numbers through incentives. In contrast, certain higher-priced private colleges frequently offer tuition discounts to the students they want. Interestingly, Ivy League colleges have a set policy that all financial aid they offer is need-based (that is, available only to people who can't otherwise afford college). We discuss need-based discounts in greater detail later in this chapter.

Eligibility-based tuition discounts

Colleges often offer to reduce tuition as part of a benefits package or as part of their general policy. For this sort of tuition discount, you can't negotiate for a better deal, and eligibility tends to be strictly defined. You either qualify or you don't. Here are a few examples:

- **College employees often get tuition discounts.** If you're the spouse, child, or (rarely) grandchild of a faculty or staff member, you're often entitled to a tuition discount or a tuition exemption. We discuss these discounts in more detail in Chapter 17.

- **Some colleges also offer discounts to alumni and their dependents.** Colleges often do this as a way of keeping a tradition alive or rewarding return business. Stanford University, for example, offers a 20 percent tuition discount to alumni returning for Continuing Education courses.

✔ **Eligibility may be based on age.** Some colleges offer discounts to seniors. Tulane University, for example, offers a 50 percent discount for students aged 60 years and older.

✔ **Discounts may be offered to students with siblings attending the college.** Seton Hall University, for example, offers a 10 percent discount to students whose brother or sister attends SHU.

✔ **Tuition discounts are often tied to employment.** George Washington University in Virginia operates liaison programs with various corporations, offering a 10 percent tuition reimbursement to employees who complete a course of study with them. Like many similar programs, the reimbursement amount is capped at a set figure. In GWU's case, the maximum that can be claimed is $1,000 per year per student.

✔ **Some employee tuition discount programs also apply to the rest of the family.** The State of Tennessee offers employees of the executive, judicial, and legislative branches of government a fee waiver for one course per semester, and tuition discounts of 25 percent on all college courses taken by their dependents. Specific restrictions apply — generally the dependant must be under 24 — but they're easy to follow.

Programs for state employees and their dependents exist in most states, so definitely investigate this possibility if your parent, or even your grandparent, works for (or used to work for) the state. While you're at it, don't forget to check on discounts available if your parent works for the city in which a college is located.

✔ **Some programs are tied to religious institutions or organizations.** At Rosedale Bible College, active ministers and their dependents are offered a 75 percent tuition discount if they're members of the Conservative Mennonite Conference. Ministers *outside* the Conference receive only a 25 percent discount, and the rate for their dependents falls to 15 percent. Also, several other religious institutions offer discounts to groups.

✔ **Some tuition discount programs may not be for college tuition.** Instead, discounts for a private school, a daycare, or other similar institution may be offered to the children of those attending or working at a particular college. For example, Children's World Learning Centers offers Johns Hopkins University employees a 10 percent tuition discount on published tuition rates at any of the Children's World Centers.

✔ **Some discounts are offered for non-peak school times.** Pennsylvania College of Technology has initiated an Early Start program, offering students a 25 percent tuition discount on specific courses if they take them in the summer term, which typically has lower enrollment than the rest of the year.

Incentive-based tuition discounts

Some colleges use these incentives to meet their enrollment objectives of increasing the quality or diversity of students, or to ensure that they acquire a sufficient number of students for the year. The effect for you, the student, is that the college offers you a discount to register with it. In effect, the college waives all or a portion of your fee because it believes that you'll make a significant contribution to the college environment.

The college itself funds this amount through internal budgets, endowment funds, and income. Generally, a certain amount is set aside in the college admissions budget for these incentives. You can try to negotiate for a better financial aid package or ask for the financial aid officer to work with you to obtain extra financing through other sources.

To make the terminology even more confusing, sometimes this discount is also known as an *entrance scholarship*. If you receive one, take special note of whether or not the award is recurring or renewable. As we mentioned, many entrance scholarships only apply to your first year. Then, after you're a registered student, happy at the college with friends and enjoying an established relationship with your professors, the amount you must pay in subsequent years effectively rises dramatically.

Other Ways Your College Can Help You Pay Less

Colleges have other resources to help you reduce the amount of tuition you pay. Most financial aid officers will work to help you apply for everything that may be available, but you must take the first step by asking for their help. Sometimes, asking for help is as easy as checking a box on the applicable financial aid form. Students who win more money go the extra mile by asking college financial aid officers for help and advice.

College-based scholarships

These awards are funded by an existing endowment that's been given to the college by alumni or other interested parties. These scholarships may be need-based, merit-based, or a combination of the two. They may be available to anyone attending the college or limited to individuals in specific departments or years. These scholarships may also be renewable, recurring, or a one-time award, depending on the endowment and college rules. We discuss these awards in greater detail in Chapter 13.

External scholarships or grants administered by the college

These awards are funded by an endowment held by a third party, typically outside the college. It may be an organization, a foundation, an individual, or a company that's decided to give a specific amount to a student who will attend a particular college.

The college administers the scholarship, but you may need to apply for it separately from your general admission application. Many colleges simply add boxes in the specific applications for you to check if you wish to apply for these scholarships. Always check the boxes — you have nothing to lose and free money to gain!

Federal Work-Study

Okay, we know, if you have to work for the money, it's not exactly free. However, Federal Work-Study is frequently offered in your package. Here's how it works.

Colleges and the federal government set up arrangements within the school and with local businesses and community service organizations. The college pays your wages, which can go directly to you or which may be credited to your student account at the college. You're paid by the hour, but you're usually not paid *much*. The job must pay at least the federal minimum wage, and most are hardly more lucrative.

There are, however, three distinct advantages to Federal Work-Study jobs:

- ✔ These jobs are supposed to be associated with your field of study, and, therefore, they help you gain relevant experience. Of course, this can mean that a chemistry major will get a job washing out test tubes — not necessarily great to put on the ol' resume!

- ✔ Unlike an off-campus job delivering pizzas in which you're fully taxed on your wages, income from Work-Study jobs is eligible for deduction from your *modified adjusted gross income* (MAGI). The end result is that Work-Study jobs let you keep more of your hard-earned money than a regular off-campus job.

- ✔ Work-Study jobs are usually based around your class time; the same isn't always true with off-campus jobs that often interfere with your schoolwork or study time.

The Ivy League: It's All about Need

Colleges in the Ivy League (Brown, Columbia, Cornell, Dartmouth, Harvard, University of Pennsylvania, Princeton, and Yale) have standardized on a simple practice regarding aid. These colleges only give need-based financial aid. But what if you have the top GPA and SAT score in the country? They only give need-based funding. But what if you're the most sought-after quarterback in the world — the NFL is begging for you, but you want to go to college first? They only give need-based funding. But what about . . .? *Hey, they only give need-based funding!*

The thinking behind this practice is that *all* students who get accepted at these prestigious institutions are meritorious. That's another thing the Ivy League schools have standardized: All admissions are *need-blind*. That means that you get *in* based on your merit and nothing but your merit, and you get *financial aid* based on your need and nothing but your need.

Most Ivy League schools have a policy to meet 100 percent of a student's need, while others are unable to make this assurance but work hard to help students get what they need. Harvard, with an endowment of over $17 *billion*, can easily afford to make this guarantee.

International students should take note that this policy applies only to U.S. citizens and, in very particular cases, to citizens of other countries. Columbia University, for example, offers need-based funding to *Canadian* citizens. This restriction does *not* mean that international students can't receive need-based funding, but it does mean that the financial aid officers will consider them on a case-by-case basis. We discuss international options in Chapter 15.

Note that "meeting 100 percent of a student's need" does not mean that the college will waive *all* your tuition, fees, and expenses if you're needy. The total cost first gets reduced by any federal funding you may receive, then any state funding, external scholarships and grants you bring with you, your estimated family contribution (EFC), and any savings you may have. Only then will the college offer you a package that may combine grants, loans, and Federal Work-Study.

Also keep in mind that colleges may not apply the same formula as the federal government to determine your EFC. Your college may choose to define your need based on information from your FAFSA, PROFILE, or any other information they may request of you. For more on this topic, see the section, "Negotiating a Better Deal," later in this chapter.

An average undergraduate year at Harvard will set you back $39,000, but about 50 percent of the undergraduate student population receives need-based funding from the college. Columbia costs about $40,000, and about 30 percent of Columbia students receive financial aid specifically from

Columbia. So how do the rest pay for college? Most get some form of financial aid from other sources. The greatest source is, of course, the federal and state governments. However, many students also bring their merit-based scholarships with them.

Another myth going around says that a college that doesn't provide merit-based student aid also doesn't allow students to bring it with them. This myth isn't true at all. Frankly, most students admitted to an Ivy League school have a tremendous shot at winning merit-based awards because they need top grades and SAT/ACT scores to even be offered a first-year spot.

Negotiating a Better Deal

So you've been accepted, you filled out your financial aid forms, and your colleges have offered you their packages. What can you do to get more?

First of all, think about it from their perspective. The financial aid office has a set amount of need-based and merit-based funding that they can disperse, and they want to know that they're getting the best possible students for the money.

Getting more need-based money

Getting more need-based money is generally your best option. This strategy isn't as much negotiating as it is *appealing*. To put it in a slightly better light, you're reinterpreting your financial information or introducing new financial information to explain why you have a greater need than the amount you received.

You may qualify for more need-based funding for all sorts of reasons, including the following:

- ✔ **Your circumstances have changed.** The FAFSA and most college financial aid applications base their assessments on your financial situation months before you enter college. In that time, a supporting parent may have lost his or her job, someone in your family may have required an expensive and non-insured medical procedure, your parents' retirement fund may have been devastated by the stock market, or any number of other events may have occurred that renders you more needy.

- ✔ **The financial effects of certain parts of your information may not be properly understood.** For example, it may not be clear that your grandparents who live in another country are dependant upon your parents. Or the extent of a medical impairment and its future financial implications may not have been fully explained previously.

✔ **Your assessment may not take into consideration other factors.** A good example relates to retirement funds. Colleges may assess a student's EFC differently from the federal government. Columbia University, for example, *includes* the value of the family home but does not include retirement savings that are kept in a retirement savings plan. If your parents are approaching retirement age and have no retirement savings plan but expect to live off the equity in their home, the college assessment doesn't recognize the home as retirement savings. However, if you explain this situation to your financial aid counselor, you're likely to have your financial aid situation reassessed in your favor. In this situation, your family's home equity may be reassessed to zero, which would significantly *increase* your demonstrated need.

When appealing your financial aid package based on need, make sure that you bring along as much documentation as possible to prove the points you're making. A financial aid officer can't simply take your word for it that your sister needs back surgery that will cost upwards of $50,000. In this case, you must bring a letter (on official letterhead) from a doctor stating the details, necessity for the surgery, and the costs.

Not all changes in your financial position will warrant a revised need assessment. The fact that you blew your savings on a trip to Europe won't induce the financial aid officer to give you any more aid.

Getting more merit-based money

In a strictly need-based school, showing off your science prizes and honors and SAT scores in hopes that the college will suddenly change its policy just to entice you won't do any good. Most financial aid officers, however, are very willing to help guide you toward *external* merit-based scholarships. After all, it's in a college's best interest that you find extra money.

Negotiating for more merit-based money is a challenge because most financial aid officers pledge almost all their money when they send out admissions offers. Still, convincing a financial aid officer that you truly should've been offered a greater entrance scholarship based on your vastly improved final marks or SAT/ACT scores is possible, depending on the school. If the officer has any discretionary budget left, your position may be reassessed. If not, the officer can certainly help you apply for other sources of funding, including departmental scholarships and external scholarships.

We discuss merit-based money in Chapter 13, but, generally, the sources are

✔ **College entrance scholarships:** These scholarships are usually fixed by a predetermined college formula. What you're offered is what you get.

- ✔ **Departmental scholarships:** These awards are rarely included in the financial aid packages, and you must apply for them separately.

- ✔ **External scholarships:** Although we discuss these scholarships in detail in Chapter 16, many financial aid officers are knowledgeable about them, and some colleges have separate offices specifically set up to help students apply for these types of scholarships.

Of course, any money you bring along in the form of scholarships will be included in your need assessment. Yes, this may reduce the amount of need-based funding you receive. However, because the purpose of the funding is to get you to 100 percent of what you need to attend college, factoring in scholarship money makes sense. After you hit the full amount, you have no further need. If you were given more, you'd be *making* money, and that's not the purpose of need-based financial aid.

You can, however, request that the scholarship money you receive be directed toward the *loan* portion of your financial aid package. This strategy won't always work, but you're far better off bringing this option to the attention of the financial aid officer. If you don't ask, you won't get!

Demanding more money

Being *demanding* just doesn't work. No matter who you are, the financial aid officer will react negatively to threats and demands. Think about it. At UCLA, the admissions office receives 55,000 applications per year for about 8,000 freshman spots. The University of Miami expected 13,000 applications for 3,450 spots in the 2003/2004 year. In 2001, Columbia admitted 1,637 students from 14,137 applications — and received about 16,000 applications for the 2002/2003 year for about the same number of spots. If you believe that the deal your college offers isn't good enough and threaten to turn it down, the college can just as easily fill your spot with someone else.

Some colleges are, however, willing to *match* the deal you were offered elsewhere, especially if the other college is recognized to be at par or even better in terms of reputation. If the other college is considered sub par, however, the financial aid officer will frankly tell you that the college doesn't need to offer more to get a student of your caliber.

Some financial aid officers have told us horror stories of hostile students coming into the office screaming and throwing a tantrum, demanding that they receive a better financial aid package. Not only are their requests denied, but also, some students have even been hauled off by police and landed in jail or a psychiatric ward. Not exactly a great way to start off one's academic career.

Getting to know the decision makers

Many colleges are setting up systems in which students are assigned a specific financial aid officer who will deal with all their concerns throughout their college life. Naturally, the officer will deal with several students at once, but the theory is that he or she will be able to give more personalized service than if a student simply walked in and talked to whomever was available.

This way, the officer can get to know more about the particular individual and can watch for specific opportunities. The officer will also become more wary if the student has tried to bluff or scam his or her way to more money.

Lying to your financial aid officer

Some students approach financial aid officers with bogus claims, forged documents, and financial statements that neglect to mention several thousand dollars in awards. Be warned that most financial aid officers have seen it all and are particularly astute at catching frauds.

Getting caught intentionally misrepresenting yourself to the financial aid officer can have a devastating effect on your educational career. Not getting the extra money you want will be the least of your problems. Most colleges have codes of ethics, and students have had their admission offers rescinded or have been expelled for fraudulent misrepresentation. It's not worth it.

Correctly approaching your financial aid officer

Get to know the person in charge of your financial aid as soon as possible. Even before you apply for admission, make an appointment with the appropriate financial aid offices while visiting your prospective colleges. We strongly advise that you conduct a personal visit whenever possible, but if you can't make it in person, call the office and ask to discuss your financial situation.

Try to chat with them well in advance and let them choose the time. Late August through the end of September, as well as late December to mid-January are busy times for most financial aid offices because they process payments during this time. Find out when applications are due for the particular college because that will likely be a busy time as well.

After you've received your offer of admission and financial aid package, consider your options and then contact your financial aid officer to discuss how you can get a better package. You'll most likely have to do this in person, unless you simply want to correct a clerical error that can easily be supported by faxing an appropriate document.

Make an appointment and bring all your supporting documentation. Ensure that you have a compelling case that you can state clearly and succinctly.

Bring a letter explaining your situation in detail, along with copies of all your documentation that you can leave behind. In fact, you often must leave the originals, so be prepared to do so.

Providing proof is necessary because the financial aid officer may have to justify his or her position to other divisions of the college, and especially to the deans and directors. The officer's job is to ensure that you get the money you're entitled to receive, but also to keep the school within its budget.

Matching offers

Some colleges are willing to match the offers of competing colleges, although most have worked out their offers by using their own particular formula and are unwilling to make changes. As well, some colleges don't have the extra money available to match the awards offered by other schools.

However, it's always worth a try to show the financial aid officer of College X that you have received a better offer from College Y, but want to do everything possible to attend College X because it's your first choice. Financial aid officers feel a loyalty toward their school like anyone else, and they're more likely to try to help those students who feel that same loyalty. The officer may want to go the extra mile and help you track down other sources of funding or perhaps take another look at your need assessment.

The saying goes that you can catch more flies with honey than you can with vinegar. No matter what, be nice to your financial aid officer. Keep in mind that this person makes decisions that *directly* affect your financial situation, and many of these decisions are up to her personal discretion. Besides, financial aid officers generally have to deal with problems all day long, and they're often unappreciated for the efforts they make.

Be pleasant, be prepared, and thank your officer for her assistance. And, if some extra funding comes through, go back and let her know how much you appreciate the help.

How Do Colleges Decide How Much to Offer?

Financial aid officers work together with admissions officers, college administration, and the various departments to come up with their own unique formula for offering financial aid packages. Each college may have its own formula, and no one wants to share the precise secrets, but most of the elements are pretty obvious to figure out.

The formula that each college uses depends on the unique situation and goals of the particular institution. The most competitive colleges don't have to worry about attracting enough freshman students for the year. Some don't even need to worry about attracting enough *high-quality* students. That's why Ivy League schools don't offer merit-based financial aid — they don't need to.

Some institutions focus on specific subjects, and they try to attract the best students in their fields. The Massachusetts and California Institutes of Technology (MIT and Caltech) attract some of the top scientific minds in the country, and they invest in their excellence by hiring top professors and buying state-of-the-art equipment.

Other colleges focus on liberal arts, religious studies, and any number of other topics. Some colleges emphasize their athletic competitors or their arts departments. Each college will use its financial aid packages to entice the students who are best able to enhance the college's particular reputation.

Enrollment and cost balancing

People sometimes quote the old refrain that "buying a college education is a lot like buying a car." College administrators universally cringe when they hear this phrase, so you're advised *never* to repeat this phrase in the admissions or financial aid office. Okay, now you've been warned.

Despite the disgust college administration feels at the comparison, the fact remains that colleges *are* businesses. They're regulated by the government and must comply with a lot of laws. Some are heavily financed by state tax dollars, and all colleges benefit from federal and state college financing programs. In fact, without the financial assistance that governments offer students, most colleges wouldn't be able to stay in business.

There's that word again: business. Colleges all have budgets, and they want to get the best they can for their money. Educating students is a cost for the college. Tuition, alumni and corporate donations, and government financing pay for these costs and (hopefully, for the college) generate a profit. This profit can either go toward expanding the scholastic programs at the college, toward the investors if it is a private college, or toward the *endowment* — the chunk of cash the college retains for a rainy day. Harvard has more than $17 billion tucked away, but other colleges are struggling to retain any funds in this difficult economy.

The balancing part comes when college administrators try to figure out how much of their profit or endowment dollars should be spent on enticing specific students. As the student in question, you have to determine how to portray yourself as someone who brings added value to the college.

You can do so by emphasizing your personal abilities and talents that can enhance the college during your attendance — perhaps through winning awards, publishing, or your athletic performance. You can also add value to the school by becoming a prestigious or successful alumna. The college hopes that you'll turn around and donate some of your income to your alma mater, but even if you don't, having a list of successful alumni makes for good promotional material to attract more top students in the future.

Budget

Colleges must keep to their budgets. The more they put toward financial aid, the less they have for educational programs, upkeep, salaries, and other costs that directly affect the quality of education. If a college's quality diminishes, it becomes less competitive, and it must offer more financial aid to attract better students. If not checked, the downward spiral continues.

Sometimes, financial aid decisions simply come down to how much money the college has in its coffers. Perhaps the endowment income is down because the economy is in a slump, alumni aren't donating much, and the college investments aren't making the usual income. If this is the case, the college will simply have less money to offer.

Budgetary constraints are especially important to understand when you appeal your financial aid package. You want to contact the financial aid office as soon as you possible after you receive your package because, if you delay, the discretionary budget for appeals may be gone by the time you call. In this case, no matter how compelling your case, you won't get any extra funding. The college just doesn't have the money in its budget to offer you any more.

Geographic diversity

Colleges like to be able to claim that their student populations represent all fifty states. It shows that they're well rounded, open, and accommodating to a diverse crowd, and that they have nationally-appreciated reputations.

A college will *not* lower its standards just to admit a student from an under-represented state. However, if a college has to choose between students from a well-represented state and an under-represented state, all other attributes being equal, students from the under-represented state usually win out. Similarly, students from under-represented states may be able to call upon their status to attempt to draw out more funding. You can point out the greater challenge in overcoming the educational deficiencies in your particular state, greater expenses in traveling to the particular college, or any number of other justifications. The point is to offer up a reasonable explanation for the financial aid officer to use to help you get more funding.

Which states are under-represented? Think about it logically. The least represented states will fit any or all of the following criteria:

- ✔ **The least populated states:** Understandably, those states with a lower population have fewer students entering college. Lower supply equals greater demand for those students who are highly qualified.

- ✔ **States with GPAs and test scores below the national average:** For whatever reason, certain states tend to turn out students with lower-than-average GPAs and SAT/ACT scores. This deficiency means that the few students who *have* high scores are going to be highly attractive to colleges.

- ✔ **States that are geographically distant from the particular college:** As you can imagine, most students at the University of Washington are from the state of Washington. The school also has quite a few students from the neighboring states of Oregon and Idaho, but there are relatively few students from Florida, Alabama, and Arkansas. Most students look to the colleges that are geographically near their homes unless they have a specific reason to look elsewhere, either due to the quality of education offered or due to the college's reputation in a particular field of study.

The most competitive colleges rarely have to look long and hard to find qualified applicants from all fifty states. However, even some of them admit to some careful searching to ensure that the entire country is represented in every year, although they deny having quotas.

Racial and ethnic diversity

Certain colleges use tuition discounting to increase the racial and ethnic diversity of their student population. They want to diversify the student body for purposes of public relations, to help them keep up appearances that they're racially tolerant and open to all parts of society. They also want to help the student population be more racially tolerant and to include different perspectives, different backgrounds, and different "voices."

A focus on racial and ethnic diversity is rarely an issue for colleges based in big cities such as New York, Los Angeles, and Chicago. However, it can be a selling factor for colleges in less diverse states and cities.

Several independent and college-administered scholarships and grants are offered based on ethnic and racial heritage. Talk to your financial aid officer about what may be available for you.

Checklist: Getting the best financial aid package

Before you apply:

❑ Talk to an admissions officer, financial aid officer, and scholarships counselor (if the college has a scholarships office) to determine what types of financial aid are available, including:

  ✔ Tuition discounts and entrance scholarships

  ✔ College-wide scholarships and grants

  ✔ Departmental scholarships and grants

  ✔ Need-based financial aid

  ✔ College-supported loans

  ✔ Work-Study programs

❑ Talk to administrators of every department with a field of study that interests you (even remotely), and find out what departmental scholarships are available.

❑ Collect details about eligibility requirements, deadlines and award dates, degree of competition, and application requirements.

When you apply:

❑ Send in all financial aid applications that are available, including your FAFSA, PRO-FILE, and any college-based applications.

❑ Don't forget to send all supporting documentation, including tax returns, if required.

❑ Be clear about your need-based concerns, pointing out details of exceptional circumstances.

❑ Apply for any college-based, departmental, and external scholarships for which you're eligible and have any likelihood at all of winning.

❑ Emphasize your strengths, including how your particular characteristics will add to the diversity of the school, and how your personal excellence will add value to the school.

❑ Respond to any inquiries or requests for information immediately and truthfully.

After you receive your package:

❑ Work out the total cost of all years of college, taking into account any awards that won't renew in subsequent years, and compare the total costs of each prospective college.

❑ Determine what need-based grounds you may have to appeal your package, including:

  ✔ Clerical or mathematical errors — they do happen!

  ✔ Change in financial circumstances

  ✔ Factors that bear reassessment

  ✔ Special circumstances that render you more needy

❑ Determine what merit-based grounds you may have to appeal your package, including:

  ✔ Matching the package of another college

  ✔ Vastly improved performance in grades or after retaking SAT/ACT

❑ If grounds exist, make an appointment with the financial aid office to appeal your package.

❑ Collect and bring along all supporting documentation to your appeal.

❑ Follow up to make sure that all monies due to you arrive.

Chapter 13

Qualifying for Merit Scholarships

*O*nly people with the top grades across the country win merit scholarships, right? Wrong. It's surprising, considering that merit-based awards are, by definition, supposed to award the most meritorious students. But the concept of "merit" means more than just high grades.

Besides, even those awards that grant prizes to the students with the top grades *in the applicant pool* don't necessarily have the country's top students *in* the pool. Most awards start off whittling down their applicant pool through eligibility requirements.

Getting Free Money without SAT Scores of 1600 and a GPA of 4.0

We don't want to downplay the importance of excellent grades and high test scores. Winning awards is much easier if students have top marks. For instance, when it comes down to the final determination, if the selection committee is looking at you and nine other students, all of whom are fully eligible, have submitted all that's necessary, and demonstrated the qualities that the prize is designed to reward, the committee will usually choose the student with the highest marks. In fact, students with the highest marks and test scores across the country often find that certain awards come to them.

Keeping in mind that good grades are always a worthy goal, our point in this section is that you can still win awards even if you don't have the best grades. One of the most popular scholarships at UCLA, for example, has two very basic eligibility requirements: You must have a minimum 2.5 GPA, and you must come from a California high school. After that, the selection committee gives the award to the student who can best demonstrate how he or she has overcome obstacles. This scholarship is just one of the many merit-based awards for which you don't need a high GPA — but for which you do need special character.

Here, in this section, we show you how to get to that sought-after final judging before the committee decides on who wins. We also outline how to find the scholarships that think of merit as something *other* than just GPA.

Hunting for scholarships

Some colleges operate scholarship offices separate from the financial aid office. Inside, you find helpful individuals who work with students to assist them in applying for scholarships. You can find all sorts of resources available at these offices, including computers and software for Internet-based scholarship searches, all the directories listing who offers what, application forms, templates for application letters and resumes, and maybe even *this* book!

Other colleges may have a few of these resources available, but they basically decide that finding scholarships is the student's responsibility. Regardless of which sort of college you eventually choose, you can visit the scholarship office of *any* college when you're prospecting. Use the resources, work with the counselors, and apply for all the scholarships that are appropriate for you.

The financial aid office of your prospective college should let you know what sort of scholarship resources exist, so be sure to ask. A couple of great scholarship offices are the Student Aid Resource (STAR) Center at Florida State University, and the Scholarship Resource Center at UCLA.

Remembering the basics

In this chapter, we focus on college-based award scholarships. In Chapter 16, we concentrate on scholarships given by organizations that are *not* tied to a particular college. The same general principles apply to both:

- ✔ **Think about eligibility first.** Top grades and a fantastic essay won't do you any good if the award is limited to a student with a racial history that's different from yours, for example.

- ✔ **Quality is more important than quantity.** The point is to win the award, and you win only if you wow the selection committee.

> ✔ **Give yourself plenty of time.** *Every* scholarship advisor we interviewed emphasized the importance of being on time! Missing deadlines is not an option if you want to win scholarships.
>
> ✔ **Be careful.** Rushing to finish applications often leaves them sloppy and full of mistakes.
>
> ✔ **Keep perfecting your entries.** Winners of multiple awards find that the process gets easier over time because their materials become more polished each time they review (and use) them.

Meeting eligibility: Even "average" or "below-average" students may qualify

Initial eligibility is the first hurdle to overcome. When searching for scholarships, first look for the restrictions. Some scholarships are aimed only at freshmen, while others are for other undergraduate years. Still others are for graduate students only. No matter what you do, no matter how interesting your essay, a freshman won't win an award that's designated for a graduate student. Move on to the next award, and keep that one in mind for when you begin grad school.

Similarly, check for other restrictions that you can't overcome, including gender, ethnic heritage, left-handedness, residency, and a long list of others. Some students think that they can overcome these objections by claiming that the process is biased and unconstitutional. It doesn't work. Move on.

On the other hand, don't count yourself out too quickly. One scholarship counselor told us of a student whose mother was Latina. She was reluctant to apply for scholarships designated to those of Latin heritage because her last name, from her father, was obviously Scottish. After she was convinced to apply, however, she found that she *easily* qualified for several scholarships!

Most committee members are accustomed to such circumstances — the student may be adopted, the parents may have changed their names when they came to America, or she may be of mixed heritage. This is not a strange occurrence so, as long as you can show evidence that you *are* eligible when you first submit your application, you'll be considered.

Evidence of eligibility is a necessity. Even if the girl's name were Sanchez, she still would need to provide copies of a birth certificate, naturalization papers, or other evidence that demonstrates her Latina heritage. If official documents aren't available, a letter from a Latin heritage organization may do the trick. And, if written correctly, the letter may have the double benefit of *endorsing* her as well!

Winning by improving

Your overall GPA may be low because you did abysmally in your first two years of high school. But now, you've turned yourself around and are getting all *A*s. Congratulations! Various scholarships await you.

Both departmental and private scholarships award students with the top mark in a particular course — usually a core subject, but not always. Note that the winner does not have to be a student with *overall* high marks, just the student who did the best in, say, algebra.

Some scholarship committee members we spoke with said that they might be more inclined to offer a scholarship to an individual who has improved drastically, rather than someone with grades just barely above average all through high school, even if the latter student has the higher overall GPA.

Working the financial aid system

Merit scholars of any sort are considered more attractive to colleges because, statistically, these students are the ones who are more likely to succeed financially in life. Understandably, the individuals who succeed financially in life are more likely to make donations to the college that got them started.

It always pays, however, to know your competition. Departmental scholarships in English literature are more competitive at Vassar than at a state college in the Midwest. Not that there's anything wrong with the Midwest college, but Vassar is known for its English programs. Thus, the top students in the field want to attend college there.

If you had a fantastic mark in English but want to study history, why not take the English department scholarship from that Midwest college with a reputation for excellence in American history? You can take an English course and declare your major later.

Similarly, a National Merit Scholar will be offered entrance scholarships to excellent colleges across the country, but *not* at some of the very top colleges. Ivy League schools and other top colleges, such as Notre Dame and Stanford, don't offer merit-based scholarships, and other top colleges that do offer merit-based scholarships already get the applications from the rest of the National Merit Scholars. You'll be more treasured (and offered more money) at the University of Kansas or the University of Arkansas, which have statistically fewer National Merit Scholars in attendance than the other colleges we named. Always try to stand out wherever you are!

Asking the right people

Whom should you approach when searching for scholarships? The simple answer is: everyone! You never know who may have information that you can use. Because you have a limited amount of time, focus on the people in the financial aid office, scholarship office, admissions office, and departments appropriate to your field of study, as well as librarians and high school counselors.

These people work with scholarships all the time, so they're familiar with the ins and outs of the system. Use their knowledge to your advantage and get to know them, and what they *know*.

With a little research in the catalogs, guidebooks, and Web sites, you can likely find a stack of scholarships tied to your major, your ethnicity, or your religion. But the *right* people may be able to direct you to scholarships relating to your hobbies. The Director of the Scholarship Resource Center at UCLA, for example, has pointed students to scholarships for people who participate in dog shows and people who like surfing. The lesson? Talk to the scholarship professionals about your specific situation!

Searching online

Most scholarship offices and librarians use a variety of different search sites, as well as EXPAN software from the College Board. It's sold institutionally rather than commercially, so you can't get a copy at the local computer store.

Dozens of Web sites offer scholarship search services. Always be wary of any site where the claims sound too good to be true. We talk about how to spot scholarship scams in Chapter 4, but some of the more reputable Web-based scholarship searches are the FastWeb Search (www.fastweb.com) and SallieMae Wired Scholar (salliemae.wiredscholar.com).

When conducting your searches, always verify with the originating source. No, we don't mean the first place you saw it. Rather, if you find information about a scholarship offered by Big Brothers Big Sisters of America, for example, go to the Big Brothers Big Sisters of America Web site and verify that the information you saw on the other site is true.

You also want to verify that your application arrived and that you're correctly in the system. Without confirmation, you never know if all your hard work preparing the application went down the tubes, or up in smoke.

What Scholarships Are Available?

Some financial aid offices are relatively centralized. This means that all financial aid at the college must go through one office. Unfortunately, finding a college that has a single source for all *applications* for financial aid is rare. For example, Notre Dame has a centralized system, but the individual coaches determine their athletic scholarships. The financial aid office must approve them, but they have little or no involvement in choosing the recipients.

Colleges that have only need-based financial aid generally have a single office that handles all financial aid requests. On the other hand, these colleges rarely have supplementary scholarship offices that can help you find private scholarships.

At most colleges, the financial aid office deals with all governmental and college-administered need-based aid, plus major college-based scholarships. The rest — departmental scholarships, athletic scholarships, and private scholarships and grants — are administered independently.

Typically, the financial aid office requests that you submit your financial aid applications with your application for admission. To make the process more confusing, the manner of applying for aid can vary from college to college.

Some colleges simply request that you submit the FAFSA and check a box on your application indicating you want the college to consider you for financial aid as well as college-based scholarships. Other colleges request lots of supplementary documentation, including the PROFILE, a separate college-based application for financial aid that we discuss in Chapter 12, and individual applications for every college-based scholarship. Still others fall somewhere in between these two extremes. You never know unless you ask.

Discovering what scholarships are available throughout the college takes a lot of work. Nevertheless, if you follow the basic steps we outline in the next section, you can collect the information you need.

College-based scholarships

Most financial aid officers know about their own college-based scholarships, but you *do* have to ask them about how to apply. In general, college-based scholarships are available to anyone at the college, depending on specific eligibility requirements. They may be specifically offered to women, African-Americans, in-state students, out-of-state students, the physically challenged, or some other defining criteria. As usual, ask what's out there for you.

Scholarship applications may come automatically with your college application or may require a separate application form plus a submission of a specified essay. Some are available to anyone who qualifies, but they're offered in a limited number. Washington State University, for example, offers a scholarship to every state resident with a GPA of 3.6 or higher — but these scholarships are available on a first-come, first-served basis until the money runs out.

A quick search at the STAR Center at Florida State University found a host of college-based scholarships offered to top high school students, top minority students, or students of *any* sort and *any* GPA that can get into FSU and have an International Baccalaureate diploma from a Florida high school. FSU has awards for passing Advanced Placement exams, for transferring from a community college, private scholarships for orphaned or adopted students, need-based funding, athletic scholarships, talent-based scholarships, departmental scholarships, community service scholarships, and the list goes on.

Our point is that hundreds of opportunities exist. All you have to do to find out about them is ask your friendly financial aid officer and do some research.

Departmental scholarships

After you've talked with the financial aid office and every scholarship office that exists on the campus of your choice, visit the particular departments where you intend to major and start asking about scholarships.

Don't limit yourself. Remember that students change their majors all the time, so approach any department that's even relatively interesting to you. If you are interested in statistics, don't limit your inquiries to the math department. Instead, look to studies involved with quantitative methods used in cryptography, criminology, computer science, political science, military science, engineering, or marketing.

Going Artsy: Scholarships Are Available for Fine Arts Students, Too!

Scholarships for fine arts students are somewhat different than for those students in other programs. Minimum grades are required for basic admission eligibility. Then, merit is considered based on an audition or submission of an artistic work. The assessment of this audition or entry determines both admission to the department and any scholarships that may be offered.

Typically, the professor in charge of the department has discretion to decide who gets offered scholarships and who does not, along with how much each student will be offered. Most auditions and assessments, however, are conducted by a committee of experienced individuals from the department.

Applying: It takes some digging

To find out how the process works, you need to talk with the particular department and even the particular *section* of the particular department.

Scholarships may be available for music, but they'll be divided into each different instrument (including vocal). The music department may have a variety of scholarships available depending on how committed you are to honing your musical skills.

At Washington State University, scholarships are available for music majors, music minors, and those that want to play with the ensemble. Naturally, more money is available through the music department for music majors, but music minors can also apply for scholarships at other departments where they study.

Other types of artistic scholarships are available for dance, drama, painting, drawing, and sculpting. Dance may be subdivided into modern dance, jazz, ballet, and even folk dance.

Auditioning: Time to perform

If you've seen the television show *American Idol,* you have an idea of the audition process. You stand in front of a committee and perform. Judges (or the review committee members) will likely be gentler than the biting sarcasm you've seen on TV, but the process is, nonetheless, equally nerve-wracking.

Auditions generally take place on a specific day or series of days. If you can't make it, special arrangements *may* be made for another day. If you can't visit the college at all due to geographic or other reasons — this situation happens a lot at the University of Hawaii — arrangements can be made so that you can offer an audition on video.

All of these arrangements take time to set up. Don't expect to call on the audition day and ask to be rescheduled unless something extreme has come up. A death in the family or a doctor-supported serious illness are acceptable excuses. Bad planning, lack of preparation, or a movie opening don't cut it.

Regulating the arts

Various organizations regulate how art schools and scholarships operate. Similar to athletic regulatory bodies, these organizations enforce guidelines on maximum offers, harassment, and attempts to poach students from other schools.

All these organizations are administered through the National Office for Arts Accreditation (www.arts-accredit.org). At the Web site you can find related associations that administer music, art and design, theater, and dance.

Making an impact

Every artist or performer knows the importance of preparation and practice. The same is true for your audition. Most colleges have a standard application form that must be received before the audition. Savvy students make sure that their application gets to the right person on time.

Bring a copy of your application form as well as your resume, references, portfolio and perhaps a video or audiotape of your performance. Find out the *precise* details well in advance, including the exact location and directions, the physical characteristics of the room, and whether you're supposed to bring an accompanist. Always dress appropriately and take time to warm up.

You're trying to impress the committee with your talent, but you're also trying to impress them with your desire to be a student at their school. Don't forget to thank each member of the committee and follow up to find out if you need to supply any further information.

Counting the coins: How much to expect

How large a scholarship you may receive varies widely depending on the college budget and your ability. Some colleges offer full scholarships, but others offer only partial scholarships for the arts. Most art department members have told us over the years that the amounts offered are usually final: Take it or leave it. Some, though, will match funds offered at other colleges. You're more likely to get more funding by applying for need-based grants and for the variety of private scholarships available for the arts. We list some of these private scholarships in Chapter 20.

Just because you are offered a scholarship or other award doesn't mean that the particular college has accepted you. You still must qualify *academically.*

Checklist: On the money trail

When looking for merit-based financial aid, follow this path.

First, start with the financial aid office.

❑ Collect applications for federal, state, and college based financial aid.

❑ Ask for information about any college-based scholarships.

❑ Ask for information about any scholarship offices that may exist, resources, guides, and other advice about tracking down private scholarships.

❑ Ask for contact information regarding departmental scholarships for all the departments relating to anything you may wish to study.

Next, move on to the scholarship office, if one exists.

❑ Work with one of the helpful people who work at the campus scholarship office to figure out what scholarships are best for *you.*

❑ Search online, in guidebooks, and use all other resources available.

❑ Come back periodically to find out if anything new is being offered.

Continue to the individual departments.

❑ Ask about any and all scholarships, grants, fellowships, bursaries, and other forms of free money that may be available to students.

❑ Find out about eligibility, application requirements, how frequently the awards are given, who chooses the winners, and exactly how the winners are chosen.

❑ Don't limit your questions to information about freshman awards. You need to consider your *entire* college career, so make a financial plan that will address all four (or more) years.

❑ For fine arts scholarships and grants, find out how the audition process works and where you'll be playing (or singing, or dancing). Visit the actual room, if possible, to familiarize yourself with its equipment, size, acoustics, lighting, and other factors.

Repeat the process at all your prospective colleges.

❑ If you find one with an excellent scholarship office, use it for all its worth!

❑ Always thank people for their help and let them know if they helped you get any money!

Chapter 14

Playing the Game: Understanding Athletic Scholarships

- -

In This Chapter

▶ Researching athletic programs and scholarships with the NCAA

▶ Figuring out who funds the less popular sports

▶ Showing the coach what you've got

▶ Looking at other options, such as the NAIA

- -

*C*an your sport pay your way through college? Football and basketball players may get the news coverage and the top dollars, but free money is available for other sports as well. Surprised?

The amounts you can obtain vary drastically, depending on the sport, the college, and your own ability. You may not be able to get *any* money from a top sports college with a great reputation. At another school trying to develop its team, however, a free ride may be just an application — and recruitment drive — away. The problem is that most high school counselors don't know which colleges need your talents or which ones will pay for your proficiency at badminton, wrestling, or archery, for example.

This chapter helps you figure out where to go based on your athletic abilities and your sports prospects. We can't personally assess your talents, so we spell out how you can figure it all out for yourself.

Introducing the NCAA

The *National Collegiate Athletic Association* (NCAA) was spearheaded by President Teddy Roosevelt back in 1905. It was established to safeguard student athletes from injurious team play. Since then, it's developed into the organization that regulates all aspects of competitive college athletics, including recruiting and scholarships for athletes offered by hundreds of colleges across the United States.

Every college that wants to compete in athletics with all the other NCAA colleges must abide by the NCAA's long list of regulations. Its excellent and well-organized Web site (www.ncaa.org) is full of resources, neat facts, and other useful information. This Web site is *the* place to find out information about the sport of your choice — and how athletic scholarships work.

The first thing to do is to call the NCAA publications hotline at 1-800-638-3731 and ask for a free copy of the *Guide for the College-Bound Student-Athlete*. The *Guide,* which you can also view online, has information about the different functions of the NCAA, including the functions of the NCAA Initial-Eligibility Clearinghouse.

After your junior year of high school, you must register with the NCAA Clearinghouse before you can be recruited for a college athletic scholarship. The registration forms and a Clearinghouse brochure are included in the *Guide* and are available at www.ncaaclearinghouse.net.

If you've been home-schooled or are from another country, you can still be eligible for athletic scholarships, but you must provide extra qualifications to prove that you're eligible. These qualifications are fully itemized at the NCAA site, but they're often assessed on a case-by-case basis. The NCAA must be satisfied that your education has met the minimum standards of the core education of an established American high school. The sooner you begin to compile the extra materials for qualification, the better.

The screwy world of college divisions

The NCAA has established three different divisions, and Division I football is further divided into Division I-A and Division I-AA. The divisions aren't defined by sport or geographic region. Instead, they're defined by the regulations, which vary somewhat for each division and section. Individual colleges choose where they fit, depending on their goals and the availability of scholarship funds. Overall, Division I teams are considered the best of college sport, and these teams are the most competitive for athletes. Football is only played in Division I, and Division I-A football even has requirements for *fan attendance* at its games. That means that if a Division I-A football team can't get enough fans to attend its games, it loses its I-A status and has to move down to Division I-AA.

Colleges don't have to choose one division for all their teams. For example, a particular college may be in Division I for basketball and in Division II for swimming. The issue is which set of rules the college follows for each particular sport. Colleges qualify for a division by sponsoring a minimum number of both men's and women's sports, and by following the rules governing how many games must be played, restrictions on which teams can be played (generally colleges must compete against teams in their own division), and how scholarships are administered.

Division 1

To qualify for Division I, colleges must offer minimum financial aid awards for their athletics program, and they cannot exceed specific maximum amounts. These amounts vary from sport to sport, but they're set out in detail at the NCAA Web site and are summarized later in this chapter.

Division 11

Fewer scholarships may be offered at Division II, and *full tickets* (also called *free rides*) are rare. However, administrators work with hot prospects to help them apply for other forms of financial aid to beef up the scholarship offerings. Division II colleges are actively involved in recruiting, and they're important considerations for any student athlete.

Division 111

Division III institutions offer no athletic scholarships. However if you're unable to acquire an athletic scholarship from a Division I or II college, you may wish to play for a Division III school to improve your abilities and then attempt to transfer in later years.

Sport categories

College sports are divided into two categories: *head-count* and *equivalency*. We also talk about *emerging sports* in this section.

Head-count

Head-count sports are limited by the number of scholarships that can be awarded, but the award amount can be anywhere from $1 to a complete free ride. Because of the limitations on how many players the team can acquire using scholarships, most colleges award free rides to all those that get an award. Anyone who gets an award is called a *counter*.

Numbers are always subject to change, but as we go to print, the head-count sports in Division I are men's football (25 initial counters at Division I-A, 30 for Division I-AA, but for each, there are a *maximum* of 85 players in total), men's and women's basketball (13 players for men's and 15 for women's), women's volleyball (12 players), women's gymnastics (12), and women's tennis (8). Whew!

Equivalency

Equivalency sports are all other NCAA sports, including rowing, fencing, track, wrestling, swimming, and others. For these sports, the college has a maximum amount per sport that it's permitted to spend overall, and that amount is equivalent to a set number of free rides. The number of these free rides varies by the particular sport, and can be found at Section 15.5.3 of the NCAA by-laws.

Colleges divide up their budgets depending on their focus and their financial resources, and the coaches offer scholarships accordingly. If they have $1,000, they can give it all to one athlete, or they can give $1 each to 1,000 athletes. That decision is entirely up to the coaches. It's rare that the entire budget for the year won't be spent, but many coaches will hold back some funds to be used in the spring term.

Some sports have both head-count and equivalency restrictions. For example, colleges involved with ice hockey can offer the equivalent of 18 free rides to a maximum of 30 students.

Emerging NCAA sports

Emerging sports are those in the process of becoming recognized by the NCAA. At present, the sports that are emerging are archery, badminton, bowling, equestrian, rugby, squash, synchronized swimming, and team handball.

Because the NCAA doesn't yet regulate these sports, you're entitled to obtain athletic scholarships *outside* of the NCAA regulations. The flip side is that the competitions in these sports don't draw the kind of funding that the more popular college sports do. You're far less likely to get a free ride for competing in these sports. You can, however obtain funds from a combination of sources, including college-based athletic scholarships, external grants and prizes, loans, and other recognized sources.

You can track the results of college teams at the NCAA site, follow outside competitions, and find out which colleges are interested in these sports in the same manner as tracking NCAA regulated sports. From the NCAA Web site, click on the site index and find "Emerging Sports." You can also choose to generate a list of schools that sponsor a particular emerging sport by clicking the appropriate link. The colleges are sorted by institution name, division, conference, and region.

If you want a scholarship for women's archery, for example, your options are Columbia University-Barnard College, James Madison University, and Texas A&M University, College Station. Click on the school of your choice and find out more details, including address, the names of the people to contact, and what other sports are supported with scholarships at that college.

Women are athletes, too

It really goes without saying, but just in case you had any doubts, female athletes can win scholarships for their sports. No one will claim that there's complete gender equality in college athletics, but the situation has improved markedly since the U.S. government passed Title IX of the Education Amendments of 1972. Title IX requires equitable sharing of athletic aid and resources between both genders.

For more information about gender equality in sports, you can order or view online the NCAA's guide to Title IX. It's located in the General Interest category of NCAA Publications.

Athletic Scholarship Basics

Colleges offer and administer athletic scholarships separately from all other financial aid. Coaches recruit students based on their athletic ability, and the coaches have close to free rein over who gets offered the prizes. However, *all* colleges have minimum scholastic requirements for any student athlete, generally including a minimum GPA and SAT/ACT score. Although key prospects may receive some tutoring assistance to help them qualify, the fact remains that any student who can't meet minimum academic standards won't get a scholarship. Period.

The minimums vary per school, but many average at a 2.5 GPA and 1100 combined SAT. The minimums at your chosen colleges may be higher (or lower) than these, so always check with your particular prospective college.

Show me the money

Known by the NCAA as a *full grant-in-aid,* the maximum amount that you can receive is also called a *full ticket,* a *free ride,* or the *full cost of attendance.* Whatever you want to call it, a student receives all tuition and college fees, room and board, required course-related books and supplies, transportation, and any sport-related expenses such as uniforms, travel to games, and other regular expenses. Cool huh?

If more money is necessary, based on specific need-based grounds (for example, for the support of a child), the amount can be assessed on a case-by-case basis. However, NCAA regulations are extremely strict about the limitations on how much a player can receive. No matter how good you are, colleges can't give you a car or a fat chunk of cash, despite the rumors.

If a college is caught giving a student more than the regulations allow, the college is fined, the entire team may be disqualified from play that year, and further repercussions are likely. Being out of team play may also adversely affect you and your teammates when trying to get into the major or minor leagues. In short, if you don't follow the rules, you put your entire team at risk. So don't!

You still have to study, Einstein

One of the perks of playing a college sport is that the coaching staff gets involved in your life. Of course, that may be considered a downside by some, but student athletes do get special attention that other students have to pay for or work to obtain. Coaches know that their athletes can't play unless they keep up their grades, and the NCAA has relatively new regulations setting minimum requirements for hours spent studying by student athletes. If your grades slip or you don't fulfill your academic requirements, the team can suffer.

In response, coaches are ever vigilant to make sure that their players study hard to ensure they can play even harder. Florida State University, for example, has a six-to-seven-person team focused on ensuring that players study by obtaining tutoring, mentoring, special educational resources, and supervised study halls.

Try the combo

Students who don't receive a free ride may get any combination of scholarships, grants, tuition waivers, loans, work-study, book allowances, room and board, and other regular elements of college financial aid. However, the institution isn't permitted to offer more than the full cost of attendance for any student athlete.

You need to recognize that any outside financial aid you receive will be included toward your total grant-in-aid. Because the college can't give you a package that would put you over the full grant-in-aid limit, bringing outside awards with you may bring down the amount that the college would've awarded you if you didn't have these other sources of financial aid. So if you're offered a full ticket by a college, you're best off to reject any loans offered by other sources. Whenever possible, accept grants over loans.

Some specific government grants, such as Federal Pell Grants, AmeriCorps benefits, Veterans Educational Assistance Program (VEAP) benefits, and others listed in section 15.4.2.1 of the NCAA by-laws, are not included toward your total grant-in-aid.

Can a college pull your scholarship away?

Athletic scholarships are generally awarded for one year but are renewable. The NCAA has very specific limitations on pulling them or refusing to renew them. Read on for details.

Getting cut

Your award can be reduced or cancelled if

> ✔ **You make yourself ineligible for competition.** For example, if you fall below the minimum scholastic level required for competition, your funding can be cut.
>
> ✔ **You quit the team or sport.** However, the college can't transfer your award to someone else in this case.
>
> ✔ **You engage in serious misconduct that requires disciplinary action.** Cheating on an exam is one example of serious misconduct; so is an on-campus assault or a drug conviction.
>
> ✔ **You commit fraud on your application or any other information you submit to the school.**

The NCAA requires colleges to offer the opportunity for a hearing before they reduce or cancel any athletic-based financial aid. It also requires the opportunity for a hearing to appeal the non-renewal of your scholarship.

Getting hurt

If you suffer an injury or illness while on scholarship, whether during participation in your sport or otherwise, you retain your scholarship at least for the year. At certain institutions, the scholarship remains for the rest of your college life regardless of whether or not you can play again; however, the coach can't guarantee that this will be the case for you beyond the one-year term. The college doesn't include an injured player receiving a scholarship in the head-count for subsequent years if it is determined medically that the player won't be able to play again.

Your athletic financial aid can't be reduced or cancelled because of your athletic ability, or lack of it. As long as you show up at practice and competitions and try your best, avoid disciplinary misconduct, and keep your grades above the minimum requirements, your scholarship is safe for that year.

Your coach may decide not to renew your athletic scholarship because you can't keep up to the team, but coaches don't like to do this because it negatively affects the morale of the team. This is why so much time and effort is spent on the initial recruitment process. Still, every year, some athletes' scholarships aren't renewed due to poor performance. Athletes have the right to appeal the decision, but playing poorly *is* a legitimate reason for nonrenewal.

Getting Started: Researching Your Sport

If you think that you have a chance at an athletic scholarship, you can find information on the schools of the various divisions and geographic locations by searching the NCAA and NAIA (discussed later in this chapter) Web sites.

For simplicity, we refer to the NCAA site, but student athletes are best advised to track both organizations in their particular sports. On the main page, click on "Sports and Championships" and then choose a sport and click on "Polls and Rankings." You'll find the leaders in all the regions in all the divisions. To discover which schools sponsor all the different sports, start at the main site and click on "Administration and governance" to find links to colleges, conferences, and lots more information.

Another good site for tracking teams, players, and results is www.ncaa sports.com, where each sport is covered in detail in a sports journalist style. As soon as you can, start tracking the teams in your sports, watching for which teams do best, which teams move from one division to another, and which are gradually moving up in the rankings. These indicators tell you the top teams, as well as the teams that are making a concerted effort to improve in the sport of your choice.

After you've identified the key colleges in your sport, check out the Web site for each college and track the information about the particular teams. Take note of the stars in the team, their positions, and their particular year.

If you're a defensive lineman while a junior in high school and you see that the defensive linemen at the college of your choice are both juniors, they'll likely have graduated when you enter as a freshman. This is an important selling point to the coach and will certainly work in your favor.

Thinking Like a Coach

Always put yourself in the coach's shoes. He or she wants the best possible players, of course. But you must understand a few other factors as well:

✔ The team requires players for all positions, so you want to track which teams or colleges may be weak in your position or sport.

✔ The team will need to *replace* the players that graduate, so you want to track which colleges have players in your sport or position that will graduate as you want to enter.

✔ The number of scholarships a school can offer under NCAA regulations is a total amount for all years of college, not just entering freshmen. That means that only about a quarter of the scholarships they offer are for new blood. Always remember that you're trying to enter an existing team, likely comprised of players from all four years.

✔ The coach has a limited amount of space and a limited amount of money. Remember that the coach is always trying to balance the needs of the team with the set budget she has been allocated. If you're in an equivalency sport, you make it easier for the coach to meet your financial need by bringing with you scholarships and prizes from other sources.

✔ The better your grades and the better your attitude, the easier you'll be to place and keep. Coaches tell us that if they have to choose between two equally good athletes, they let the grades make their decision. As well, coaches told us that even the best players aren't worth the hassle if they continually get in trouble due to criminal activity, drug use, or slacking.

Beyond their own needs, coaches think about their players all the time. They know the odds are low for any individual student to make the team, lower still to win a scholarship, and even lower to become a successful professional athlete after college.

Every coach and athletics administrator we talked with emphasized two things: Be realistic in assessing your abilities, and remember that you're going to college to get an *education*. Most coaches advise choosing a college based on which one will give the best academic education and *then* see if you can get an athletic scholarship at that school.

Athletes dreaming of the major leagues should recognize how few spots are available for top players. Currently, there are about 20,000 basketball players in U.S. colleges — and only 58 will be drafted this year by the NBA!

The Scouting and Recruiting Process

It starts earlier than you think. Most recruiters start looking at prospective players in their *freshman year of high school*. Some start even earlier than that. Recruitment is a year-round job that never ends. Recruiters look at thousands of players year in, year out, and you want them to remember *your* name and *your* talent. So the sooner you can get on the radar of the recruitment network, the more likely you'll be considered a viable candidate when your turn comes to play for real.

You can get ready by preparing the materials we list in the section "Being seen" later in this chapter.

The *recruitment network* is made up of professional recruiters, college coaches, sports journalists, and others involved in high school and amateur youth sporting events. Naturally, coaches at the various colleges are in competition with each other to get the same players, but they still get their information the same way from the same types of sources. With a few exceptions, all the coaches know all about the best players in all their sports.

The two main exceptions are

- ✔ **Walk-ons:** Once in a while, a player who's never distinguished himself will change drastically in his final year and surprise everyone. JD Drew wowed onlookers at a baseball camp in the summer between his junior and senior year of high school, although he hadn't been a recruitment candidate before. Coaches at Florida State University hustled to acquire him and help him qualify academically. He went on to set records for home runs and stolen bases, became player of the year at FSU, and was drafted by the St. Louis Cardinals in 1998 where he still plays.

  Similarly, Andre Wadsworth was a walk-on, trying out for the football team when he was a freshman at FSU. He won a full scholarship in his second year and later became the third pick in the NFL draft in 1998, going to the Arizona Cardinals. Since then, he's won ACC Player of the Year and has become a member of the All-American team.

  Walk-ons occur because students are changing physically during high school. Someone who may have been too small to play Division I basketball in eleventh grade may shoot up 6 inches by his senior year. If this happens to you, make sure to let the coaches know.

  Walk-ons also happen because the recruiters simply miss certain players. Andre Wadsworth was from a small Christian high school in Miami, and the recruiters didn't expect a powerhouse such as Andre to come from this school. He didn't expect it himself, choosing FSU for its *business* school and trying out for football almost as an afterthought. Happily for fans, it was a good thought.

- ✔ **Special connections:** Every school has a network of alumni and concerned friends. If they discover a dynamo player who may not be involved in the recognized competitions, they often send the word to their alma mater. Naturally, coaches will be curious (and possibly skeptical) about why they haven't discovered this athlete through normal circumstances, but they certainly investigate each prospect.

  Whether the student simply hasn't bothered with competitions or is located in a place where he or she is unlikely to be noticed, the statistics generally tell the tale of eligibility. Regardless of an athlete's background, someone who can run a four-minute mile is valuable for the track team.

Brigham Young was established and is administered by the Mormon church, so Mormons around the world send the "BY" athletics department information about Mormon talent. This special connection is unique to Brigham Young; however, other colleges have other associations that may be religious, historical, or simply through an interested alumni.

Being seen

College coaches and recruiters are always looking for promising talent. They track the regional, state, and national high school competitions. They watch the nonscholastic competitions — playing on a nonscholastic team is often more challenging than playing on a high school team, which is obviously limited to players who attend a particular school. Coaches also drop by the summer sports camps, read the sports sections of local newspapers, and keep in touch with reputable pre-college coaches across the country and even around the world.

If you want a coach to see you, you have to compete at the top levels. You have to attend the important camps, meets, and competitions for your sport. You also have to self-promote, hopefully with the assistance of your existing coach. In a perfect world, getting an athletic scholarship is considered a team event, with a team made up of you, all your coaches, and your parents.

During the summer between your junior and senior year of high school, coaches will hold camps and clinics and will attend tournaments relating to your sport. It's in your best interest to be there, too. If you don't show yourself, you won't be seen! And you know the old expression, *out of sight, out of mind.*

In the autumn of your senior year, if coaches are interested in you, they'll correspond with you as well as all the other athletes they consider to be hot prospects, whittle down their list, and eventually visit those students who are considered worthy of the time and expense required for a trip. You may also be requested to conduct an official visit to the college, so that the coaches and other staff can compare you to their existing lineup. During the visit, they want to watch you in action, so now is your big chance to wow them.

Coaches, however, also want to get to know you as a person to determine if you'll fit with the rest of the team, and with the personality of the college. Remember that recruiting is a two-way street — ask a lot of questions about life on campus, the camaraderie of the rest of the athletes, and what makes the college unique. These questions are important because this college may be your home for the next four years.

Registering with online recruiters

Student athletes can register with various online recruiters or other agencies. Basically, you register with them by paying a fee. You enter your name, school, height, weight, position, and a few statements you want to make. Then anyone who happens to come to the site can check you out. As well, most agencies will send your stats to your top college choices, and other services are available that vary depending on the particular company.

Some of the better-known online recruiters and agencies are the College Bound Student Alliance (www.cbsa.com), the international College Prospects of America (www.cpoa.com), Football Prospects (www.footballprospects.com), Scout USA (www.scoutusa.com), The Sport Source (www.thesportsource.com), and StudentMVP.com (www.studentmvp.com).

Is it worth it? Well, the top scouts are using the established networks, including professional recruiters that they hire, so they really don't need an agency to send them your details. Also, you can send your information to the coaches as easily as the agencies can. Although we can't speak for all college coaches, *few* of the coaches and athletic administrators we interviewed claimed that they even glanced at the materials sent by these agencies. Many said they were leery of any organization that would charge high school students for such a service. However, some said that they were open to information regardless of how it was offered.

Using the services certainly won't hurt your prospects. As always, however, you have to be realistic. Using an agency to send your stats to a winning Division I-A football team is probably a waste of time and money. The team already uses its *own* resources to find you. Using an agency to help you find a lesser-known Division II college, however, *may* work for you.

Besides, the Web sites of some of the agencies do have useful information, including sample resumes and cover letters for student athletes. We caught a number of inconsistencies in the statistics posted at some of the flashier sites, though, so be wary of quoting them. As always, buyer beware.

Here's an example: Brigham Young has a strict honor code and doesn't allow drinking, smoking, drugs, or premarital sex on campus. Before you sign up there, you need to realize that this policy isn't just lip service — the college means it! Depending on your personality, these rules can make BY the perfect choice for you or the worst choice that you can make. Other colleges have gained reputations for steroid use or lax academic standards — you need to investigate all the implications of choosing a college before you get there.

Okay, so no one is pounding on your door begging you to join his or her team. Or perhaps you *have* received a letter of inquiry asking you to send more information about yourself to the coach of a particular team. Whether you're being solicited or you want to promote yourself independently, you need to show the coach the same things.

Introduce yourself

Send a cover letter expressing your interest in the specific team and college, outlining why you'd be an asset. It pays to know details about the team and the coach — always address your letter to the coach after confirming the spelling of the coach's name!

Let the coach know your key strengths and explain briefly how they can benefit the team. For example, if you're not the biggest player, explain that your speed and dexterity helped you run in the three touchdowns to win the state championship. Tell the track coach that your ability to run 100 meters in 10.2 seconds can help the team continue its tradition of excellence *after* winning seniors John and Jane Doe graduate.

Don't forget to include your contact information (*especially* your phone number), citizenship, and Social Security Number.

Show 'em your stats

Provide your height, weight, position, history, and special qualifications. Statistics are mostly numbers, so you need to show that your numbers are up there with the best in the country. List your times, your game point averages, your runs batted in, or whatever numbers are appropriate to your sport. Let the coach know if you're a switch-hitter, if you compete in other sports, or if you've been trained by named professionals.

The college will consider you to be more valuable if you can compete in more than one sport because it will, in effect, be getting two players for the price of one. Naturally, this only applies if you're actually good enough to qualify and win in each sport. Note that you're counted toward whichever sport is considered the *dominant sport*. The most dominant sport is football, followed by basketball, men's ice hockey, women's volleyball, women's field hockey, men's swimming, and men's water polo. If your two sports aren't among this list, you can choose which is the most dominant.

Most coaches tell us that they know if an athlete is worth seeing after a quick glance at the stats sheet. This is the first place for you to face reality.

If you are 5 feet 11 inches and trying out for Division I basketball, you probably won't be considered. It's just that plain. Sure, there are exceptions, but you'd better be an outstanding player that leads your team to national competitions. (Of course, in this situation, you won't need to promote yourself. The coaches will come to you.)

The individual timed sports are easier to gauge than the team competitive sports — your time for the 100 meter butterfly stroke can easily be compared with everyone else's time, but knowing that your team won the state finals doesn't necessarily mean that you had much to do with that win. You need to make it clear that you're a vital part of any team you're on.

Don't forget to include your academic standing, GPA, and SAT/ACT scores. You are *far* more attractive to coaches if they know that they don't have to worry about your eligibility from an academic point of view.

Show 'em your recommendations

Hopefully, your existing coach will be part of the recruiting network known by a coach at your first choice college. College coaches value the judgment of those who have helped them in the past and steer clear of those who have previously misrepresented players. Even if your coaches are unknown, a good word — make that *several excellent words* — from your coaches is a necessity when trying to get an athletic scholarship.

Notice that we said "coaches" because you're expected to compete for your high school and another external team or organization. In fact, most college coaches value youth or league play over high school teams.

Getting you a scholarship should be considered a team effort, so work with your coaches as much as possible. They're far more likely to know college coaches than most other people around you. They're certainly familiar with the scouting and recruiting process. They should be able to help you pull together and perfect your materials and write you some inspirational recommendation letters. The letters can compare your style of play to a recognized player, especially others that played for the particular college.

Show 'em that you're a playa

Most athletes are asked to send a videotape demonstrating themselves in action. The better your video, the more desirable you appear. If possible, start collecting tapes of your games or competitions in your freshman year and edit together the best moments in a final tape.

By "moments," we don't mean that you should string together several two-second clips of you catching a ball. Let the coach see at least one entire play to demonstrate how you anticipate, react quickly, run fast, catch the ball, and share the play with the rest of your teammates.

Mind your manners when coaches visit

Coaches will want to meet you *if* you've impressed them with all that came before. This piece of advice should be obvious, but we'll say it anyway: If a coach comes to visit, be nice! Say please and thank you a lot and be eager to join the team. Remember that recruiters are people, and so are you. Coaches need to know that you'll be an easy fit with the rest of the team, and that you won't be a discipline problem. If you appear surly or uncaring, coaches have hundreds, if not thousands, of equally good prospects to choose instead.

Getting recruited

Good recruiters are always looking for talent, but coaches start compiling their lists as early as your freshman year. By your sophomore year, the recruitment network is actively scouting top players, so you want to be visible by then. NCAA member colleges must follow a lot of rules about how and when to contact players during the recruitment process, so make it easy for them by providing all your information. NAIA colleges (discussed later in this chapter) have fewer restrictions and have more flexibility in getting to know you.

If you feel that members of either organization are harassing you, contact the organizational headquarters, using the contact information on the Web site — also located in Chapter 20 of this book. Both organizations are committed to the welfare of student athletes and don't tolerate harassing behavior.

The recruiting process goes into full swing in the autumn of your junior year. Coaches can contact you starting September 1st. At that time, you may receive questionnaires from prospective colleges. If you get solicited, respond immediately, fully, and accurately! Lack of a timely response tells coaches that you aren't interested in their college, so you may be moved off the main list. Anyone interested in free money would be silly to do that, right?

Getting recruited by a coach doesn't guarantee your entry into the college. Each institution has minimum requirements for students — even athletes. If your GPA and ACT/SAT scores don't qualify you for the school, you won't get your scholarship.

Also remember that getting scouted does *not* mean that you'll be offered a scholarship. Many football coaches send out more than 2,000 recruitment letters per year, asking prospects for more information about themselves. They can offer scholarships to only 25 of those prospects. You do the math.

Getting an offer

If the coach of a NCAA member college decides to offer you a scholarship, he or she will send you a *National Letter of Intent* (NLI). This letter is a binding agreement between you and the college — the college offers you financial aid for one academic year as long as you're admitted to the college and are eligible under NCAA guidelines, and you agree to attend the college and participate in the athletic program.

If the package contained in your NLI doesn't contain a full scholarship, you may wish to try negotiating for more. To do so, contact the coach or assistant coach who contacted you and ask to discuss your package. You're more likely to be successful in obtaining a better offer if you can demonstrate that you're being sought by other teams that are willing to pay you more for your skills.

Recruiting terminology

During the recruiting period, you'll start to hear some different terms that refer to the degree of *contact* that coaches and other athletic staff are allowed to have with you. The times for each period vary, depending on the sport, but generally, the contact period starts in your junior year. Recruiting calendars that explain the dates for each sport are available on the NCAA Web site.

✔ **Contact period:** Coaches and other authorized members of the college athletic department can contact you in person and off campus.

✔ **Dead period:** No contact is permitted by athletic staff whatsoever.

✔ **Evaluation period:** Athletic staff can watch you and participate in off-campus activities to give them a chance to evaluate your talent and determine if you're likely to be eligible to play for their team and qualify for their college. However, they can't contact you directly to negotiate.

✔ **Quiet period:** Athletic staff can discuss your prospects, but only on their campus. They can't contact you at home or in your high school.

You'll need to *prove* that you've received competing offers, so don't try to create a bidding war with nothing but your say-so. Most coaches have worked in the industry for many years, and they know the coaches on the other teams. Although they're certainly in competition for top players, they know what other schools are likely to need in terms of players, and they'll have a fairly good guess of what any team is likely to offer someone of your caliber. Coaches are *very* tough to fool, so don't bother trying.

Many coaches keep some of their budget available to pull in fresh talent for sports that start in the spring. If you didn't sign a contract with a team prior to the fall term, you still have time to approach teams that may not have covered all their positions.

Signing day

The NCAA designates a particular first day that Letters of Intent can be signed by student athletes. The day varies from sport to sport, but generally, the first Wednesday in February is the signing day for football, and other sports are often in April. However, there's also a weeklong early signing period in November for sports other than football.

After you and your parents have signed the NLI, other NCAA colleges that participate in the NLI program must stop recruiting you. If you wish to rescind the agreement and break your contract, you'll probably be barred from receiving another such NLI for one or two years.

For more information about the NLI program, log onto `www.national letter.org` or call 205-458-3013.

Other Sources of Athletic Scholarships

By far, the most scholarship money for athletes is available through NCAA-regulated teams. However, other funding is available through other organizations and private sources.

The National Association for Intercollegiate Athletics

Though lesser known than the NCAA, athletic scholarships are also available from colleges that are part of the *National Association for Intercollegiate Athletics* (NAIA). A total of 309 colleges are member institutions of the NAIA, including a few Canadian universities.

The NAIA's Web site (`www.naia.org`) contains information about the organization, member teams, and its own *Guide for the College-Bound Athlete*. This guide explains eligibility, scholarships, recruitment policies, and more.

The maximum financial aid limits for any individual student athlete are similar to those outlined by the NCAA; however, issues of head-count don't factor into the equation. The recruitment process is also less regulated, allowing coaches to contact you more frequently and enter into an ongoing dialogue. NAIA members scout in much the same manner as NCAA members, using professional recruiters and a network of high school and team coaches, sports journalists, and others.

The NAIA is devoted to enhancing "the character-building aspects of sport." It's known for its commitment to sportsmanship, and both racial and gender equality. Teams are divided into two divisions, as well as conferences and regional groupings, and they engage in national championship competitions.

Junior colleges

Junior colleges and other colleges that don't particulate in the NCAA or NAIA programs offer some scholarship aid for athletes. These schools typically compete against other junior colleges in their local area or region.

Just like emerging NCAA sports, the funding available from these other sources is much less than for the more competitive teams that draw large crowds of paying viewers. The funding sources are also less organized, so they're more difficult to find. Your best bet is to approach junior colleges in your area directly to find out what sort of local networks exist.

Chapter 15

Free Money for International Study . . . and for International Students

. . . .

In This Chapter

▶ Discovering life in a different country

▶ Accessing the organizations that can help you find financial aid

. . . .

*T*his chapter deals with two international components of college education: how American students can get free money to attend international institutions and how international students can get free money to study here.

Part of our job in this chapter is to set your expectations appropriately low. The discouraging reality is that most students studying abroad are entirely self-funded, meaning that they and their parents foot the bill entirely for their schooling. Similarly, most international students aren't eligible for the vast majority of American student aid — and, thus, pay the full sticker price when studying here.

This bad news aside, there are some important free money resources to know about, and we explain where to search and how to apply for all things *gratis*. (See, you're speaking a foreign language already!)

Before You Go

Both American students studying abroad and international students studying here have a lot to consider before going this route. Studying abroad can be a rewarding experience, allowing you to appreciate a new culture, gain some knowledge about different histories and political systems, and possibly learn a foreign language. Also, studying Chaucer at Cambridge, learning French at the Sorbonne, or researching international trade at the University of Tokyo somehow seems more authentic. It's certainly far more exotic.

Before you book your flight, however, be advised that living in a foreign country can be as challenging as it is fascinating. The things you take for granted, including telephone access, healthcare, banking, shopping hours, and transportation may be vastly different in another country. Even if you choose a country where you speak the language, the idioms and culture of the people may pose a challenge.

Doing the prep work

Besides psyching yourself up for the inevitable cultural and language challenges, you need to do some legal paperwork. Your passport must be up to date, for example, and you'll most likely need a student visa. If you want to work while going to school, you'll probably also need a work permit. Many countries prohibit students from working at all (or price work visas too high for many students), thereby eliminating any source of (legal) local money.

Obtaining a student visa and a separate work visa can take *months* to acquire. Students coming to America should understand that restrictions have been tighter and immigration bureaucracy more problematic since the September 11, 2001 terrorist attacks. Smart students get organized long before they plan to start their overseas studies. Many colleges help students obtain the necessary paperwork for student visas, and some larger schools even have special departments to speed the way for international students.

Getting admitted

To be admitted to a college or university, all students must apply through the regular application channels. International students, however, must meet a few other requirements. For instance, you may have to provide evidence of your language skills by submitting results of a foreign language test.

Students coming to the United States (whose native language isn't English) must usually submit results of their *Test of English as a Foreign Language* (known as TOEFL). American students wishing to study in a language other than English must take similar tests.

International students applying to study in the United States also need to be more proactive than American students about writing the *Scholastic Aptitude Tests* (SATs) or the *American College Test* (ACT). If your prospective college requires either of these tests, you must submit your results, whether you are an American or an international student. Finding information about the tests can be difficult outside the United States, and students may have to travel some distance to find a testing center. Check out the College Board's site (www.collegeboard.com) for information about SAT testing dates and centers outside the United States. For the ACT, go to www.act.org.

An organization that can help

The Department of Education's *U.S. Network for Education Information* (USNEI) performs many functions for the college bound. Its most important role (at least as far as we're concerned in this chapter) is to provide information for American students wishing to study abroad as well as for international students wishing to study and live in the United States.

Subjects on the USNEI Web site (www.ed.gov/NLE/USNEI/index.html) include international information sources; regional information sources; institutional directories; foreign diplomatic and consular services; and other details, such as immigration procedures and custom allowances when you return home. Also covered are U.S. study-abroad programs, including those at both the undergraduate and graduate levels, as well as additional financial support for students living abroad. Teaching opportunities for international workers coming to the United States are also discussed.

The USNEI site also has useful articles outlining the American education system, various U.S. institutions and programs, student visas and financial assistance. In addition to logging on to the Web site, you can also call them at 1-800-424-1616. If you have specific questions about material on the Web site, you can also e-mail the USNEI folks at USNEI@ed.gov.

Going Away? Get Free Money!

Most colleges and universities abroad charge international students higher fees than citizens of their own country. This rate difference is because tuition is often subsidized by taxes that non-citizens don't pay. You can see this principle in action here in our country: State colleges charge out-of-state students far more for tuition than in-state residents.

Despite these higher fees, many international institutions are still lower priced than equivalent institutions in the United States. Canada is a good example, where annual tuition for an international student at the esteemed University of Toronto (sometimes referred to as "Harvard of the North") is only about $6,200 in our money. This price is a far cry from private colleges in the United States, charging upwards of $25,000 a year!

Free money from American sources

Most of the need-based grant money that you can get by going to an American college won't be available to you if you choose to attend an institution in another country. However, read on for a few exceptions.

Study-abroad programs

The most accessible option for free money is to connect with an international institution through an affiliated institution or "sister college" based here in the United States. Many American colleges offer study-abroad programs affiliated with international schools. Check with all your prospective colleges and find out what's available.

If you have your heart set on a particular college or university in another country, contact the admissions department there and ask if it's affiliated with any schools in the United States. In particular, ask if the institution works with Title IV programs in the United States. Title IV is the part of the *Higher Education Act* that authorizes federal loan, work, and grant education financial assistance programs. In short, it deals with financial aid, and is the means through which funding for your education can take place.

When you engage in a study-abroad program through a school in the United States, your governmental and institutional financial aid is generally fully portable. In other words, you can study abroad and take your federal, state, college and third-party awards with you.

American Universities abroad

You may also want to look into *American Universities* located in a host of foreign cities, including Paris, Beirut, and Cairo. The education is conducted in English, but you get the benefit of experiencing life in a foreign land. As we discuss later in this chapter, students may access U.S.-based *loan* programs when attending one of these universities. Government *grants,* however, are generally not available.

Although these institutions are called "American," they aren't in any way affiliated with the American government, nor are they necessarily up to American educational standards. Accreditation relies on the standards of the particular country in which the university is situated. Some such universities are excellent while others leave a lot to be desired, so check out these schools well before you need to make other plans, in case things aren't to your liking.

Scholarships for your international education

Various private organizations support students studying abroad through scholarships. These organizations include Rotary International, the Henry Luce Foundation and the international organizations listed at the end of this chapter. Use the sources listed in Chapter 20 to search for more organizations.

Obtaining loans

The *International Education Finance Corporation* (IEFC) administers the Federal Stafford Loan program, Federal PLUS Loan program, and the private *International Student Loan Program* (ISLP) for U.S. citizens studying at eligible institutions abroad. More than 400 international institutions are eligible for the federal programs, and ISLP is available on an even broader basis. Check out all the details at www.iefc.com/us/us-ug-fully-enrolled.php.

The IEFC also administers programs for graduate students studying abroad and for undergraduates studying abroad for a short period who'll receive their degrees from a U.S. institution. For more information about these opportunities, access the links at www.iefc.com.

Free money from international sources

Very few foreign governments or organizations offer money to Americans or nationals of any other country besides their own. Why should they? Supporting people who aren't their own citizens isn't in their best interests financially or politically. To be fair, the U.S. government and American colleges don't offer a lot of assistance to students from Bolivia, Bhutan, or Brazil, choosing to help their own native sons and daughters from Boston and Boise instead. To varying degrees, every country takes care of its own.

Reciprocal trade agreements have made it possible to access *some* funding in Canada and Mexico, as well as Germany and Japan. Individual institutions in these countries are the best sources for information about these programs.

The best place to start looking for this type of information is, of course, on the Web. After you find out all you can online, write, e-mail, or telephone the appropriate office at each university to confirm any key facts and ask any questions not answered on the Web site.

Dual citizenship has its advantages

Holding citizenship in a country where you wish to study can make the entire process much easier. You'll probably be entitled to the (often) lower tuition rates offered to citizens. You won't have to obtain student or work visas, and you can be employed while attending school if you wish. You'll also be eligible for more scholarships and grants from within the country.

Look into your family history and do a little research to find out if you're eligible — if one of your parents was born in the United Kingdom, for example, you're probably eligible to become a British citizen. This citizenship will give you a European Union-compatible passport that's recognized in fifteen countries across Europe, and possibly ten more countries after they join in May 2004.

Be aware, however, that becoming a citizen of another country can have certain drawbacks. Many foreign countries have mandatory armed forces service that kicks in when a citizen reaches anywhere between the ages of 17 and 21. You may find yourself pressed into service as soon as you enter the country under your non-American passport.

AP courses at international schools

We discuss the value of taking *Advanced Placement* (AP) courses and tests in Chapter 21. Many American colleges and universities accept these tests in lieu of taking certain freshman courses. Passing sufficient AP tests with high enough marks allows you to start college as a sophomore!

Besides saving you up to a year of college time, taking AP courses can save you lots of money. AP courses are *a lot* cheaper than full-blown college courses, so, as we discuss in Chapter 21, it makes sense to consider taking AP courses if at all possible. Those headed overseas will be happy to know that AP courses can be applied at colleges and universities in 22 other countries around the world! Check out the list of schools outside the U.S. with formal AP policies at `www.collegeboard.com/ap/colleges/international`.

Along with advanced standing, a passing grade (usually 3 or more out of 5) in the native language of the country where you wish to study is usually accepted as proof of your ability in that language. This means that successfully passing AP German, Spanish, or French can serve both as your language test and work toward giving you advanced college standing!

Coming to America? Get Free Money!

Now, don't get too excited. There's no big pot of gold available for international students who wish to study in the United States. In fact, the vast majority of students from abroad pay for the privilege through sources they've obtained in their own country. Current estimates show that about 80 percent of international undergraduate students get no U.S.-based funding.

So what's the point of this part of the chapter? We have two points actually:

- About 20 percent of international undergraduate students *do* get some U.S.-based funding, and you may be part of this group.
- Resources *may* be available in your home country for funding your U.S.-based education.

U.S.-based aid for international students

Before even thinking about obtaining free money to attend an American college, savvy international students find out what it takes to be accepted as a student in the United States. One excellent source of information comes from the College Board (www.collegeboard.org) as a condensed version of its huge directory of American colleges.

Called *The College Handbook Foreign Student Supplement*, this resource can be found in selected major bookstores in countries such as Canada and Australia as well as the European Union countries. If you can't find it locally, write to College Board Publications, Box 886, New York, NY, USA, 10101.

The College Board also operates the Overseas Educational Advising Centers. You can locate the center closest to you by going online, locating apps. collegeboard.com/cbsearch/center/searchOverseasAdvCenter.jsp and clicking on your region.

After investigating the College Board, check out EduPASS (www.edupass.org), a site that provides information for international students interested in studying in the United States. Begun as the international section of FinAid, this extensive site covers more than just financial aid. You can find information about admissions, visas, culture shock, and more. One page lists which U.S. colleges that give financial aid to international undergraduate students, and another page offers scholarship links and resources available to international students. We list a bevy of other resources for international students in Chapter 20.

From the government

We're not going to beat around the bush: Most government-based aid is *not* available to international students. This actually makes a lot of sense because government-based aid is paid for through citizens' taxes. If you aren't an American citizen, you (and your parents) aren't contributing to tax revenue. The thinking is, why should you then reap the benefits of the system?

One major exception is for foreign nationals who have been granted refugee status for humanitarian and compassionate reasons. These individuals are generally treated as U.S. residents when applying for financial aid.

Note that anyone born in the United States is entitled to U.S. citizenship and all the federal aid and private scholarship money you can get. Even if you've lived most of your life outside American borders, looking into your citizenship options is definitely worthwhile.

From the college

Like the federal government, most colleges don't make need-based funding available to international students. Merit-based funding, however, is sometimes available regardless of citizenship for *certain* programs. Each college is different — in fact, each *program* of each college is different — so international students must do extensive research to find the scholarships for which they may be eligible. Happily, a simple e-mail request to the financial aid department of each prospective college usually results in most of the information you need.

Be advised, however, that most college financial aid offices don't directly administer departmental or athletic scholarships. For these awards, you must contact the specific departments or coaches individually. On the bright side, athletic and departmental scholarships are more likely to be available to international students than any other type of college-based scholarships. Indeed, the athletic recruiting network travels throughout the world looking for top athletes from every continent. We talk more about the athletic recruitment system in Chapter 14.

For departmental scholarships, on the other hand, contacting the college directly and applying to the department is the student's responsibility. A drama recruiter, for example, is unlikely to bang on your door to offer you a scholarship — despite your renowned acting talent.

Generally, private colleges are the ones most likely to give funding for international students. State colleges are heavily subsidized by state taxes, so their policies preclude them from giving much funding to out-of-state students, let alone out-of-country students.

Graduate students from foreign countries are much more likely to obtain funding than undergraduate students. We quoted a statistic earlier in this chapter that found that 80 percent of international students don't get financial aid. This number drops to only 50 percent for graduate students, so the odds of finding some free money definitely get better the further you go in school!

From private sources

Because U.S. citizenship tends to be a key qualifier for most awards, only a few private U.S.-based scholarships and grants are available for international students. To find awards that don't require U.S. citizenship, perform Web-based searches, using such resources as www.finaid.org, www.fastweb.com, and studentawards.com.

Loans to international students

Certain colleges and private organizations will help international students obtain student loans to study at U.S. colleges. The most extensive program is the *International Student Loan Program* (ISLP). The ISLP is jointly administered by the International Education Finance Corporation (IEFC), The Education Resources Institute (TERI), the Bank of Boston, and Educaid. Under this program, TERI guarantees the loans, while the Bank of Boston and Educaid provide the actual funds.

Students may borrow from $2,000 per year to the full cost of education, and they have up to 25 years to repay the loan. Interest applies at the prime rate, and a 5 percent "guarantee fee" is applied for undergraduate loans. The final catch is that a qualified U.S. citizen or permanent resident must co-sign the loan. For all the details, go to www.iefc.com/international or call 1-888-296-IEFC (4332) or 781-843-5334.

Another option is the *Global Student Loans program* (www.globalslc.com), which provides comprehensive education loans for international students without requiring an American co-signer. The Global Student Loan can cover the full cost of attendance, including transportation.

Special status for Canadians and Mexicans

Some American colleges have chosen to extend grant and scholarship eligibility to Canadian or Mexican students. For example, Columbia University is committed to meeting the full need of entering students as long as they're citizens or permanent residents of the United States, citizens of Canada, or visa refugees. Since the passage of the North American Free Trade Agreement (NAFTA), more colleges are offering special status to Canadian and Mexican students.

This special status is more likely to be offered at private colleges, especially those in the northeast (for Canadians) or in the southwest (for Mexicans). Canadian and Mexican students are advised to consult individual institutions to find out if this situation applies to the colleges of their choice.

Financial aid in your home country

Because 80 percent of international undergraduate students receive no financial aid from U.S.-based sources, these students are best advised to look to *local* sources. The extent of these sources varies widely depending on their home country, and it would take several books to cover all the options available to students from around the world.

Tapping your own government

In general, use the same advice that we provide in the rest of this book and modify it for your own situation. The College Board's Overseas Educational Advising Center in your home country is likely to have information about what resources may be available to you.

The U.S. embassy in your country will also have information about studying in the United States. Also, *your* country's embassy in the United States may have information about the students from your country that are already studying in the United States. It wouldn't hurt to contact them and find out what works (and what doesn't) when pursuing scholarships and grants.

Discovering international organizations

Finding an international organization that will fund undergraduate students who wish to study abroad is rare, but several have highly competitive programs for graduate students. These organizations include the United Nations, the Organization of American States (OAS), America-Mideast Educational and Training Services, Inc. (AMIDEAST), the International Maritime Organization, the International Telecommunications Union, the League of Red Cross Societies, Rotary International, the Soros Foundation, the World Health Organization, and the World Council of Churches.

As well, the *Fulbright Program* offers about 4,700 Fulbright scholarships per year to graduate students from around the world. For more information, you can obtain particulars of the application process at your country's U.S. embassy, Fulbright offices worldwide, the Institute of International Education (www.iie.org), the College Board's Overseas Educational Advising Centers or by contacting the United States Information Agency, Office of Public Liaison. You can reach this agency at 301 4th Street, SW, Room 602, Washington, DC 20547. You can also e-mail the office at inquiry@usia.gov, call them at 202-619-4355, or send a fax to 202-619-6988.

Most funding sources available to international students must be applied for before you come to the United States. After you arrive, you often become ineligible — so make sure that all your paperwork is done, received, approved and processed *before* you leave home. Bon voyage!

Part V

I Didn't Think of That! Lots More Sources of Free Money

The 5th Wave   By Rich Tennant

"My uncle agreed to fund my college education under the condition I change my major from Byzantine Art and Philosophy to Financial Management and Fund Raising."

In this part . . .

Many students have no problem applying for government grants or even asking their college for scholarships, but that's where they stop. They never realize that the additional free money they need might be available from the people they see every week, work with every day, and even serve with in the U.S. Armed Forces.

You may be surprised to discover how many organizations close to you offer scholarships or other sources of free money. These organizations may include a service club to which you belong, a church or religious institution that you attend, or even the company for which you work.

A little research here and some well-written application letters and essays there can add a bundle to your college aid package. Tons of sources are out there. You just have to discover what's waiting for you!

Chapter 16

Getting Free Money from Organizations

In This Chapter

▶ Finding the organizations that want to give you money

▶ Focusing on what makes you special

▶ Thinking like a scholarship committee member

▶ Creating a winning package

*M*ost people are aware that colleges give out scholarships, and that money for college can also be obtained from the government. Organizations, on the other hand, are often a mystery to college-bound students. Most students don't think to turn to organizations for help with college costs, even though they're some of the best sources for free money.

Meet the Groups that Give Away Money

Undoubtedly, you have an inkling that some organizations offer scholarships, but you might not know *which* organizations to approach, *how* to approach them, or *why* they give their money away.

By the way, the term *organization* is the all-encompassing word that we use to include every entity that offers free money for college, excluding government bodies, colleges, and employers, all of which we discuss in other chapters in this book. Some organizations give away money based on merit, and some based on need, and some use a hybrid assessment formula based on both need and merit.

Who are these generous organizations?

We're glad you asked. The organizations include the following:

- ✔ **Service and social clubs:** The Elks Club, Lions Club, Rotary Club, 4-H Club, Boy Scouts and Girl Scouts, and Greek organizations (college fraternities and sororities) are just a few examples of service and social clubs.

- ✔ **Foundations formed by corporations, groups, or individuals:** These foundations include large organizations with multiple awards (such as the Coca-Cola Scholars Foundation, that gives away 300 scholarships annually worth $1,000 to $20,000), mid-sized organizations (such as the Barking Foundation that gives 14 awards ranging from $1,000 to $3,000 to Maine residents — and, no, dogs need not apply), and small organizations offering as few as one scholarship a year (such as the SuperCollege.com Student Scholarship worth $500 to $2,500).

- ✔ **Employment or trade groups:** Professional organizations (the Screen Actors Guild or the Airline Pilots Association), trade unions (AFL-CIO, Teamsters), and military service organizations (the American Legion, ROTC, Fleet Reserve Association, the National Guard, Air Force Aid Society and many others) fall under this category.

- ✔ **Various religious, historical, and interest-based organizations:** These include your church, synagogue, mosque, temple and many others.

It seems so overwhelming. Where do you start? That's easy — you start with yourself.

In Chapter 1, we ask you to put together lists of your family history, affiliations, and whatnot. Well, now you get to put these lists to good use. Use all the categories that we suggest, and add anything else that comes to mind. Then look up the appropriate organizations in Chapter 20. After you figure out where to apply, use the information in the rest of this chapter to make every application that you send a winner.

And the categories are: (Drum roll, please. . . .)

- ✔ **Your state:** This one's pretty self-explanatory.

- ✔ **Your intended college(s):** Contact the financial aid office and ask what scholarships are offered. Also, check out your parents' colleges and any college fraternity or sorority that your parents may have joined.

- ✔ **Your ethnic heritage:** Particularly plentiful are scholarships for African-Americans and Native Americans, but something's available out there for almost everyone. Don't be afraid to go back a few generations or dig around in your family's past.

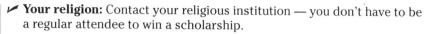

- ✔ **Your religion:** Contact your religious institution — you don't have to be a regular attendee to win a scholarship.

- ✔ **Your (or your parents') employers, trade organizations, or unions:** You may need to look under the trade name instead of the more recognizable commonly used name; for example, lawyers are listed under the American Bar Association, the Trial Lawyers Association, and a variety of other listings.

- ✔ **Veterans:** If you, a parent, or even a grandparent served in any part of the U.S. military, a scholarship (or several) may be waiting for you.

- ✔ **Disability:** If you, a dependent, or even a parent suffers a physical or mental disability, including a disease such as cancer, you probably qualify.

- ✔ **Special circumstances:** A variety of scholarships have been set up for victims of the World Trade Center bombing, but, on a lighter note, awards are also available that are limited to tall people (Tall Clubs International Foundation), so brainstorm *anything* about you that is even slightly different from everyone else.

- ✔ **Your talents:** If you can play an instrument extremely well, sing, dance, scuba dive, or perform any number of other abilities, enter a contest to win a scholarship.

- ✔ **Your interests:** Some scholarships list as a criterion that the applicant must have an interest in the subject matter, be it writing, another language, or community activism.

- ✔ **Your (or your family's) associations:** If anyone in your family is a member of *any* organization, find out what sorts of scholarships are offered. Don't limit yourself to the local chapter; go right to the national headquarters. In fact, even if no one in your family is a member, you can still apply to most service organizations, such as those listed earlier in this section.

- ✔ **Essay-focused awards:** This final category applies to everyone because there's no eligibility restriction. These awards are offered by such institutes as the United States Institute of Peace, offering scholarships to the writer of the best essay on international peace and conflict resolution.

As you collect information and decide which organizations to contact, you should assess the priority of each and mark it in your notes with a system of stars. Assign one star for those organizations that you want to approach if you have the time, and assign five stars for those organizations that offer an award you have a good chance of winning. (Organizations with two, three, and four stars obviously fall somewhere in between.) This way, if you get short on time, you can quickly target your most important awards.

Are you eligible?

Before you get to either the merit or the need assessment, you have to look at the question of eligibility. Just because an organization offers money for the college-bound doesn't mean that you're automatically eligible to receive it. Most scholarships have some sort of eligibility criteria that you must meet before you'll even be considered for the award. Nicely, organizations tend to explain the criteria upfront, and the scholarship directories we list in Chapter 20 contain brief explanations on student eligibility for each award.

The standard evaluation categories consist of the following:

- Background (ethnic, religious, family history, employment)
- Intended field of study
- Geographic location (home or college)
- Impairment (physical, learning, visual, hearing)
- Talent (sports, arts, languages)
- Community service (the voluntary kind, not the kind the judge orders you to do when you've been bad)

You can't do anything to change your ethnic heritage, but you *can* do something to qualify for the talent or community service awards. Of course, a few awards have no eligibility limitations; they're available to anyone entering college and are generally assessed by highest marks or performance in a contest.

Why Would They Give Me Free Money?

A better question is, why wouldn't they? These organizations have a mandate to give out money to the students who best fit their standards. You simply have to demonstrate that you deserve the award.

Knowing your audience

Every marketer understands the concepts of targeting and spin. *Targeting* is focusing your product on a particular audience, and *spin* is the way information is presented. Applying for scholarships is a lot like marketing, and what you're marketing is *yourself*. To market yourself well, you need to understand the various scholarship committees and customize each application to the interests of the particular organization. You do that by spinning your materials to target the goals and purposes of the organization.

The spin for an essay sent to the Ayn Rand Institute for the *Atlas Shrugged* essay competition for business students, for example, should be markedly different from the essay sent to the AFL-CIO scholarship program. One group is staunchly anti-union, while the other *is* a union, so you obviously can't use the same essay for both. Similarly, your essays for the Catholic Aid Association, the American Liver Foundation, and the Garden Clubs of America would all be different, not because they're in conflict with each other but because each has different goals. If you want to win a scholarship from an organization, your materials must reflect their purposes.

Now, we aren't telling you to pander to every organization and to be untrue to your principles. In fact, you're far better off targeting those organizations that represent your principles. You're more likely to compose a convincing essay if you actually believe what you're saying. Go figure.

The other important point is to show your best side to each organization, recognizing that you probably have many sides. You can be a devout Catholic fascinated by liver research who just happens to grow prized begonias, but you can't focus on everything in a short essay or bio. Instead, tell each organization about the part of you that they'll best understand (and want to hear). You want the scholarship committee to identify with you because its members want to give their money to students who are just like they are — students who'll represent them well and, hopefully, carry on their legacy.

Applying yourself

After you've researched a variety of organizations, investigated all you can about them, and collected your materials, you're ready to apply.

One thing we cannot stress enough is to start early! Deadlines for these awards are usually in December or January, but they may be as early as *September* prior to your freshman year. Some scholarship committees only review the first few hundred applications that arrive. If you wait too long to apply in these cases, even if your application is stunning, you won't have a chance because your application won't be opened.

Also, creating winning applications is an art that you can't rush. Your essays must be *thoughtful.* Your other materials must be complete and perfect. Applications that are hastily scribbled or riddled with errors don't win awards. Start early — in fact, start now!

The procedure

Start out by choosing and identifying the organizations you want to approach. Collect information about the scholarship application process for each organization, including the details we outline in Chapter 1. If you have to fill out any printed forms, make several copies of each of them so that your final submission is flawless.

Categorize your collection of scholarship applications in terms of the different types of materials you must produce for each. That way, you can reuse essays, bios, and application materials with only slight customization. Generally, you can figure out the interests of the scholarship committee by reading the mandate for the scholarship and for the organization.

For example, you may have one group of organizations focusing on your intended field of study, say biochemistry, for which you must write an essay outlining why you've chosen this subject. Another group of organizations may reflect your mother's Italian heritage, for which you must focus your entry essay on your experiences as an Italian-American. Still another group of organizations may be interested in your father's history as a veteran with a heritage in the Deep South. Another group may focus on your public service activities.

You may decide to complete all the application forms at once and then turn to the bios and essays (which we discuss later in this chapter). Don't forget to use the information you've collected in your college applications folder (see Chapter 1) to your best advantage.

The format

Make sure that you follow the award rules *to the letter*. If the organization asks you to send a printed essay, don't send a video hoping to wow the committee with your originality and creativity. All you end up demonstrating is that you can't follow simple instructions.

Sure, a few people may actually enjoy your deviation from the norm, but they won't be able to award you a prize because they also have to follow the organization's own guidelines. If you absolutely must send that delightful and enthralling video, send it *in addition* to the required materials.

The application form

It's short, it's easy, it's factual. You can breeze through this part and spend your quality time on the essay, right? Wrong. We do want you to spend quality time on the essay, but don't shrug off the application form. The scholarship committee makes its first, and deepest, cuts when reading the applications. Committee members separate out any applications that don't demonstrate eligibility, and any that don't *appear* to offer anything special.

The kind of information requested includes identifying and contact information (be accurate and use your full name), employment experience, community service, organization memberships, academic achievements, awards and honors, and other facts.

The application provides you with your first opportunity to spin yourself. For example, don't just list your memberships; enthusiastically explain your role as a the organization's *leader.* You don't have much space, so you'll have to be short and pithy, but impressing them with one or two achievements is better than boring them with a hollow list.

And don't forget to sign the application form!

The cover letter

Organizations rarely come out and ask you to include a cover letter, but it's assumed in any business correspondence that a cover letter will be sent, and this *is* business. It needn't be long. Include the date and address (naming the contact person if possible), along with your contact information, preferably built into a letterhead format.

Thank the committee for the opportunity to apply, list what materials are enclosed, and end with a couple of sentences about why their organization is important to you. Print it and sign your name with a blue pen. Black ink is okay, but it may give the appearance that the page has been photocopied.

Whatever you do, don't get cute and use pink, silver, or any other wild color of ink. It's just not appropriate for this occasion.

The bio

Here the committee reads about your personal history and finds out who you are. Your bio is similar to a resume, but it has better sentence structure. Not all organizations request a bio, but many do, and some ask the biographical questions in the application form. If your biographical information is requested in the application, you don't need to send a bio as well unless it's specifically requested. If the application doesn't have a section for biographical info, send a bio, regardless of whether it's requested.

No matter how tempted you may be to do so, never lie on your application! Before the prizes are awarded, almost all organizations check to make sure that the facts presented are true.

You can, however, present yourself in the best possible light. This is no time for modesty because the only way the committee can know how great you are is if you tell it. Here you have the opportunity to spin all the extraordinary things you've done — go for it! Just don't go overboard; limit yourself to a single page. Keep in mind that brevity is effective, too.

The essay

Your essay should be interesting and have a flow that makes readers want to know what you'll say next. It should contain a central theme that you demonstrate by examples or personal vignettes. And it should serve your overall purpose of selling yourself to the committee.

Some scholarships simply request an essay, while others ask for a demonstration of your schoolwork. Knowing these requirements in advance allows you to create an essay for one of your classes that you can later use in scholarship applications. This brings up an important point: What topics are appropriate for scholarship applications?

A few scholarships define the topic for you, but most do not. You have to figure out what people whom you've never met want to read, and you usually have about 500 to 1,000 words to get your point across. But what point do you want to make?

As always, look to your audience. Here are a few examples:

- ✔ If you're applying to the National Organization for Women for a scholarship to pursue a degree in women's studies, you can recall your first experience with discrimination, explaining how it made you feel in your youth and how it affected your decision to enter your chosen field. But don't leave it at that. Compare your experience with topical events of the day or a recognized theme that you're likely to study in your first year at college. Demonstrate that you've done your homework, and that you pursue this field because you have a passion for it.

- ✔ If applying for a Haskell Award for students in architectural journalism, you can discuss the attempts to cover the new designs for the World Trade Center without sentimentalizing the tragedy, tying in your personal opinions about what should be done or even expressing your confusion over it. There's nothing wrong with knowing what you still need to learn and recognizing the necessity to continue learning throughout your life. You could tie the essay together with a final statement about the importance of architecture on our collective well-being, giving hope for new buildings and new minds to develop in the future.

- ✔ If the award or the organization giving it has no clear focus, discuss a favorite book and the impact it had upon you, how it shaped your actions and goals. Relate the themes in the book with instances from your own life, and generalize what you've learned into a comment, belief, or wonder about humankind.

The selection committee doesn't expect you to be an expert in any field. That's why you want to go to college — to study and, hopefully, become an expert. However, the selection committee *does* expect you to be fascinated by the topic you've chosen, and to address clearly the following questions:

✔ Why are you so fascinated by your chosen field of study?

✔ What triggered your interest?

✔ What do you intend to do in the future?

✔ How are you going to get there?

Your essay can be lighthearted and even funny at points; however, it should also demonstrate that you have undertaken a serious and meaningful task. You can use a simple voice; in fact, attempting to sound too scholarly may put off some committee members, some of whom are *real* experts in your chosen field of study.

We provide a sample application form and essay at the end of this chapter, but for more detailed information, check out the recently published *College Admission Essays For Dummies,* by Geraldine Woods (John Wiley Publishing, Inc.).

The reference letters

Most scholarships sponsored by organizations require references. Some students make the mistake of merely sending the contact information of people who can be used as references. Instead, you want your references to provide letters that explain why they think that you're worthy to win the particular scholarship. The letter should reveal your finest qualities, explaining how this particular reference learned about you while, perhaps, working with you on an academic, charitable, or other endeavor.

There are two basic tips when gathering reference letters:

✔ **Find the best references:** Teachers are often good choices for references — after all, the point of getting a scholarship is to get an education, and who knows more about your education than your teachers? However, you also want a reference from someone who will impress the committee, if possible. Who would impress them?

Try to think about it from their perspective. If the organization is political, how about getting a reference letter from the mayor or your congressman (from the same political party as the organization, of course). If the organization is religious, talk to your minister or rabbi. If the scholarship is aimed at people pursuing a career in creative writing, get to know a published author or a columnist at the local newspaper. A respected member of their own organization is always a good choice. Just remember that these people must be able to write knowledgeably about you, so make sure that you get to know them well in advance.

✔ **Get the best letters:** You've been doing all sorts of research on various organizations, so it stands to reason that you'd be better able to compose an appropriate reference letter, right? Well, don't sell your references short. You've chosen these people to be your best references because they're intelligent, respected, and know you well — so writing a letter shouldn't be too great a challenge for them.

That said, these people are probably quite busy, and, after all, you do have the inside scoop on the organizations where these letters are going. Help out your references by handing them a list of significant points about you that you wish to emphasize. They can phrase the letter in their own words or leave it in yours. Just make sure that you don't give the exact same list to all your references. A scholarship committee may get mighty suspicious if they receive letters from different references for you that say exactly the same thing.

Don't forget to tell your references a precise date when you need to have the letters in your hot little hands or sent off to the scholarship committee, and remind them periodically as well. You may want to ask them to finish the letters about a month before you plan to send them, in case one of your references requires extra nagging.

Other stuff

Almost all scholarship applications require transcripts, so have those ready and photocopied.

Some applications also request financial information to demonstrate need. You can use the information you already collected for your FAFSA and spin it in a more attractive light, perhaps emphasizing your daily efforts caring for your mentally challenged brother and the financial burden of the medical bills on your family.

Particular scholarships may require other materials that are attuned to their purposes, such as a portfolio for artistic or fashion-related scholarships. For others, there may be a contest, such as the National Solo Competition offered by the American String Teachers Association. Some scholarships narrow down the competition and then conduct an interview for the final stage. The Beverly Hills Theater Guild sponsors the Julie Harris Playwright Award in which applicants send in an original play, while the Concert Artist's Guild Competition requires two tapes from students of classical music.

Frequently, scholarship committees require you to send a self-addressed stamped envelope (SASE), so that they can respond to your application.

Less frequently, you're required to send a photo. A photo helps committee members remember who they're discussing, so try to make it a picture where you appear earnest, studious, diligent, and worthy.

The look and feel

It's all about packaging. You can make your application inviting to the reader by using an attractive folder, a printed label, and good quality paper. Smudges from your printer or pen blotches look messy, so be careful to avoid them. Printing from a computer looks neater than printing by hand, and you can make sure that your materials are error free before you print.

If you must use a pen, use block letters and make sure that every word is legible and correct. If you make a mistake, use another page — crossed out sections or white goo on your application will make the scholarship committee think that you're messy, lazy, or unprofessional, and we don't want them to get the wrong idea.

When assembling your materials, always think about the person who has to read your application. Put everything in the order that they are listed in the application outline; that way, the committee members don't have to search for the appropriate page. Finally, if you use large envelopes, you won't have to fold your applications, so your lovely package will remain untarnished.

The delivery

We say it many times throughout this book, but it bears repeating: Be on time! In fact, make sure that your application gets there well before the deadline. That way, you have time to confirm that it arrived with the office staff at a time when they aren't deluged by a mountain of new arrivals.

By mail

Many organizations only receive applications by mail, so you'll likely mail most of your applications. Mailing is a wise choice even for those that accept e-mail solicitations because it lets you create your masterpiece in a hardcopy that's formatted the way you like, and you can be certain that it will appear exactly the same way to the person who opens your package. You can create a production line to mass-mail several applications at a time by assembling envelopes, stamps, printed labels, and, of course, your applications.

By e-mail

E-mail is effective when sending applications that request absolutely nothing personal. If you need only send your contact information, field of study, grades, and other factual information, applying online is fine. In fact, some organizations prefer this method because it makes your application easier to process. If you choose e-mail, make sure that you get a confirmation that your application was received.

However, if the application requests an essay, written bio, or other personalized materials, you're better off sending your application by mail. Sure, e-mail is easier, but printed materials make a better impression on the committee. Sending your own printed materials allows you to format your masterpiece the way you like, using an attractive font, snazzy cover, and quality paper.

In person

In-person delivery is the preferred method for organizations you know personally and that are within relatively easy travel distance. Call ahead to ensure that you can present your materials to someone on the committee and talk with them briefly at the same meeting. Even a brief chat with the committee member's secretary or assistant can have a significant impact on your chances. Personal interaction means that you're far more likely to be remembered during the selection period.

When you arrive at the office, be presentable, well dressed, polite, and gracious. Thank *everyone* you speak with for their time, and try to impress upon them your knowledge of and appreciation for their organization.

Afterward, send a thank-you card to the organization for spending the time meeting with you and considering your application. The card will likely be placed in your file and be seen by everyone who reads your application. A thank-you card demonstrates that you're thoughtful, gracious, and well mannered — qualities that scholarship committee members like to see. If you're chosen to win one of their scholarships, you'll be associated with their organization, and they don't want to have to worry about the behavior of *their* students having a negative impact on the organization.

Being sponsored

Someone within an organization may decide that you deserve a scholarship before you even apply. Depending on the size of the organization, he or she may need little more than your permission to sponsor you for the award, and maybe your transcripts, or that person may need to provide a full application, including essay, bio, and the works. Regardless of what's required, this application should immediately become a priority because the sponsorship significantly increases your chances of winning.

People within organizations rarely think to sponsor someone on their own; most need a little push. Don't be shy about telling everyone you know that you're looking for scholarships and asking if they know of any.

Distinguishing yourself

You may look at your list of achievements and think that you sound pretty impressive. Perhaps you do, but, once again, you need to put yourself in the scholarship committee's shoes. They read hundreds or thousands of applications, looking for a handful that really stand out.

Here are a few tips to give your application that extra zip:

- ✔ **One big achievement is better than several mediocre ones.** You may have been a member of 20 different clubs and teams, but that doesn't have nearly the impact of being the founder and leader of the Young Entrepreneurs of your town, who created a Web-based student-run business pulling in $20,000 in revenue from around the country and donated half the proceeds to the local soup kitchen. That may sound like too much of a challenge to achieve, but the point is to be the founder, leader, or creator of something. It can be an adult literacy program, a food drive, your high school chapter of the ASPCA, or just about anything, as long as it demonstrates your commitment, drive, and *leadership*.

✔ **If you can't be a leader in your group, find another group.** If most of the other people at your high school or from your town are part of a particular organization, you won't stand out simply by being a member of it. Find another, perhaps smaller, organization that needs your help and energize it.

✔ **Highlight your awards and honors, explaining briefly the award's significance and why you won.**

✔ **Highlight anything that sets you apart.** If you grew up in Africa when your parents were Peace Corps volunteers, use that to demonstrate your commitment toward racial harmony, your understanding of diverse cultures, and your aptitude with languages. If you worked in the mines every summer during high school, use that to emphasize your commitment to the environment, your dogged work ethic, and your willingness to get your hands dirty to accomplish a task.

✔ **Apply where others like you will not.** It's up to you to research farther than anyone else from your area.

✔ **Create your own letterhead and labels with a logo, slogan, and contact information.** Doing so is fairly easy with off-the-shelf design software. The point is to look polished and professional, so be conservative in what you create.

✔ **Edit.** We know, it seems like we keep telling you to add stuff, and now, we're telling you to trim it down. The hard truth is that most application forms have woefully little space, and your essay is typically limited to a low word count. Professional writers can trim an article by half while retaining the impact, and so can you given a bit of time. Happily, you'll appear more elegant if you can be succinct. You'll also please the scholarship committee member reading your application.

Receiving Graciously (Will I Owe Anything if I Take Their Gift?)

You might. Some organizations request (or require) a report on how you're benefiting from the scholarship funds, to be sent midway through your year at college. Many ask you to attend a presentation ceremony, get your picture taken with the scholarship committee and possibly be interviewed for the newsletter or even for the local newspaper. Whether or not a report or appearance is required is not as readily evident when researching scholarships, but you can often see what previous winners went through by looking on the organization's Web site.

Paying your dues

Instead of looking at writing a report as a chore, think of it as your opportunity to pitch the organization on giving you more money for next year. A report rarely needs to be formal; in fact, a letter is often sufficient. You may, alternatively, be asked to speak at a meeting of the organization. Again, use this meeting as an opportunity to demonstrate that the funds have been put to a worthy cause, and to subtly imply that renewing the scholarship would bring even greater glory to the group.

Following up whether you need to or not

Even if the organization doesn't require, or even request, follow-up materials, send something anyway. Sending a thank-you note to someone who gives you a gift is simply good manners, so the organization deserves one as soon as you receive your check. The kind people who wrote your reference letters should also get a thank-you note when you receive their letters, and you should send them another note after you receive your scholarships to let them know that they were effective.

As well, you may want to send a brief monthly note, telling the organization how much you appreciate their gift and how much you're learning at college. You can use the same note for each organization that gave you a scholarship and simply change the contact info, so sending these updates won't take a lot of time. Not only will you make the people in the organization feel appreciated, you'll also keep yourself in their thoughts when they're determining where to spend next year's scholarship money. Both thoughtful and smart — that's your style!

Sample Scholarship Application Form

Name: <u>Jennifer Clare Smith</u>

Address: <u>101 Main Street, Pleasantville, Great State, USA, 11111</u>

Telephone: <u>555-555-5555</u>

Social Security Number: <u>555-555-5555</u>

High school: <u>George W. Bush High</u>

Intended college: <u>Brilliant College</u>

Academic achievements, awards and honors:

<u>National Merit Scholarship award winner</u>

<u>Regional Math League champion 2001, 2002, 2003</u>

<u>Achieved top grades in Algebra and Calculus throughout Pleasantville, 2003</u>

Extracurricular activities:

<u>Led Bush High Senior Math Team to the State finals, winning city and regional championships</u>

<u>Co-created Math tutorial program with Miss Hill (Algebra) that educated more than 50 Juniors</u>

<u>Published article, *Why Math Matters*, in Pleasantville Times — picked up by national online service MSN on October 4, 2002</u>

Employment experience:

<u>Founder and director of MathMen Tutorial service, managing a staff of five</u>

<u>Web programmer, creating commercial sites for local businesses and government (summer only)</u>

Community service/Organization memberships:

<u>Organized annual Thanksgiving Day Food Drive through Rotary Club, feeding over 200 people</u>

<u>Funded Teen Help Line servicing more than 1000 calls from desperate kids, as director of school-based fundraising activities</u>

<u>Programmed Web sites for numerous charitable organizations such as Rotary Club, Kiwanis, and 4-H Club — initiating online fund-raising capabilities, new communication and promotional benefits</u>

Education and career goals:

<u>To study the fascinating field of applied mathematics and cryptography and enter this burgeoning profession in the service of my country, eventually working with National Security forces to help protect Americans by creating enhanced safety measures for online communications.</u>

Signature: _____ *You sign here* _____

Sample Scholarship Application Essay

Professional associations offer many scholarships for students that want to study their chosen profession. Here the task is to write an essay about why you want to be an architect. The author could have simply answered the question, but that would be uninteresting and would fail to keep the readers attention. Instead, she takes us on a journey of architecture she has seen, explaining what it means to her.

Every Brick

Although I felt a slight mist of spittle on the back of my neck, I didn't dare move.[1] The subway was raging as everyone hotly debated the new designs for the World Trade Center. Sure I had my opinions but a girl from Chicago quickly learns not to offend the sacred symbols of New York — at least not in a New York City subway car.[2]

It recalled to me the profound effect the loss of those two buildings had upon all of us. No, no, it's the loss of the people, I am reminded. Perhaps, but far more people die on the roads every year in America than were lost in that horrible day. This is a focused grieving and part of that grieving is for the buildings.[3] We remember the magnificence, the defiance of standing so tall in a city we consider the center of the world.

They were a symbol of the American people. And that is the loss we feel most sharply. I had heard before that architecture is a barometer of society, but this was the moment I understood why.[4]

Mies van der Rohe's bronze and glass Seagram's building on stilts ushered in a time of invention and industry, when we believed we could create *anything.* Earlier, after the West was won, our hearts needed a new vista to explore, and we looked to the skies. In the birth of the Art Deco[5] movement, our eyes were swept upward in admiration and in hope.

In Florence, a young doctor had told me that the mystical effect of Michelangelo's statue of David was purely scientific. In close proximity to so immense a figure, the eyes look upward, strain and trip a nerve where the swoon reflex kicks in. Sure it was a great sculpture, he told me, but nothing to faint over.[6]

Notes:

1. The first line grabs your attention. The writer could be in serious danger. We soon find out she is not but by then we are hooked.

2. The writer makes the moment personal by telling us a bit about her in a slightly teasing way, as if the reader is an old friend.

3. It is clear that the topic of the essay is the buildings and not the tragedy, which is good because the target for the essay is "why I want to be an architect."

4. After laying the foundation, the writer is building to her point, just like an architect. In this sentence, she outlines the framework of her thesis and in the following paragraphs she will fill in the substance.

5. The writer mentions one of the most famous architects of the Twentieth Century but, pointedly, not *the* most famous, and makes observations that are well known to architects but might not be as generally known in the public at large. The writer shows she has some understanding of architectural history but does not come off sounding pretentious.

6. Another personal moment that demonstrates a certain worldliness. It would be out of context had the author not made *looking up* so clear a theme.

Later, I had walked the Italian streets, so tastefully bedecked with carved marble, the elegant, ancient city pumping with life and drawing my eyes in every direction. But in countries bereft of cultural integrity you see only slabs of gray, so stark and utilitarian, placed unnaturally amidst the background of the blue and white sky.[7]

It was more than just a reflex. The buildings talked to the people and the image of the structures reflected upon society.[8] Architecture, I realized, is the only profession that mixes art and science with such an exquisite balance that those who enjoy the effect barely notice it at all. On the other hand, what we think of as pure art tends to be locked away, placed unnaturally in galleries and museums, and we must seek it out, make it conspicuous, in order to enjoy it.

Architecture is just there, all around us. And as I emerged from the subway station that day in New York my eyes were drawn upward, to the buildings, to the sky.[9] They say that every brick wants to be a skyscraper, and this living city shouted out the delight of every brick that got its wish, and the anguish of every brick turned to rubble. In this new ancient city I knew that I wanted to build the skyscrapers, to build the pillars of hope that inspire the minds of the future.[10]

Notes:

7. The author further ties the roles of the buildings with the city and the people.

8. She rejects the doctor's belief and chooses her own. She is demonstrating independence and conviction, traits so often associated with architects.

9. We are brought back to the beginning to tie the essay together.

10. The essay ends on a positive note, looking up like the skyscrapers the author wants to build. The reader feel the passion the author has for her chosen profession. Since the audience for this essay is a group of professional architects, the essay allows them to return to a time when they felt nothing but awe, hope and drive at the prospect of becoming an architect.

Chapter 17

Asking the Boss for Free Money

• •

In This Chapter

▶ Riding on your parents' coattails

▶ Understanding college faculty and staff benefits

▶ Finding out about government worker programs

▶ Demystifying organizational educational assistance programs (EAPs)

• •

*O*rganizations know that having an educated workforce is key to remaining competitive with other firms, whether these firms are in the United States or overseas. Thus, keeping employees up-to-date on the various new technologies and trends is obviously in the best interest of the firm.

Perhaps surprisingly, many organizations (especially those in educational, financial, and high tech areas) have active employee tuition discount programs aimed at the *dependent children* of employees. Children of government employees, especially employees at the federal level (including those who work for the U.S. Postal Service), also have a few options for scholarships and grants, usually based on merit.

In this chapter, we explain how to get free money for college from the workplace (even if the workplace is a college) and how to profit from the many workplace programs that provide such benefits. We also give you a heads-up on some of the caveats associated with these programs.

Because employer-related education assistance programs can work for you *directly* (if you're a working, independent student) or *indirectly* (if you're a dependent student, and your spouse or parents are working), we switch freely between these options in this chapter.

Free Money from a College?

For some prospective college students, colleges themselves are the first place to look for free money in the form of education assistance programs, tuition discounts and tuition exemptions.

Colleges are full of smart people, and not surprisingly, some of these smart people are in the school's administration. These people know that to lure (and keep) the best staff and faculty, they must do everything in their power to make their particular school attractive to existing and prospective employees.

Working at a college or university can have many benefits, not the least of which is free or low-cost tuition for both the workers *and* their kids. Many colleges — especially private ones — grant dependent children of employees (staff members) and faculty (teachers, instructors, and professors) free or low-cost tuition. Under these programs, the college waives or reduces tuition costs, usually under specific employment benefit plans.

Some faculty benefit programs are so good that colleges even extend tuition discounts to dependent children who are going to *other* colleges, not just the one where the father or mother teaches! Cool, huh?

For some colleges, the benefits don't stop there. In a few rare cases, schools also give *residency* discounts, so that the child of a faculty member can stay on campus for a reduced rate. Students are usually on their own for food expenses, however, as well as for books, equipment, and transportation. So, although a tuition discount doesn't pay for everything, getting your courses for free certainly makes your financial life a lot easier.

How much does my free ride cost the college?

The true cost of letting the dependent child of a staff or faculty member go to college for free is pretty close to zero. True, if *lots* of students were added to a given course or section, there would undoubtedly be additional costs associated with marking the extra papers, answering more questions, and grading exams. That many extra students might also mean that a college would have to hire an extra teaching assistant or even an instructor. Adding one or two "free riding" students, however, accounts for little, if any, additional cost to the college after the school is operating, the teachers are hired, and the classrooms are heated.

In some colleges where space is particularly tight, certain programs (especially professional programs) are restricted to traditional tuition-paying students, but this situation is rare. Obviously, if *all* the students at a particular college received this preferential treatment, the college wouldn't survive for long. That said, employee- and faculty-based tuition discounts and exemptions are increasingly popular at colleges across America, and show no signs of diminishing. Why is this trend increasing?

Free (or reduced cost) tuition is a win-win-win situation. The college wins by attracting top-notch faculty and staff for very little real cost; the faculty and staff win by not having to worry about paying huge tuition bills as their kids get to college age; and students win by getting a free ride (or, at least, reduced or exempt tuition), thereby freeing up money that would otherwise be used for tuition payment.

Understanding the college hierarchy

The higher your parents move up the college or university ladder, the more their benefits increase. This fact should come as no surprise because employees in other sectors are frequently given more perks as their experience, seniority, and rank increase over time.

You may, however, be surprised to know that the actual *job function* of your father or mother also plays a big part in whether you're able to receive a tuition discount and, if you are, how much of a discount.

To figure out your tuition discount eligibility, you need to know where you (or, more to the point, your parent who works at the college) stand in the college hierarchy.

Officers and directors

These people run the college or university. They can include the school's provost, chancellor, principal, deans, and other people who have decision-making power at the college or university. Frequently, these officers were once professors at the college and usually still retain their educational rank.

Officers and directors, therefore, often are considered to be the pinnacle of the particular educational institution — especially by *themselves*. Not surprisingly, colleges award the highest benefits available (usually including full tuition discounts for dependent children and other perks) to officers and directors.

Faculty

Depending on the school, "faculty" is usually defined as teaching staff who are professors, instructors, and department heads. Within the designation *professor,* further distinctions are usually made to include *full professor, associate professor,* and *assistant professor.* Often, library administration personnel and faculty research staff are included under the "faculty" designation for tuition exemption or tuition discount purposes.

Visiting professors are usually *not* eligible for many benefits, including tuition discounts (although they may still be eligible at their original college). If the faculty member is part-time, he or she may not be eligible for the full set of benefits, including tuition discounts for dependent children. It depends on the institution.

Staff

These people are the "worker bees" at the college and include various administrative positions (such as secretaries and assistants), technical positions (such as computer operators and A/V staff), and safety and security positions (such as janitors, mechanics, and campus police officers).

Interestingly, teaching assistants — usually graduate students who conduct student tutorials and mark much of the students' work — are considered *part-time staff* (and not faculty) by many colleges. Although many schools use teaching assistants (especially large colleges where first-year class sizes can swell to 500 or even 1,000 students), they afford the fewest benefits to these people, arguing that teaching assistants are students themselves and thus don't need more benefits. Yeah, right.

So how does the hierarchy affect me?

Most colleges and universities offer a sliding scale of benefits to employees, based on where they fit into the hierarchy. As the son or daughter of a college dean, for example, you'll likely be able to get more free money than if you were the son or daughter of the assistant janitor.

Depending on where you end up on this scale of potential free money, you may feel that this system rewards the most deserving (in other words, the people who've made the most important contributions to the school) or that it unfairly maintains the status quo of rich and poor — and unfairly discriminates against *you.*

However, the important aspect of employee tuition discounts is that most colleges in America use them to motivate and reward their employees. If one or both your parents work for a university, you definitely want to find out how large a tuition discount you may be eligible to receive, and what you can do to get what's coming to you. Even if the discount's not as big as you'd like, a little free money is better than no free money.

Finding out more

Universities typically don't advertise these discounts — probably because the school doesn't necessarily want to draw attention to the fact that it gives free or reduced tuition to kids of its faculty and staff, while the rest of the student body is asked to pay higher prices. Information about these tuition discount programs can therefore be difficult to find, even on the college's own Web site. If your parent doesn't know the details, discreet inquiries made at the financial aid office by you or your parents, may yield the desired results.

If you think that you may qualify for a staff or faculty discount, speak with your parents immediately. They might have to check with their department head, union representative, or school official to determine your eligibility for the program.

When applying for the tuition discount, you have to fill out a waiver form and send it to the college admissions or financial aid office. Plus, the college will require some paperwork from your father or mother (whoever is working at the school); he or she can likely go to the college's human resources department to get it.

Frequently, your parent must obtain a signature on these forms from his or her supervisor or other higher administration official. Getting this signature may take some time. Thus, our usual mantra of doing your research long before you need the information also rings true in this situation.

What else can the college offer dependents?

Working in the education field definitely has its advantages when it comes to getting a free ride. Sometimes, colleges even offer tuition discounts when the dependent children of their faculty go to other colleges to study. New York's Columbia University, for example, offers a 50-percent deduction in a dependent's non-Columbia tuition if one parent is full-time faculty and 100 percent if both parents are faculty at Columbia. (Keep in mind, though, that this type of discount is rare.)

1 (or My Parents) Work for Uncle Sam. How Can 1 Get a Free Ride at College?

President John F. Kennedy once proclaimed in a speech, "Ask not what your country can do for you; ask what *you* can do for your country." Fact is, a lot of people are doing something for their country these days, and nicely, the country can give something back to them — reduced tuition.

According to the U.S. Census Bureau, 17,567,100 people worked for the government in 2000 (the last year for which government worker figures are available). This number includes people who work at the federal, state, and local levels. At the same time, the Census Bureau reported that 135,800,000 people (not counting those in the military) were gainfully employed in the United States. These numbers mean that the government employed roughly 13 percent of the workforce of the United States in the year 2000.

We discuss options available for *civilians* who work for the federal, state, and local government in this chapter. In Chapter 18, we discuss tuition options and college payment plans for the members of the U.S. Armed Forces.

Conjunction junction, what's your job function?

Lots of tuition programs are available for employees of federal, state, and local governments, although these benefits are often restricted to the higher, professional job classifications. However, most of these programs only provide some tuition benefit if the courses are directly applicable to the worker's job description.

For this reason, professional development courses can be more available to employees rather than traditional (general) college degree courses. So although an advanced accounting or math course would be eligible for an accountant or other financially oriented employee, a course on French Impressionist painters probably would not. However, it may be possible to get a discount on a few general college courses if those courses allow that person to complete a college degree, provided that the degree is important for promotion or other job advancement. It really just depends on one's job.

Pay now; get reimbursed later

Unlike college tuition waivers or fee exemptions, where no money changes hands, government-based employee tuition programs are usually *reimbursements*. The worker pays for tuition and is reimbursed after the class is completed — provided that he or she earns satisfactory marks in the course and provides proof of payment and official transcripts. Usually, a certain mark is required (typically at least a "C" average or higher, or a "pass" in a "pass/fail" course) for reimbursement.

Program requirements and qualifications can vary widely from agency to agency and from department to department. Further, program criterion seem to change all the time, so ask your supervisor, section head or human resources representative how to get more information about these programs.

Dependents need not apply (most of the time)

The good news is that if you're a current, active government employee, many tuition reimbursements are available for you. The bad news is that if you're the dependent of a government employee, very few tuition programs are available for you.

Unlike the encouraging tuition programs set up by colleges and large corporations (we discuss the latter in the next section), the government doesn't exactly pave the way for dependent students of employees looking for free money.

Politics likely play a role here. The public perception can sometimes be that all government employees make wads of money for doing next to nothing. However, the fact is that most people who work at government jobs make salaries that would qualify their kids for college financial aid. Sure, they're working, but the vast majority of government workers are members of the middle class, struggling to make payments on the house, the car, and their kids' college tuition.

A little help from your friends at the FEEA

One organization is very useful to dependent students of federal workers: the *Federal Employee Education and Assistance Fund.* According to the organization, FEEA has awarded more than $2.75 million in college scholarships exclusively to federal and postal employees and their family members — but it doesn't get one cent from the federal, state, or local governments!

If governments don't sponsor the program, who does? Well, it turns out that a small group of retired federal employees are responsible for the administration of the FEEA Fund. The FEEA scholarship program is also partly underwritten by corporate sponsors.

The majority of the funding for this program, however, comes from federal employee contributions. The amount of money donated in each region directly determines how much is available for scholarships in that particular area.

Applying

First of all, you're eligible to apply for the scholarship if you or a parent is presently employed as a civilian member of the federal government or works in the United States Postal Service. The worker must have at least three years of federal service before he or she is eligible. If the worker is eligible, all dependent family members (including spouse and kids) are also eligible.

Although *employee applicants* are likely to be part-time students, *dependent applicants* must attend school full time. All applicants must be enrolled or plan to enroll in an accredited post-secondary school in a course of study that will lead to a two-year, four-year, or graduate degree. Further, all applicants must have at least a 3.0 grade point average on a 4.0 scale.

This means that if you're a high school senior, the organization wants proof of your cumulative GPA score (on a 4.0 scale). If you're already in college (either as an undergraduate student or a graduate student), the organization wants to see your cumulative GPA score for whichever level of college you're enrolled.

If you've been working for ten years (and consequently out of the academic world), the organization wants to see the last set of academic scores you have: If you already have a college degree and are headed back for more, this means your *college* GPA; if you entered the workforce directly from high school, this means your high school GPA scores. Unlike many other scholarships, your SAT or ACT scores don't play a factor in the FEEA awards.

According to the organization, FEEA scholarship applications are available from January through March for each year. During those months, the application is available for downloading from the organization's Web site at www.feea.org. We've reprinted the 2003/2004 application on the following pages. Detailed instructions also accompany the form.

Applications are usually due back at FEEA headquarters by the end of March each year, although each year's application shows the year's specific deadline. Awards are announced in August in time for the fall school term and are paid in two installments: half in the August/September period and the balance in the December/January period. Because the FEEA awards (like many other competitions) are given out pretty close to the start of the school year, you're best off working toward lots of other awards as well, just in case this one doesn't come through. According to FEEA, awards generally range from $300 to $1,500.

Doing what it takes to win

After meeting the eligibility rules, all FEEA awards are purely *merit-based*. The organization considers the academic achievement record of each applicant, as we've mentioned. However, applicants also need to submit a personal recommendation letter, evidence of extracurricular and community service activities, and a written essay. The essay topic changes each year and is printed on the application.

FEEA scholarship awards are good for one year. Winners must reapply every year and are given no preferential standing in subsequent years' competitions. Applicants not selected for awards in one year may also reapply. Like other pure merit awards, applicants don't supply any financial information.

FEEA 2003-04 Scholarship Program
Eligibility and Application Procedures

BASIC ELIGIBILITY REQUIREMENTS:

- The FEEA Scholarship Program is for current civilian federal or postal employees and their dependent family members (spouse/child). Adult children and other relatives are eligible if claimed on the sponsoring employee's tax return. Active duty military members and civilian and military retirees (unless currently a civilian federal employee) are not eligible nor are their dependents.
- The applicant or the applicant's sponsoring federal or postal employee must have at least three (3) years of federal service by August 31, 2003. Past active duty time will count toward this requirement if included in service comp. date on the Standard Form 50.
- The applicant must be at least a college freshman by the fall 2003 semester.
- All applicants must have at least a 3.0 cumulative grade point average (CGPA) unweighted on a 4.0 scale. Current college freshmen must have a minimum 3.0 GPA for the fall 2002 semester.
- All applicants must be current high school seniors or college students working toward an accredited degree and enrolled in a two- or four-year post-secondary, graduate or postgraduate program.
- Applicants who are dependents must be full-time students. Applicants who are federal or postal employees may be part-time students.
- All applicants must submit a complete application package postmarked no later than March 28, 2003. Incomplete or late applications will not be considered.

A COMPLETE APPLICATION PACKAGE SHALL INCLUDE:

- **A FEEA Scholarship Application Form:** A photocopy of the scholarship application form is acceptable.
- **Essay**: Typed, double-spaced, essay not exceeding two pages on the topic: "Are the civil service laws that protect federal employees important? Why or why not?"
- **Written Recommendation/Character Reference:** Please submit a written recommendation/character reference from a supervisor, coworker, community leader, teacher or counselor.
- **Transcript:** The transcript must show a CGPA of 3.0 or higher.
  High School Seniors: Submit full high school career transcript that includes fall 2002 grades. (Report card is acceptable for fall grades)
  College Freshmen: Submit a transcript that verifies at least a 3.0 for the fall 2002 semester.
  Applicants not currently enrolled: Submit a transcript from the last school attended.
  All other applicants: Submit full post-secondary career transcripts that include fall 2002 grades.
  NOTE: If your transcript is being mailed directly by the school, the transcript must be postmarked by the application deadline of March 28, 20032. An official transcript is not required; photocopies of transcripts are acceptable.
- **List and Briefly Describe Awards, Extra-curricular and Community Service Activities:** Please provide this list on a separate page. Include dates and other relevant information that will help committee members understand your contribution.
- **Copy of ACT, SAT or Other Examination Scores:** This is required for applicants who are high school seniors but optional for all other applicants.
- **Copy of Most Recent Standard Form 50 "Notice of Personnel Action" (PS 50 for Postal Employees):** You must provide a form that is **no older than 1/01**.
  If applicant is a federal or postal employee, submit the employee's own form.
  If applicant is a dependent of a federal or postal employee, then the sponsoring employee's form should be submitted.
  If a current SF-50 is not available you must submit a current pay stub and a letter from personnel identifying your duty station, grade and service comp. date.
- **Two Self-addressed, Stamped, #10 Business-size Envelopes with First Class Postage Properly Affixed.** The first will be used to acknowledge receipt of your application and the second to provide results of the competition. All qualified applicants will be notified by 8/31/03.

MAILING INFORMATION:

- Place all of the above materials **unfolded** in the same 9" x 12" (or larger) envelope.
- **Please:** No Staples, No Paper Clips, No Folding.
- Mail the complete application package to: FEEA Scholarship Award
  Suite 200
  8441 W. Bowles Ave.
  Littleton, CO 80123-9501
- **Make sure that your application package is postmarked no later than March 28, 2003.**

> The FEEA Scholarship Program is made possible by you and your fellow employees' contributions to FEEA
> Pledge #1234 in the CFC and, in part, by contributions from the Blue Cross Blue Shield Association and other
> FEEA sponsors.

FEEA 2003-04 Scholarship Application

Please check the boxes to make sure that your application is complete:

| | **All applications must be postmarked by March 28, 2003.** |

☐ **This Application Form:** A photocopy of this form is acceptable.

☐ **Essay:** Typed, double-spaced, essay **not exceeding two pages** on the topic:
"Are the civil service laws that protect federal employees important? Why or why not"

☐ **Written Recommendation/Character Reference:** May be from a supervisor/coworker, community leader, teacher or counselor. Must be submitted together with the application package.

☐ **Transcript:** *High School Seniors:* Submit full high school career transcript that includes fall 2002 grades. (Report card is acceptable for fall grades)

College Freshmen: Submit a transcript that verifies at least a 3.0 for the fall 2002 semester.

Applicants not currently enrolled: Submit a transcript from the last school attended.

All other applicants: Submit full post-secondary career transcripts that include fall 2002 grades.

☐ **Check here** if transcripts are being mailed separately by the school. (If checked, transcripts still must be postmarked by March 28, 2003.) An official transcript is not required; photocopies are acceptable.

☐ **List and Briefly Describe Awards, Extra-curricular and Community Service Activities**: Please provide this list on a separate page. Include relevant dates and average time spent at activity. Clearly and briefly explain your contributions.

☐ **Copy of ACT, SAT or Other Examination Scores:** Required for applicants who are high school seniors; optional for other applicants.

☐ **Copy of Most Recent Standard Form 50 "Notice of Personnel Action" (PS 50 for Postal Employees):** You must provide a form that is **No Older Than 1/01.** If applicant is a federal or postal employee, submit the employee's own form. If applicant is a dependent of a federal or postal employee, then the sponsoring employee's form should be submitted. If a current SF 50 is not available, you must submit a current pay stub and a letter from personnel identifying your duty station, grade and service comp. date.

☐ **Two (2) Self-addressed, Stamped #10 Business-size Envelopes with First Class Postage Properly Affixed.**

Please do not fold or bind any pages with staples or paper clips.
Place all materials unfolded into a 9 x 12 in. (or larger) envelope postmarked no later than March 28, 2003.
MAIL TO: FEEA Scholarship Award, Suite 200, 8441 W. Bowles Ave., Littleton, CO 80123-9501

Please complete the following. Incomplete applications will not be considered.

Applicant's Name: _____

Complete Home Address: _____

City, State, Zip: _____

Social Security #: _____ Home Telephone #: ( )_____

Federal Employee's Name: _____
Relationship to Applicant: ☐ Father ☐ Mother ☐ Spouse ☐ Self ☐ Other (specify) _____
Federal Agency Name: _____
Federal Employee's Work Telephone #: ( )_____
Length of Federal Employment: _____ Duty Station: _____

Applicant's **Unweighted** Cumulative Grade Point Average (CGPA)
Must have at least a 3.0 CPGA unweighted on a 4.0 scale: _____
College/University (attending or planning to attend): _____
Class Status as of fall term 2003 (Must be at least a college freshman by fall term 2003):
☐ Freshman ☐ Sophomore ☐ Junior ☐ Senior ☐ Graduate Student

About the FEEA Fund

FEEA is a private, not-for-profit 501(c)(3) tax-exempt corporation, which provides educational benefits and emergency assistance exclusively to all civilian federal and postal employees and their dependent family members. FEEA receives no government funds. Virtually all its operating revenue is derived from federal employee contributions specifically pledged to FEEA #1234 in the Combined Federal Campaign (CFC). FEEA is truly "Federal Employees Helping Federal Employees."

Source: Federal Employee Education Assistance Fund

Will My Boss Send Me to College?

So far in this chapter, we've outline some free money ideas for people who work for colleges and universities (and whose *parents* are staff or faculty). As well, we offered up some leads for people looking for free money who work at the federal government or the U.S. Postal Service (and whose parents work there).

In this section, we outline some options for getting free money from your corporate employer. That's right, your boss (or, if you're not yet working, your parents' bosses). Depending on your organization, you may be eligible for tuition assistance from your or your parent's employer.

Organizations typically offer tuition assistance to entice educated and talented people to work for them. Many larger companies offer some form of tuition assistance for their workers, and some offer programs for the *dependent children* of workers.

If you're already working, your boss should consider sending you off (or back) to college for many reasons, including the following:

- ✔ Making you ready for possible promotion
- ✔ Wanting to keep you happy as a particularly promising member of the company
- ✔ Having you upgrade your skills to keep up with technology

Employer-based tuition programs are great if you want to finish off your degree by completing a couple of courses. However, if you're starting an entirely new degree, this option may not be the best one for you because of the potentially overwhelming time commitment of working full-time and going to school part-time.

Sure, perhaps you and your family can put up with a year or two of missing family events, birthdays, and maybe little Chris' soccer games so that mom or dad can take the necessary classes, do homework, and study for exams. But it takes a dedicated employee (not to mention a committed family) to maintain this pattern for the several years it takes to get a full degree.

Reality check

Okay, okay, if you're working at a summer job or an entry-level full-time position, such as the corporate mailroom, your chances of getting the boss to open up his checkbook and pay for four years at Harvard are limited.

That said, many, many companies across America offer some kind of tuition assistance to their employees. The first place to check eligibility is usually your supervisor, department head, or the human resources representative. If you or your parent works in a unionized company, the shop steward or other union representative is the best person to ask about any tuition benefits.

What can you get? It really depends on the company and your (or your parent's) position within the company. Generally speaking, the larger the organization, the better the chances of a tuition program. Both Ford Motor Company and United Technologies Corporation, for example, offer excellent plans for employees. Similarly, the higher you are on the totem pole (that is, the higher your position within the organization), the better your chances for education benefits.

The rules of corporate learning

Tuition discount programs within large organizations are usually called employee *education assistance programs* (or employee EAPs for short). In general, EAPs are far more common in larger organizations than they are in small ones because larger companies have bigger budgets for this purpose.

Although each company has its own policies and procedures regarding EAPs, you need to consider a few points when researching your options:

- ✔ **EAP options are dependent on seniority.** Organizations involved in EAPs often set minimum seniority levels for employee learners. Usually, the more time you've spent at a company, the more options you have. Similarly, employees usually have to wait a specified number of years before they're eligible to participate in the corporate EAP.

✓ **Corporate EAPs are typically based on reimbursement, not payment.** Only in a few notable exceptions do corporations pre-pay the tuition of a college-bound worker. Usually, the worker registers her intention to take the course with the company's HR department (or directly with her boss). Next, the employee registers at the college and pays tuition money (and buys the necessary books). After successfully completing the particular course, the employee files the appropriate paperwork with the company to recoup the costs of both tuition and books.

✓ **EAP reimbursement usually requires a minimum grade.** Companies involved with EAPs often require employees to attain a minimum grade for the course, usually a "C" average, or a "pass" in a pass/fail course.

✓ **EAPs can require supplementary service contract agreements.** Often, the worker must sign a contract to remain with the company for a certain number of years, usually between two to five. If the worker leaves before the specified lock-in period, he or she usually has to pay the employer back the amount spent on the college tuition.

✓ **Distinctions are made on employee status.** Full-time employees are usually given far more latitude with EAPs, and in many companies, part-timers are completely excluded from participating in EAPs.

All in all, EAPs are generally worth the trouble — especially if you intend to work at the particular company for a few years. Not only are they a valuable perk for the worker, but they are also a way for employers to keep skill levels high in the workplace.

Chapter 18

Joining Up: You're in the Army (or Navy or Air Force or Marines) Now

*H*ey, have you heard that there are large organizations that send qualified students to college for free (including room and board), give them a part-time job while they're at school so that they can earn some pocket money, and then dispatch them overseas to exotic places — all at no charge? As an added benefit, these students are *guaranteed* to find a job after graduation. That's right: These organizations boast nearly 100 percent career placement. And, get this: Not only will these organizations get you started on your chosen career, but the job is guaranteed to be in your field of study.

Sound too good to be true? Surprise! We're talking about joining the U.S. Armed Forces. Not only does Uncle Sam want *you,* he also wants to send you to *college.*

In this chapter, we discuss some of the *many* military options available to get free money for college. As it turns out, Uncle Sam is glad to pay for your college education *and* guarantee your after-college employment for a few years. If you're already in the military, you may be able to get him to pay for your college *after* you leave the service or even pony up the money for you to attend school while you're still serving.

We also outline the real-life consequences of joining up to serve your country. Although joining the military is a great way to get a free education, it's certainly not a free ride. Not only are you under substantial service obligations when you become a member of this country's military forces, but the experience will also certainly change your life. Whether the change is right for you is a major life decision that only *you* can make.

We can only scratch the surface here in explaining the various education benefits relating to military service. Each branch of the military has its own particular education programs. In addition, you may want to look into *state* programs, such as the National Guard, that also offer opportunities for free money for college.

If You're In High School . . .

Depending on where you are in your life, you may have several ways to get free money using a military option. If you're a high school freshman or sophomore student, you can join the Junior Reserve Officers' Training Corps (ROTC).

If you're in your junior year of high school, you probably want to look at the various college-based ROTC programs, such as the AFROTC (the Air Force's program), AROTC (the Army's program), or the NROTC (the program used by students headed into the Navy and Marines).

Selected applicants for the NROTC Scholarship Program, for example, are awarded full scholarships through a highly competitive national selection process. They receive full tuition, books, fees, and other benefits at many of the country's leading colleges.

Upon graduation, students are commissioned as officers in the Air Force, Army, Navy, or Marine Corps. You can also serve some of your obligation in the *Reserves,* units that continue to train and stand ready but are only activated in times of national emergencies.

The list of ROTC schools is too large to list in this book, but every state has at least one approved school. And don't think that ROTC-approved colleges aren't prestigious. Massachusetts Institute of Technology (MIT) and Harvard University just happen to be two schools on the list.

Okay, so what do I get?

Each service has its own separate college-based ROTC program, along with its own program benefits. The Army's ROTC Scholarship program, for example, offers different college tuition awards of up to $17,000 each year. In certain cases, the Army will pay up to $20,000 per year and, rarely, even your full college tuition (if your fees are higher).

Like some other scholarships, ROTC scholarships *cannot* be applied toward room or board. Army scholarship winners, however, also receive a tax-free *stipend* or subsistence allowance (ah, *more* free money) of up to $400 per month for up to 10 months each year the scholarship is in effect. The monthly subsistence allowance is currently $250 for freshmen, $300 for sophomores, $350 for juniors, and $400 for seniors.

What's required of me?

Various ROTC programs have different requirements, but in general, you study an ROTC-approved program, usually taking much the same courses as your friends in the same college (who might not even realize that you're in a ROTC program). Every semester, you also take one or two courses directly related to your future role as an Air Force, Army, Marine, or Navy officer.

In the Navy's ROTC program, for example, *midshipmen* (that is, student-officers) are required to complete the traditional course of study required by the college or university they attend as well as several naval science courses, usually dealing with leadership and other related subjects.

In case you're thinking that these courses are a breeze, NROTC students are also required to complete the equivalent of two semesters of *calculus* before the end of their sophomore year and two semesters of calculus-based *physics* before the end of their junior year. Hardly a walk in the park.

Sounds good. How do I qualify?

Each branch of the military has its own specific requirements for entry into its particular ROTC program. All the programs have some common elements, though, including high academic scores, impressive physical ability, and, in a perfect world, dedicated community service. The Army ROTC program, for example, requires that students meet the following requirements:

- You must be a United States citizen.

- You must be 17 years of age by October 1st of your freshman year and younger than 23 on June 30th of that year. (In addition, you must not reach your 27th birthday by June 30th of the year in which you graduate from college and receive your commission.) If you have prior active duty military service, you may be eligible for extension of this age requirement.

- You have to satisfactorily explain any record of arrest and/or civil conviction.

- You must have a minimum high school GPA of 2.5.

- Your SAT score must be least 920 points, or your ACT composite score must be at least 19 points. (You don't have to take both tests; one or the other is fine.)

- You agree to accept a commission in the United States Army.

- You must meet required physical standards.

- You can have no moral obligation, personal conviction, or other reservations that will prevent you from "supporting and defending the Constitution of the United States against all enemies, foreign and domestic," or conscientiously bearing arms.

- For a four-year scholarship, you must be a high school graduate or have an equivalent certificate (such as a GED) before the September of your college freshman year. If you're currently taking or have taken college courses, you must be considered a beginning freshman and have four academic years remaining for a bachelor's degree.

- If you're in an accelerated program and will complete your senior year of high school and first year of college concurrently, you must have four academic years *remaining* in an approved bachelor's degree program upon enrollment in the fall of the combined academic year.

- If you're a college freshman in a five-year college program with four years remaining before graduation, you must submit an official college letter verifying that your course of study is a five-year program and that you have four full years remaining.

The Army ROTC scholarship program changes periodically. For the most current information about eligibility, applications, and deadlines, call 1-800-USA-ROTC (1-800-872-7682). You can also contact the Army ROTC department at the college you plan to attend, or the school closest to you that has an Army ROTC on-campus program.

When do I apply?

If you're in high school, you should talk to your counselor about earning a military scholarship no later than midway through your junior year. You can apply to the Army ROTC program, for example, from March of your *junior* year to November 1st of your *senior* year.

For traditional college admission (that is, for a program that starts in September), your complete application must be received by November 15th of your high school senior year. Letters to scholarship winners are typically sent out on March 1st of that year. Like some colleges, the Army ROTC program also has an early admission option. Here, the application is due by July 15th of your junior year, and scholarship winners are notified by October 15th of the same year.

In case you were wondering, students not admitted under the early decision option will automatically be considered for the traditional, regular admission. The Army says that only a small number of scholarships are awarded under the early decision option; most are awarded later on during the regular admission period.

What happens next?

Just about every scholarship we discuss in this book has either a merit-based eligibility component (such as high GPA or SAT scores) or a need-based eligibility component (such as low income or non-existent savings). Sometimes, *both* components play important roles in winning a scholarship.

Although the military takes no notice of your need, it *does* take notice of your merit, which is why it considers your SAT or ACT scores. Because the number of ROTC positions in each branch of the service is limited, three specific qualification categories are considered. These include:

- **Your personal interviews**. You must attend an interview with an Army officer who will assess your skills and your ability to fit in, and will answer any questions you have about the Army ROTC. The answers you give will be passed to a *Professor of Military Science* (PMS — insert your own joke here) at the schools you listed on your application. Each PMS (or his designate) will contact you and further discuss your suitability for the Army. Depending on the distance involved, these secondary interviews can be held in person or over the phone.

- **An Army medical examination.** If you do well in the interviews, you must pass the medical exam in order to keep in the running (pun intended) for your scholarship. You can't use your personal physician for this exam. Rather, the Army will arrange an exam at the *Department of Defense Medical Examination Review Board* (DODMERB). You must pay your own way to and from the exam, and pay for any hotels, meals, and anything you need for the trip from your own pocket.

After you're cleared by the DODMERB, you can sign your service contract and start receiving benefits, such as tuition payment and monthly stipends. Congratulations, you're in the ROTC program!

✓ **An Army physical fitness test.** Well, you may be in the ROTC program but you still have to pass a rigorous physical test, called the *Army Physical Fitness Test* (usually referred to as the APFT). Although it is possible to fail the fitness test and be kicked out of ROTC, the people we chatted with at ROTC suggest that they're looking for athletic scholars who enjoy leadership. By the time they've been accepted into the program, it's a given that these people are *very* fit — so passing the actual fitness test is pretty much a done deal. Of course, if applicants need to get *more* physically fit, the regular (and grueling) physical training (PT) sessions will certainly help.

In case you were wondering, the Army *occasionally* lets students out of their ROTC contract if the student wants to leave the program. Students are usually asked to repay their tuition *loan* (after all, a lot of taxpayers' money is at stake when Uncle Sam pays for college), but no further military service is required of the student. If, however, the ROTC commander at the school has reason to believe the student is "working the system" and trying to get a free education, he or she can force the student into the Army as a private to work off the debt to Uncle Sam.

What about military colleges?

Before we leave the subject of qualifying under a ROTC program and studying at civilian colleges, we also need to mention the option of studying at *military* colleges. All three major branches of the military operate their own degree-granting colleges (as we mentioned, the Marine Corps is technically part of the Navy and thus uses the Navy's college).

Based in historic Annapolis, Maryland, the Naval Academy (www.usna.edu/) prepares young men and women to become officers in the U.S. Navy and Marine Corps. The Army equivalent, The Military Academy at West Point (www.usma.edu/), is located about 50 miles north of New York City and is *the* school for those aiming for a military career in the Army. The aptly named Air Force Academy (www.usafa.af.mil) is the military college of choice for those interested in becoming career Air Force officers or pilots, or for those students who wish to enter the astronaut program.

All three colleges are unique among American schools. For each of your courses, class sizes are *very* small, with most having no more than 25 students. In your senior year, some classes may have fewer than a dozen other students! All three colleges also feature very low student-to-faculty ratios and something the schools like to call "protected study time," a required study period that goes from 7:30 p.m. to midnight Sunday through Friday to help students keep up with their courses.

If a career in the military is on your wish list, research these colleges and visit their respective Web sites as soon as possible. Competition is *very* tough every year for the few hundred positions available, and students should expect to work extremely hard to get into their choice of schools. Far more students are rejected every year than are admitted, attesting to the high standards of each school.

Besides the usual academic and physical testing scores that accompany traditional civilian-college based applications, students wishing to study at military colleges must be *nominated* by a U.S. Senator, Congressman, the Vice President, or the President. Nominations to the Naval Academy, for example, can be a rather complex process. Each member of Congress can have five constituents attending the Naval Academy at any given time. When one constituent leaves the Academy, a vacancy is created, and the new nomination possibility exists.

Children of deceased or disabled veterans, children of prisoners of war or servicemen or servicewomen missing in action, and kids whose parent received the Medal of Honor are given special admission privileges. You can download sample nomination letters from each of the school's Web sites.

If you're successful in these schools, not only will you get free money for college, you may get an entire lifetime of learning, service, job security, and excitement — and, of course, you'll look *great* in the uniform!

What happens after I receive my degree?

Assuming that you opt for a civilian college and an ROTC program, you can figure on a period of formal military training as a junior officer and then a posting to a base in the United States or abroad. You can count on eight years of service to your country, above and beyond your four years of college.

If you entered the ROTC program on a scholarship, you can count on four of these eight years in *active* service (meaning that you'll be working full-time, in uniform, in whichever service you have chosen) and then four years in the *Reserves* (where you return and live at home, but still train on a regular basis and participate in maneuvers when obligated or when an emergency is declared).

If you decide on a career in the military, you may be offered additional positions and promotions, but after your initial eight years (not counting your four years of college), you have no more service obligations to your country.

When you graduate, you receive a posting to a specific fort, ship, or other military base. Although each service says that newly commissioned officers will be given some choice where they'll serve — this is informally called your *wish list* — you must go where you're needed. So depending on the branch of service, you may serve near your hometown at a nearby fort, on-board a ship patrolling the Pacific, or on an aircraft carrier in the Gulf.

Is ROTC right for you?

Naturally, only *you* can answer this question. First, you have to satisfy the academic requirements for the ROTC program associated with your chosen branch of service.

For Army ROTC (the largest program), you need combined SAT scores of *at least* 920. To enter the Navy ROTC program (which also includes officers headed into the Marine Corps), you need a combined SAT score of at least 1050. The hardest ROTC program (from an academic point of view) is the Air Force program. To get in here, you'll need at least an 1100 combined SAT score.

Postings in the U.S. Navy

Upon graduating from the NROTC Scholarship Program, you have military service obligations of eight years, of which at least four of those years must be in active duty. Immediately after graduating from NROTC, midshipmen attend the Navy's six-month Surface Warfare Officers' School (SWOS) located in Newport, Rhode Island. Here, you learn about your responsibilities as a ship's division officer. You also learn how to "drive" your ship as a "Conning Officer" and later as an "Officer of the Deck."

Later, the Navy says that SWOS will teach you how to control your ship's engineering plant as the "Engineering Officer of the Watch," and then to "fight" your ship as the "Combat Information Center Watch Officer" or "Tactical Action Officer." After successfully completing SWOS, you have two division officer tours of 24 months and 18 months, respectively.

As you can imagine, the Navy has many home-ports for its surface fleet around the world. The Navy says that it will give full consideration to any requests for specific postings (within the scope of your job, rank, and advancement potential). According to the Navy, the surface fleet consists of many different types of ships, including cruisers, destroyers, frigates, aircraft carriers, amphibious ships, minesweepers, patrol craft, and auxiliary ships. Anchors aweigh!

Source: U.S. Navy ROTC program

After you get in the program, staying in is hardly a breeze, and many students drop out of the program. Some students can't hack the time commitments of between 5 to 15 hours per week, depending on the program, the college, and the branch of service. ROTC students must also attend early morning PT sessions (that's physical training, for you civilians), the occasional weekend of military training, and at least one military science class each semester.

As you can tell, attending ROTC (and later the military) is *definitely* not for everyone. Some people find the clockwork running of their lives to be very disconcerting. Others have problems with the strange new rules and regulations. In the past, women and visible minorities have had a tough time of it in this traditionally white male bastion. This problem is changing (albeit slowly), as more outreach programs are designed and implemented to attract a more diverse mix of people.

Joining the military is one of the most important decisions that you'll make in your life. If you have problems dealing with authority figures, you probably won't be able to cut it in the military. You could be miserable for the four years of school *plus* the additional eight years of military service.

On the other hand, if you like knowing where you stand at all times and enjoy a solid, routine way of doing things, you'll likely enjoy your service. Plus, it's hard to beat the fact that after-college unemployment will be something you'll never have to endure with ROTC. As well, depending on the military branch you choose, you actually may see places you never would if you had attended college the "regular" way and taken a traditional job at an insurance or software development company.

Free Money for Dependents of Veterans

Americans have a proud history of fighting for their country. Likewise, the country has a proud history of taking care of the spouses and dependent children of veterans who paid a heavy price for our freedom.

At the federal level, the organization you want to research is called the *Department of Veterans Affairs* (usually shortened to *Veterans Affairs* or simply *VA*). This branch of the federal government provides health benefits and services, compensation and pension benefits, life insurance, vocational rehabilitation and employment services, burial and memorial services, home loan guaranty services, and best of all for college-bound students, educational benefits for veterans, their spouses, and dependent children.

The Survivors' and Dependents' Educational Assistance Program

One of the many programs of interest is the *Survivors' and Dependents' Educational Assistance Program.* This program provides education and training opportunities to eligible dependents of veterans who are permanently and totally disabled due to a military service-related condition, or who died while on active duty or as a result of a service-related condition.

The Survivors' and Dependents' Educational Assistance Program offers up to 45 months of education benefits, but VA limits total education benefits (from all programs) to 48 months. These benefits may be used for degree and certificate programs, apprenticeships, and on-the-job training. If you're a spouse, you may take a correspondence course. Remedial, deficiency, and refresher courses may be approved under certain circumstances.

According to VA, to be eligible for this program, you must be the son, daughter, or spouse of any of the following:

- ✔ A veteran who died or is permanently and totally disabled as the result of a service-connected disability. The disability must arise out of active service in the Armed Forces.

- ✔ A veteran who died from any cause while such service-connected disability was in existence.

- ✔ A service member missing in action or captured in the line of duty by a hostile force. These soldiers are commonly called *MIAs.*

- ✔ A service member forcibly detained or interned in the line of duty by a foreign government or power. In other words, a prisoner of war or *POW.*

Who qualifies under this program?

There are three categories of eligibility under the Survivors' and Dependents' Educational Assistance Program:

1. **Dependent.** If you're a qualifying son or daughter and wish to receive benefits for attending school or job training, you must be between the ages of 18 and 26. In certain instances, you can begin before age 18 and continue after age 26. Even if you're married, you can still receive this benefit.

2. **You, as an active service member.** If you yourself are currently in the Armed Forces, you are *not eligible to* receive this benefit because you're on active duty. To pursue training *after* military service, you must have been discharged from the service under anything but "dishonorable" conditions. Veterans Affairs can extend your period of eligibility by the number of months and days equal to the time spent on active duty. This extension, however, cannot go beyond your 31st birthday.

3. **Spouse of a service member.** If you're a spouse, benefits end ten years from the date that the VA finds you eligible (rules that the veteran is officially MIA or a POW) or from the date of death or permanent disability of your veteran spouse.

What educational opportunities will the program pay for?

The Survivors' and Dependents' Educational Assistance Program pays for a variety of different educational programs, including the following:

- ✔ First and foremost, you can take an undergraduate or graduate degree. You may also take a "co-op" training program offered by a college or university, which is an accredited independent study program leading to a college degree.

- ✔ You may take courses leading to a certificate or diploma from business, technical, or vocational (trade) schools. You may take these courses from a two-year college if you wish.

- ✔ You may work and train in an apprenticeship or job-training program offered by a company or union. Most of the time, these programs are already paid for by your workplace, but if they aren't, VA pays for them.

- ✔ If you're a spouse, you may take a correspondence course (although, obviously, you can take the course on-campus if you wish).

- ✔ You may take a farm cooperative course.

- ✔ If you want to study abroad, the Survivors' and Dependents' Educational Assistance Program's education benefits are payable — but only for programs directly applicable or leading to a college degree.

- ✔ You may take secondary school programs if you aren't a high school graduate.

- ✔ You may take secondary school deficiency or remedial courses to qualify for admission to an educational institution.

What courses will the program not pay for?

There are, of course, some restrictions on training. Veterans Affairs says that training benefits are *not* payable for the following courses, types of programs, or situations:

- ✔ Bartending or personality development courses

- ✔ Correspondence courses, if you're a dependent or surviving child

- ✔ Non-accredited independent study courses

- ✔ Any course given by radio

- ✔ Private flight training

- ✔ Self-improvement courses, such as reading, speaking, woodworking, basic seamanship, and English as a Second Language

- Any vocational or recreational course not leading to a degree

- Audited courses (You must actually get grades and receive marks for your courses.)

- Courses not directly leading to an educational, professional, or vocational objective

- Courses you've taken before and successfully completed

- Courses taken by a federal government employee and paid for under the Government Employees' Training Act (You can't get money for a course already paid for by a different branch of the government.)

- Courses taken while in receipt of benefits for the same program from the Office of Workers' Compensation Programs

- Courses from a school that you own or control

How much educational assistance will I get?

Under the Survivors' and Dependents' Educational Assistance Program, you're eligible for a maximum of 45 months of educational benefits, and depending on your course load (full-, three-quarter-, or half-time), you can receive up to $680 per month. If you can only manage to study half-time at college (perhaps you're working full-time to support your family), Veterans Affairs pays you $340 per month.

In other words, if you spend nine months full-time taking college-level degree credits, VA will pay you $680 × 9 = $6,120 in benefits, provided that you qualify for the program. If you spend 24 months working half-time on your degree, VA pays you $340 × 24 = $8,160.

We summarize the education benefits for veterans (who can qualify for benefits under Chapter 30 of Title 38 of U.S. Code), dependents or spouses (who can qualify under Chapter 35 of the same legislation) as well as active reservists later in this chapter.

Applying

You must first obtain and complete VA Form 22-5490, Application for Survivors' and Dependents' Educational Assistance. Send it to the VA regional office that has jurisdiction over the state where you'll train. If you're a son or daughter, under legal age in your state, a parent or guardian must sign the application.

A state agency or VA must approve each program offered by a school or company. If you want to know whether you'll receive benefits for a program, call 1-888-GI-BILL-1 (1-888-442-4551) and ask.

Receiving payments

After selecting a school and submitting your application to VA, ask the school certifying official to complete an enrollment certification. The school official will send the enrollment certification to the appropriate VA regional office. If you have basic eligibility for benefits and your program or course is approved, VA will process your enrollment and issue payments based on your certified training time.

If you're in a degree program at a college or university, you'll receive payment after the first of each month for your training during the preceding month. In other words, you'll receive payment for a May class after June 1, for instance.

You can get all the VA forms on the Web at www.vba.va.gov/pubs/educationforms.htm.

The Montgomery GI Bill

The *Montgomery GI Bill* (MGIB) is aimed at educating enlisted men and women, both those in active service to Uncle Sam and those who've retired. Understanding the MGIB is an important step in getting free money for college. Unfortunately, the bill has so many rules and regulations (which, of course, are in a constant state of change) that *fully* understanding how active servicemen and servicewomen as well as veterans qualify is a job on its own.

Suffice it to say, you may be eligible for up to $985 per month to pay for college courses used in a degree program. The University of Maryland, the largest civilian school used by members of the U.S. Armed Forces, currently educates well over 20,000 students stationed around the world. These servicemen and servicewomen can study anything from accounting to zoology *virtually* — and Uncle Sam picks up the tuition!

These funds do, however, have several limitations on what you can receive from Uncle Sam. Generally, there are four benefit categories based on factors such as date of entry into the Armed Forces, years of active service, rank achieved, and other metrics.

You can see which benefits accrue to which service categories by checking out VA's *Publication # 22-90-2: The Montgomery GI Bill — Active Duty*. You can view this pamphlet online at www.gibill.va.gov/education or by stopping by your nearest VA office. To locate your state VA office, go to www.va.gov/partners/stateoffice/index.htm.

This pamphlet provides a great summary of various educational benefits under the MGIB, and it explains the structure of each qualification category.

Your benefits

Your benefits are dependent upon your years of active service and other conditions.

You're eligible for 36 months of MGIB benefits, provided that you've completed three years of continuous, active duty (or two years if you signed up for less than three years of service). You're also eligible for this 36-month term if you were discharged for the *Convenience of the Government* after completing 20 months if you signed up for less than three years of service, or 30 months if you signed up for three years or more. (In case you were wondering, being discharged for the *Convenience of the Government* is the same as being *laid off* in the civilian world.)

You may be entitled to less than 36 months of MGIB benefits if you separated before completing three years of continuous active duty (or two years if you signed up for less than three years), and your separation is for one of the following reasons:

- ✔ A medical condition preexisting service
- ✔ A reduction in force (in civilian terms, you were laid off)
- ✔ A hardship (this term is specifically defined by the military)
- ✔ A physical or mental condition that interfered with duty that was not due to willful misconduct
- ✔ A service-connected disability

Education and training options

According to Veterans Affairs, you may receive MGIB benefits for a wide variety of training and education programs — provided that your courses or programs are approved by VA or by a state agency. These benefits include the following:

- ✔ An undergraduate or graduate degree at a college or university. Also included are cooperative ("co-op") training programs as well as accredited independent study programs leading to a standard college degree.
- ✔ A certificate or diploma from a business, technical, or vocational school.
- ✔ An apprenticeship or on-the-job (OJT) training program offered by a company or union. Apprenticeships or OJT programs may offer an alternative to college or vocational school for helping you gain experience in the field you choose.

✔ A correspondence course.

✔ Flight training. You must have a private pilot certificate and meet the medical requirements for the desired certificate before beginning training. If your program began before October 1, 1998, you must continue to meet the medical requirements throughout your flight training program.

✔ Programs overseas that lead to a college degree.

Veterans Affairs does, however, put restrictions on which education courses and programs qualify for MGIB benefits. Consult the list of restrictions listed for the Survivors' and Dependents' Educational Assistance Program mentioned earlier in this chapter and check out VA's GI Bill Web site at www. gibill.va.gov/ for updates.

Eligibility requirements

According to Veterans Affairs, benefits end ten years from the date of your last discharge or release from active duty. However, you may be able to have VA extend this deadline. Veterans Affairs can extend your ten-year period by the amount of time you were prevented from training during your service period due to a disability, because you were held by a foreign government, or because of other specific conditions.

Application procedures

Each college has somewhat different regulations and application procedures. In general, students applying for the first time for MGIB benefits must complete VA Form 22-1990 (Application for Education Benefits). If you're applying under Chapter 30 (Montgomery GI Bill), you must attach your DD 214 (the release-from-active-duty form).

You can get lots more details about the MGIB by calling 1-888-GI-BILL-1 (1-888-442-4551). If you're hearing impaired, the number to call is 1-800-829-4833.

What about the Benjamins?

The "standard" VA education benefit program has dozens of variations, and the only way that anyone can fully understand them all is to spend some time on the VA Web site and speak to the helpful people at the VA call center.

If you just can't get enough military info . . .

Besides the information we already provide you in this chapter, you can also check out the following resources:

✔ The biggest and fullest U.S. military Web site around at is www.military.com

✔ The government's own Web site for MGIB questions can be found at www.gibill.va.gov/.

✔ Your Education Service Officer (ESO) on base if you're on active duty.

✔ Your State Veterans Affairs Office for the state where you'll attend training. Find it at www.va.gov/partners/stateoffice/index.htm.

All veterans, their spouses, and their dependents, however, should be familiar with some basic award levels. Table 18-1 summarizes these levels.

Table 18-1	GI Bill Award Levels		
Military qualification	*Full-time benefit*	*Three-quarter-time benefit*	*Half-time benefit*
Veteran, honorably discharged and qualified under Chapter 30	$900/month	$685/month	$450/month
Qualified person under Survivors' and Dependents' Educational Assistance Program (Chapter 35)	$680/month	$511/month	$340/month
Reservist, but must be still in Active Reserves	$276/month	$207/month	$137/month

Source: Veterans Affairs

Chapter 19

Staring into the Educational Crystal Ball

*D*anish physicist and scholar Niels Bohr once said, "Prediction is very difficult, especially of the future."

Don't worry, we're not going to spend the rest of this chapter describing Bohr's Nobel Prize-winning theory on atomic structure. Instead, we polish up our crystal ball and look into the future of what might happen to college costs, tuition, scholarships, and grants. We also explain how these trends might affect *your* financial situation and your ability to get free money in the future.

Costs Will Increase

Okay, okay, predicting this one may not be a big stretch. After all, college tuition prices have been going up ever since there were colleges to attend. What we're trying to get across here is the fact that costs will increase far more than most students' ability to pay for them — and certainly more than inflation. The result will be increased pressure to take on more student (and parent) debt, as well as a sudden realization that some colleges are pricing themselves out of the market, at least for most people.

That tuition fees are rising is certainly no secret. According to the U.S. Department of Education, the average cost of attendance at four-year public colleges rose 28 percent during the 1990s. Over the past ten years, however, some schools have *doubled* their tuition fees. A few colleges have raised their tuition fees even higher than that!

Some organizations that are active in college financial aid estimate that tuition will rise by 5 percent every year. Based on recent tuition increases, we think that a more realistic estimation is between 7 and 10 percent per year. Taking the worst-case scenario of 10 percent annual tuition increases means that an arbitrary $3,000 annual fee will rise to a whopping $7,074 in ten years! You can see why it's so important to start saving early and to research sources for free money as soon as you can.

Many state governments have begun to feel that schools should "carry their own weight" and have kept funding steady in the face of rising costs. In some cases, states have actually *cut* funding to colleges in their jurisdiction. States have historically carried a large part of the financial burden for college tuition, so the cutbacks mean fewer dollars into the college coffers — and higher prices for the students who attend college.

Not only will fees increase, but also, more people will be competing for the same chunk of financial aid. The amount of aid *per student* won't grow as much as the increased cost of tuition, and in some cases, might actually shrink.

The Department of Education reported, for example, that the number of Pell Grant (see Chapter 5) recipients in the decade between 1990 and 2000 increased 18 percent, but the average award grew only 2 percent. In the same period, the number of FSEOG recipients (also see Chapter 5) went up by 64 percent, but the average award *declined* 30 percent!

All this information boils down one simple piece of advice: You and your parents (if you're a dependent student) absolutely must start setting up a financial aid plan immediately to get you through school. Making a realistic plan dramatically increases your chances of attending college. Investigate *all* the government-sponsored college savings plans available to you, such as Coverdell ESAs (discussed in Chapter 8).

Demand for Higher Education Will Rise

According to the Department of Commerce, college graduates earn an average of 98 percent more income than those men and women who don't have college degrees. Plus, people with a master's degree earn 170 percent more. Further, the U.S. Bureau of Labor Statistics reports that employment opportunities will grow fastest for professionals with a college education. Already, a majority of the best, fastest-growing, and highest-paid occupations require a bachelor's degree as a bare minimum.

It's no secret that America is getting more educated. Back at the turn of the last century, fewer than 5 percent of 25-year-olds had college or university degrees. Things pretty much stayed static for a few decades and even dipped during the Great Depression.

By 1990, according to the Department of Education, 27 percent of 25- to 29-year-olds had earned at least a bachelor's degree. This number soared to 32 percent a decade later. This trend will likely continue for two reasons: First, we as a country are more affluent, with disposable income rising every decade since 1900 (it even grew in the 1930s, despite the effects of the Great Depression). Second, jobs are becoming more sophisticated and more reliant on formal education.

This increasing demand for a college education will put more competition on the mostly fixed number of spaces at colleges across America. Besides having the effect of raising the entry marks and GPA requirements for schools across America, another, more interesting effect may occur. Colleges likely will offer additional "virtual" classes, using high-speed Internet access as well as more traditional classes at night, on weekends, and during the summer.

Will the number of virtual colleges and distance-learning schools increase? Probably not in the short term. Although more people want to upgrade their qualifications and gain their first, second, or even third degree, the number of college professors and other instructors is somewhat fixed for now. Of course, colleges can train and hire more instructors, but this training and hiring takes years to complete and will thus limit the "supply" of education for the foreseeable future.

Some Colleges Will Merge or Close

It may seem strange that any colleges would close when there is increasing demand for a college education. However, due to increasing competition from larger mega-colleges and smaller specialized schools (as well as a more mobile America, able to move wherever the best education and jobs are located), some smaller, less specialized colleges are likely to merge with larger ones or become "satellite" colleges. Other schools will simply close due to increasing costs of operation.

According to one survey we've seen recently, one-third of private colleges will close by 2010. However, the overall demand for higher education will increase from 15 million students in 2000 to 20 million in 2010. In other words, more students will be trying to pack themselves into fewer colleges, and the result will be larger classes and less individual attention from professors. Can anyone say, *increased competition?*

Whether these dire forecasts come true remains to be seen. It is true, however, that smaller colleges will be increasingly pressured to differentiate themselves from other schools. Colleges that can't (or don't) specialize in money-generating programs will be forced to close down. Students attending these colleges may be left with uncompleted degrees and few options other than trying to transfer their credits to other colleges, which may or may not accept them.

Therefore, looking at a college's finances will become just as important as looking at its academic programs. In the future, a school's *financial* condition may be just as important to prospective students as its libraries, student-to-professor ratio, or football team ranking is to current students.

Prospective students can easily check into the affairs of any accredited college by contacting the appropriate college accreditation authority. The Department of Education maintains a list of accrediting bodies. You can verify your school's particular situation by calling 1-800-4-FED-AID (1-800-433-3243) or visiting the Department's Web site at www.ed.gov.

Books, Computers, and Other Supplies Will Become Cheaper

This seemingly paradoxical situation may take place if course curriculums (*curricula* for those Latin majors) become more streamlined across colleges. Currently, professors have a large degree of latitude when deciding what books to require for their courses.

In some cases, the professor has actually *written* the book and pockets a few hundred (or a few thousand) dollars from book sales every time the course is taught. In the cases of extremely popular courses, such as first-year economics or biology, the professor may make as much money from book sales as he or she does from teaching!

As colleges become more digitally aware, more on-demand printing will mean that *chapters* or *articles* rather than complete books will be used in courses. Currently, course packs (bound, royalty-paid photostats of chapters, articles, or books) are popular in certain courses. With the advent of more digital technology within campus bookstores, we might see cheaper books on the horizon. This possibility is especially good news for students who spend up to $3,000 every year on books and supplies.

Computers will obviously get more powerful, more mobile, and cheaper. They will also become a requirement at most colleges and universities, raising the bar for many less well-off students. Massachusetts Institute of Technology (MIT) has announced that, starting in 2004, all its course curricula, including textbooks, will be available free for students on the Internet.

Currently, only a few schools require their students to purchase a computer to attend college; a few others *include* a computer in their first-year students' tuition costs. Whatever new hardware and software looms on the horizon, clearly, technology will play an increasing role in college education.

Despite the fact that both books and computers will likely get less expensive, both will probably continue to increase the so-called digital divide between rich and not-so-rich students. These days, having a personal computer is pretty much a necessity, and knowing how to use one certainly is taken for granted in today's digital economy.

Many financial aid packages won't be able to cope with the added cost of computers required by some schools, so some students will find it difficult to attend these especially "high tech" schools. Other students may be driven deeper into student debt by purchasing computer and other high tech equipment that's necessary just to stay in the educational game.

The Traditional Classroom May Disappear

The science of teaching really hasn't changed much in the last two or three thousand years. Young (relatively well-off) students sit down in a large auditorium or lecture hall to listen to an older professor or instructor who writes down key points with pulverized bits of stone. If a student has a question, he or she can raise a hand.

No, we aren't glimpsing back into Ancient Greece. You can see this scene replayed over and over every day in colleges across America. This vision is changing, however, as more technology is incorporated into classrooms and lecture halls.

Already, multimedia presentation tools, such as large color projection systems linked to instructor-run laptops, have been installed in the larger or more prestigious colleges. Some graduate student lecture halls have high-speed Internet and intranet connections. Students in these classes are expected to reference class materials as well as perform on-the-spot research on issues discussed in class, using their own laptop computers.

Laptops, the Internet, and taped classes let students watch lectures from the comfort of home or the dorm room. Already, colleges, such as the University of Phoenix, are teaching in the virtual world. You can now study, learn, submit assignments, ask questions, and chat with students and instructors without leaving home. Although rare today, these futuristic scenes will grow exponentially in the next few years.

The impact of these cultural and technological changes may help level the playing field between colleges. Students who would otherwise not be able to travel to the school (and afford a place to live on campus) might be able to study and still remain at home.

Adult learners, who've traditionally been unable to attend most daytime classes due to work commitments, will also benefit from this technology. These learners will be able to watch lectures and participate at odd hours, opening a huge world of opportunities for many people. The decreasing costs involved in "attending" college — such as residence fees, travel, and the requirement to postpone employment — may just balance out the increased costs of tuition. Also, because people who couldn't take time off work to attend college or who lived too far away will suddenly be able to attend these virtual classes, a greater number of students may clamor for college spaces and for financial aid.

Scholarships Will Become More Privatized — and Personalized

A long time ago, rich people bequeathed large sums of money to colleges so that their name and legacy could live on after they themselves had passed on to their Great Reward (as some called it then). In exchange for this largesse, buildings, gymnasiums, running tracks, and even swimming pools were named for these benefactors.

If you look around pretty much any East Coast college (in general, East Coast schools were founded decades, if not *centuries,* before their West Coast counterparts), you can see this in action. The campus of Harvard University, for example, is scattered with buildings and other important structures named after their benefactors: Blodgett, Fogg, Hemenway, Newell, Sackler, Weld, and many others.

Besides buildings, *scholarships* have also been named after their benefactors. The most famous of these is the Rhodes Scholarship, named after Cecil Rhodes, son of an English clergyman. Rhodes first traveled to South Africa in 1870 where he and his older brother staked a diamond claim that eventually became the famous De Beers Mining Company.

These days, corporate sponsorships aren't only on buildings, but entire colleges, divisions, and schools. What's more, the names of various well-heeled corporations have started to adorn *professors* in college. Some colleges have professors whose salaries are paid by a corporation, usually through the one-time donation of a large amount of cash. The colleges usually couch the arrangement as a particular company funding the position (usually called *endowing a chair*), but the effect is the same: A large corporation is *sponsoring* the professor! For example, David Filo and Jerry Yang, the creators of Yahoo!, recently endowed a chair at their alma mater Stanford University. Henceforth, its Department of Engineering will have a Yahoo! Founders Professor.

Taking this scenario to the next logical step, we predict that students *themselves* will be sponsored by corporations. In the near future, a lucky student might be sent to college on a full running-shoe scholarship (provided that she's a good athlete and willing to wear the corporate emblems or branding at all times). A math major could be sponsored by a computer company, and an English specialist sponsored by the publishers of dictionaries.

Before this future unfolds, what can you do as a student looking for free money for college? Why not approach your local corporation to sponsor you through college? When you think about it, the situation isn't that much different from a little league team being sponsored by the local car dealership. Due to its novelty, personal sponsorship will certainly garner some great press coverage — exactly what your sponsor wants!

Paperwork Will Get More Complicated

If you've read very much of this book, you know the extraordinary efforts that colleges, states, and, of course, the federal government make to help you get free money for college. Of course, the result of all these different programs is hardly straightforward. In fact, it can be downright ugly.

You find it hard to imagine the free money process getting any more complex, but it will. Every tiny change in the expected family contribution (EFC) calculation, every adjustment made to the U.S. tax acts by Congress, and every helpful loan and grant application offered by the Department of Education seems to make it *more difficult* to get free money for college!

Deep down we all know that everyone is trying to help, but, sometimes, continuing to believe this good thought is difficult. Considering the amount of ever-growing paperwork, the number of intrusive questions, weird (and often illusive) deadlines, and vague instructions, it's hard to believe that we can all make sense of the entire plan.

Yet, make sense of it we must. For without all the free money programs, few American students would be able to live their dream of a higher education — and of a better life. Savvy students know that they must master the arcane rules, complete the complex forms, and meet the changing deadlines if they're to reap the rewards.

These same students also know that the paperwork is likely to get *worse*. So, take notice! In future, you'll have to work harder to figure out the forms and get the applications in on time. The good news is that you can do it — as long as you start early enough!

Paperwork Will Involve Less Paper

Although you may have to answer more questions, the Internet will hopefully streamline the application process. You can already complete and "sign" your FAFSA online, and many colleges accept digital applications both for admission and for financial aid. Even *responses* to online applications — once the sole dominion of paper — are now commonly sent via e-mail.

These online capabilities may make it faster and easier for students to send in their applications, but they have a negative side as well. A single click in error may send your files to the wrong place. Thus, students must be even more diligent to perfect their applications before sending them. As well, a single error in any one of your files (high school transcripts, financial information, residency) can easily be replicated over and over again — and you may not even be aware that the error exists!

As always, it's up to you to be attentive and make sure that the right information goes to the right places. At least the online application trend will save you money in postage!

Chapter 20

Resource Guide

. . . .

In This Chapter

▶ Finding federal, military, and state resources

▶ Checking out college-related organizations

▶ Looking for help on specific topics

▶ Meeting corporations and other private organizations with money

. . . .

*D*o you ever wish a single source of information was available that contained everything you need to know before you head off to college? Wouldn't it be great to have a resource guide with valuable listings to help you answer all those nagging questions about college applications, financial aid, military service options, and a host of other details?

Well, wish no more: This chapter is it! Here's a resource guide filled with addresses, telephone numbers, Web sites, and all sorts of information to speed your way into college. We start off this chapter by outlining the dozens of federal government resources that are useful to students. Next, we move on to military options and state resources — those offered by state governments as well as organizations. We continue by looking at the specific topics of scams, loans, international study, and standardized tests — topics everyone heading for college should understand. Finally, we list private resources that may provide options to pay for your college education.

Federal Resources

So much information about going to college is available that knowing where to start looking can be difficult. You don't know which sources you can trust and which sources may be a waste of time (or a waste of money). We think the best place to start your research is by investigating programs offered by the federal government. More financial aid is available through the federal government than all other sources *combined*. Granted, much of this financial aid is in the form of loans or work-study programs, but Uncle Sam also gives out *billions* of dollars in grants every year. Take a look at what's available!

Department of Education

The most obvious place to start your quest for free money is the government's own department charged with providing education and financial aid to millions of American students. The Department of Education gives away close to $70 billion every year to students looking for college financial aid and also runs the group that administers the FASFA (see the section "FAFSA — Free Application for Federal Student Aid," later in this chapter). You can reach the department at

U.S. Department of Education
400 Maryland Avenue, SW
Washington, DC 20202-0498
Phone: 1-800-USA-LEARN (1-800-872-5327)
Web site: www.ed.gov

Department of Education's COOL Database

You might think a government Web site can't really be that cool. But we'll bet that after looking around here for a little while, you'll begin to think the database lives up to its name. Besides, COOL stands for *College Opportunities On-Line,* and the site has lots of these. Here, you can search for a college based on its geographic location, type of institution, size of school, instructional program, or degree offerings, either alone or in combination.

Operated by the Department of Education's Institute of Education Sciences, the COOL Database can ferret out colleges to suit just about anybody's wish list. For example, the database can find all the four-year private institutions that are based in Alabama, have an enrollment of fewer than 1,000 students, and are, say, 65 miles away from a given zip code. Currently, the COOL Database lists over 9,000 colleges and universities!

After you find some colleges of interest, you can obtain further information on each school by clicking on the school's hyperlink. You can save, print the information, compare one school's costs, locations, degrees granted, and other key criteria with another, and place the results in your college applications folder. Check out www.nces.ed.gov/ipeds/cool/Search.asp for more details. You can also reach the organization at the following address:

National Center for Education Statistics
Institute of Education Sciences, U.S. Department of Education
1990 K Street, NW
Washington, DC 20006
Phone: 202-502-7300

Department of Labor's Occupational Outlook Handbook

Ever wanted to look into a crystal ball and see what jobs will be waiting when you get out of college? Well, check out the U.S. Department of Labor's Occupational Outlook Handbook and take a trip into the future!

The Occupational Outlook Handbook is a great source of career information and is designed to provide valuable assistance to students (and others) making decisions about their future careers. The handbook is revised every two years and describes what specific workers do on the job, what their working conditions are, the training and education needed for each type of job, average earnings for the profession (sometimes categorized by seniority), and expected job prospects for a wide range of occupations.

Top-level categories of studies include management, professional, services, sales, administrative support, farming and related, construction, installation and related, production, transportation, and even job opportunities in the U.S. Armed Forces!

You can check out the handbook at the Web site www.bls.gov/oco.

FAFSA — Free Application for Federal Student Aid

The place where it all starts for federal student aid is the FAFSA, available as a paper application form or a digital form you can fill out online. FAFSA (Free Application for Federal Student Aid) is administered by the Federal Student Aid Information Center (part of the U.S. Department of Education), whose friendly folks are able to help students (and their families) complete the FAFSA, answer any questions about the form, and provide technical assistance for the "FAFSA on the Web" product.

Without completing the FAFSA, you're pretty much dead in the water as far as any student aid is concerned. This application is the first necessary step to receiving not only *federal* student aid but also state-based student aid in many states. Many colleges also use the information you provide on your FAFSA as the basis for their scholarship, grant, and other free money considerations. Sure, you may have other need-based paperwork to complete, but the place where it all starts is the FAFSA! We discuss the FAFSA in Chapter 5. The organization can be reached at:

Federal Student Aid Information Center
P.O. Box 84
Washington, DC 20044-0084
Phone: 1-800-4-FED-AID (1-800-433-3243), toll-free in all 50 states
Phone: 1-800-730-8913 (for TTY users)
Phone: 319-337-5665 (for students outside the United States)
Web site: www.fafsa.ed.gov

Also check out the worksheets that can be downloaded at http://www.fafsa.ed.gov/worksheet.htm.

Federal School Code Database

To complete your FAFSA, you need to know the federal school code for each college on your wish list. Despite the fact that the paper version of the FAFSA currently lets you leave this area blank, entering the codes is a good idea because it speeds your application along to the schools of your choice. Unlike the paper version of the FAFSA, however, you *will* need at least one federal school code to complete the FAFSA on the Web, and the FAFSA site links to the federal school code database with one click of your mouse.

You can find the federal school code database (run by the U.S. Department of Education) at: www.fafsa.ed.gov/fotw0304/fslookup.htm. (Note there is no letter "l" at the end of this URL.) We discuss completing your FAFSA in Chapter 5.

Federal Employee Education and Assistance (FEEA) Fund

If you are (or if one of your parents is) an employee of the federal government, you may be eligible for education assistance. Federal Employee Education and Assistance (FEEA) is administered by a consortium of employee organizations, unions, and federations, and *not* by the federal government. We discuss this organization in Chapter 17. You can contact the organization at:

Federal Employee Education and Assistance Fund (FEEA)
W. Bowles Avenue, Suite 200
Littleton, CO 80123-9501
Phone: 303-933-7580
Fax: 303-933-7587
Web site: www.feea.org

Federal Student Gateway

This "student gateway to the U.S. government" is the definitive portal to government education programs, college resources, scholarships and other financial aid, and generally all the things students and parents want to know about going to college. This repository of government information and services is run by the U.S. Department of Education and is a cooperative effort between various federal agencies, students, and other parts of the higher education community.

Using the gateway, you can plan your education, figure out how education fits into your career plans (and vice versa), find out about military service options, check out the various federal student aid plans, and get lots of information about the various government resources for students. Many a student has started her search at this site and spent hours bookmarking other useful sites and downloading important information. In Chapter 1, we explain how to create a college application folder to organize all this information.

You can access this information on the Web at www.students.gov.

Federal Student Aid (FSA) Portal

This site, again run by the Department of Education, provides a clearinghouse for federal student aid. It offers all sorts of resources, directions, and tips about student loans, plus solid information about finding a career, facts for new financial aid borrowers, and some good loan *counseling* information. The site also describes how to reapply for student financial aid and how to maintain your financial aid eligibility from year to year.

Ever wonder what happens to your loan if you leave school early, either because you decide college isn't for you or your college closes abruptly? Find out at the FSA Student Portal. The site's NSLDS Financial Aid Review service provides access to information on your particular loan or grant requests, your outstanding balances, loan status, and disbursements.

You can reach this site at studentaid.ed.gov (no "www" prefix). A related site also run by the Department of Education is the Federal Student Aid Homepage at www.ed.gov/studentaid.

Grants.gov

This "electronic storefront for federal grants" is an excellent portal site for grants of all sorts. You can find the educational grants at www.grants.gov/education.html.

Information Resource Center

This is another great site run by the U.S. Department of Education. Here, you can find information about popular grant programs, publications and other written materials, and even a helpful directory assistance listing.

You can read about the Department of Education's priorities and recent special initiatives, search for (and order) publications online, and find out about available grants, student aid, and other forms of student financial assistance. Here's how to reach the center:

Information Resource Center
U.S. Department of Education
400 Maryland Avenue, SW
Washington, DC 20202-0498
Phone: 1-800-USA-LEARN (1-800-872-5327)
Phone: 1-800-437-0833 (for TTY users)
Phone: 202-401-2000 (for local calls in Washington, D.C., or calls from outside the United States)
Web site: www.ed.gov/offices/OIIA/IRC/secondarypage.html

Internal Revenue Service

Check out the 58-page booklet *Tax Benefits for Education* (also known to the in crowd as IRS Publication 970). You can find a copy at your local tax office or online (www.irs.gov). Numerous other IRS publications of interest to students are also available, and we discuss some of these in Chapter 8. We give additional information about other IRS-related programs in Chapter 7.

Project EASI

Project EASI is a federal government resource that helps students and parents plan for post-secondary education. EASI stands for Easy Access for Students and Institutions.

You can find it on the Web at easi.ed.gov (no "www" prefix).

Social Security

You need a Social Security Number to work as well as to apply for financial aid using the FAFSA. Check out the government listings of your telephone book for a location near you or apply online at www.ssa.gov.

The Student Guide for Financial Aid

The Student Guide is an annual publication available directly from the government, your high school counselor, and colleges across the country. *The Student Guide* provides students with just about everything they need to know about qualifying for federal student aid, including Federal Pell Grants, Federal Supplemental Educational Opportunity Grant (FSEOG), Federal Work-Study, Federal Perkins Loans, Stafford Loans, and PLUS Loans.

The Student Guide is one of the most useful (and understandable) publications from the government. We recommend that every student read through the booklet. The guide is published by the Department of Education and is available by calling 1-800-4-FED-AID (1-800-433-3243). If you're outside the United States, you can also call the organization at 319-337-5665.

Best of all, *The Student Guide* is *free* for the asking. Because the guide is revised every year, make sure that your copy is the most up-to-date edition. Besides calling the folks at the Federal Student Aid Information Center for a copy of *The Student Guide,* you can also download a copy from studentaid. ed.gov/students/publications/student_guide/index.html (no "www" prefix).

All Things Military

Many options for scholarship resources are available through the various divisions of the military. We discuss the U.S. Armed Forces in Chapter 18.

ROTC programs

To learn more about the U.S. military's Reserve Officers' Training Corps (ROTC), check out www.todaysmilitary.com/chart_rotc.html. We discuss the ROTC program (and the overall military option) for free money for college in Chapter 18. The following sections offer contact information about the ROTC for each branch of the Armed Forces:

Air Force Reserve Officers' Training Corps (AFROTC)

Headquarters Air Force ROTC/RRUC551
East Maxwell Boulevard
Maxwell AFB, AL 6112-6106
Phone: 1-866-423-7682
Web site: www.afrotc.com

Army Reserve Officers' Training Corps (AROTC)

College Army ROTC
Gold QUEST Center
P.O. Box 3279
Warminster, PA 18974-9872
Phone: 1-800-USA-ROTC (1-800-872-7682)
Web site: www.armyrotc.com

Naval/Marines Reserve Officers' Training Corps (NROTC)

Navy Opportunity, Information Center
P.O. Box 9406
Gaithersburg, MD 20898
Phone: 1-800-NAV-ROTC (1-800-628-7682)
Web site: www.nrotc.navy.mil

Military academies

If life in the U.S. Armed Forces is your career choice, you might want to attend a special military academy for officers' training. Find out all about these prestigious institutions with the information provided below.

Air Force

The Air Force Academy
HQ USAFA/RRS
2304 Cadet Drive, Suite 200
USAF Academy, CO 80840
Phone: 1-800-443-9266 or 719-333-1110
Fax: 719-333-3647
Web site: www.usafa.af.mil

Army

US Military Academy
West Point, NY 10996
Phone: 845-938-4011
Web site: www.usma.edu

Navy and Marines (including the astronaut program)

US Naval Academy
121 Blake Road
Annapolis, MD 21402-5000

For admissions:
Candidate Guidance Office
United States Naval Academy
117 Decatur Road
Annapolis, MD 21402-5018
Phone: 410-293-4361
Web site: www.usna.edu

Other military sites

The largest site for the US **military** is www.military.com, where you can find helpful articles, resources, and links. You also can perform a scholarship search at www.military.com/careers/education/scholarshipsearch. Several other resources are **also** useful if you **wish to** pursue a career in any branch of the U.S. Armed Forces. Check out the **options** listed in this section.

National Guard

One Massachusetts Avenue, NW
Washington, DC 20001
Phone: 202-789-0031
Fax: 202-682-9358
or
National Guard Advertising Support Center
P.O. Box 1776
Edgewood, MD 21040
Web site: www.ngaus.org
E-mail: ngaus@ngaus.org

For the Army National Guard
Phone: 1-800-GO-GUARD (1-**800-464**-8273**)**
Web site: www.1800GOGUARD.com

Montgomery GI Bill

For specific information about **the** benefits and **options** available under the Montgomery GI Bill (MGIB), **here's** where to turn:

Web site: www.gibill.va.gov
Phone: 1-888-GI-BILL-1 (1-888-442-4551)
TDD: 1-800-829-4833

Education Service links

This portal site is part of the **GI** Bill Web site, but **provides** excellent links to all sorts of educational resources. You can find **it** at www.gibill.va.gov/education/Links.htm.

State Veterans Affairs offices

To locate your state Veterans Affairs office, visit the Web site www.va.gov/partners/stateoffice/index.htm.

State Resources

State financial aid for education is generally administered together with federal student aid, or it is provided directly to state colleges that are able to offer much lower tuition to state residents. Some state initiatives and organizations, however, do offer college-financing options that students should investigate.

College Savings Plan Network

This network is affiliated with the National Association of State Treasurers. The Web site offers links to state-sponsored savings and prepaid tuition plans, including the IRS 529 Plans in each state. The site also has information about federal resources, information for international students, and a free scholarship search. Find out more at www.collegesavings.org.

Leveraging Educational Assistance Partnership (LEAP)

Formerly known as State Student Incentive Grant (SSIG), this is a state-run financial aid program allowing states to receive matching funds for state residents from the federal government's Department of Education. You can reach the program by contacting:

Policy Development Division
Policy, Training, and Analysis Service
Office of Student Financial Assistance
Department of Education, Grants Branch
400 Maryland Avenue, SW
Washington, DC 20202-5447
Phone: 202-708-8242

College Organizations

The organizations listed in this section have been formed by professional associations or interest groups to help them pursue their own agendas. The resources they compile and offer, however, are useful for lots of students entering the college system. They're definitely worth a look!

Professional and minority organizations

There are several more minority organizations, but we list the two that are most active. Also check out the minority organizations listed in the section "Scholarship-granting organizations," later in this chapter.

Coalition of America's Colleges and Universities

Formed by education professionals, this organization provides a vast array of resources for students, parents, and educators. You'll find information on preparing for college, choosing the right college, paying for college, and many specific topics, including returning to school as a mature student, distance learning, and more. Its Web site is www.collegeispossible.org.

Hispanic Association of Colleges and Universities

The Hispanic Association of Colleges and Universities represents more than 300 member colleges in the United States, Puerto Rico, Latin America, and Spain. Member institutions in the United States represent less than 7 percent of higher education institutions nationwide, but they're home to more than two-thirds of all Hispanic college students. Here's the contact information:

Hispanic Association of Colleges and Universities
8415 Datapoint Drive, Suite 400
San Antonio, TX 78229
Phone: 210-692-3805
Fax: 210-692-0823
Web site: www.hacu.net
E-mail: hacu@hacu.net

National Association for College Admission Counseling (NACAC)

You can find out what issues in financial aid are being discussed — they're likely to affect you in the long run. This organization also provides detailed information about college fairs, preparation for college, and more. Check it out by contacting

National Association for College Admission Counseling
1631 Prince Street
Alexandria, VA 22314-2818
Phone: 703-836-2222
Fax: 703-836-8015
Web site: www.nacac.com

National Association of Student Financial Aid Administrators (NASFAA)

This well-organized organization is a good source for statistics and research about the future of financial aid.

National Association of Student Financial Aid Administrators
1129 20th Street, NW, Suite 400
Washington, DC 20036-3453
Phone: 202-785-0453
Fax: 202-785-1487
Web site: www.nasfaa.org

United Negro College Fund (UNCF)

This consortium of 39 historically black colleges and universities administers scholarship programs for minorities for several other foundations. It also offers $500 to $10,000 scholarships to eligible African-American students studying at a college in the consortium. You can reach the UNCF at:

United Negro College Fund Program Service
8260 Willow Oaks Corporate Drive
P.O. Box 10444
Fairfax, VA 22301-4511
Phone: 1-800-331-2244
Web site: www.uncf.org

California organizations

You may be thinking, "This doesn't seem fair." Why do we list the college organizations in California and not every other state? It's simple. We want to let you know what sorts of organizations exist so that you can check out what's available in your own state. We chose California because it has a huge population, and its organizations are more extensive than most.

Association of Independent California Colleges and Universities

The AICCU represents 76 independent colleges and universities based in California. The organization's Web site contains college applications, financial aid information, and even virtual tours of many of the schools. The AICCU can be reached at the following address:

Association of Independent California Colleges and Universities
1100 Eleventh Street, Suite 10
Sacramento, CA 95814
Phone: 916-446-7626
Fax: 916-446-7948
Web site: www.aiccu.edu

California Community Colleges

This organization represents 108 statewide community (or "two-year") colleges, organized into 72 districts. These schools teach more than 2.9 million students. You can reach this organization at the following address:

1102 Q Street
Sacramento, CA 95814-6511
Web site: www.cccco.edu

California State University System

This organization represents an institution of 23 campuses, 407,000 students, and 44,000 faculty and staff. Its Web site is a valuable portal site for any student looking for admission requirements, athletic programs, and financial aid details concerning the state university school system and the particular California State University campuses.

The organization can be reached at the following address:

401 Golden Shore
Long Beach, CA 90802-4210
Phone: 562-951-4000
Web site: www.calstate.edu

University of California System

This portal site for the huge University of California System is a great place to research the various study and financial aid options at the ten UC campuses throughout the state including Berkeley, Davis, Irvine, Los Angeles, Merced, Riverside, San Diego, San Francisco, Santa Barbara, and Santa Cruz. It also provides information about three National Labs based in California including Berkeley (LBNL), Livermore (LLNL), and Los Alamos (LANL). The organization can be reached at the following address:

University of California System
300 Lakeside Drive, Kaiser Center
Oakland, CA 94612-3550
Web site: www.ucop.edu

Resources about Specific Topics

Lots of topics are of interest to students looking for cash for college, but the ones we list here are the ones we consider particularly important. Enjoy!

Avoiding scams and fraud

You've probably heard the old expression "A fool and his money are soon parted." Thousands of very smart people, however, are taken for a ride every year through phony scholarship scams, fake financial aid applications, and other trickery and chicanery.

We discuss how to recognize scholarship scams in Chapter 4, but the following resources provide additional information and people to contact if you have questions or want to report suspicious offers.

Department of Education's list of Nationally Recognized Accrediting Agencies

Make sure that the school enticing you with an offer is legitimate. The Web site is www.ed.gov/offices/OPE/accreditation/natlagencies.html.

Federal Trade Commission Scholar Scam

If you think you've been taken in a scam, these people can help out.
Phone: 1-877-FTC-HELP (1-877-382-4357)
Phone: 1-866-653-4261
Web site: www.ftc.gov/scholarshipscams

You can see the FTC's lists of known scams at www.ftc.gov/bcp/conline/edcams/scholarship.

You can check out the defendants in the FTC's most recent scholarship fraud legal actions at www.ftc.gov/bcp/conline/edcams/scholarship/cases.htm

FinAid

This free public service Web site has lots of information about scholarship scams. The Web site address is www.finaid.org.

National Fraud Information Center

P.O. Box 65868
Washington, DC 20035
Phone: 1-800-876-7060 or 202-835-0159
Web site: www.fraud.com

Various college Web sites

Many legitimate colleges include a section on scholarship scams or post alerts for known scams. Some of the better sites include Purdue University (www.purdue.edu/DFA/sandg/scams.htm) and UCLA (www.college.ucla.edu/UP/SRC/scam.htm)

Loan consolidation and information sites

Okay, okay. This book is supposed to be about free money, not loans, but it can't hurt to give you a little related information.

Department of Education Direct Consolidation Loan Program

This site is for borrowers, schools and lenders. It explains how consolidation works generally and provides details of government plans. We talk about these types of loans in Chapter 6. Here's some contact information:

Phone: 1-800-557-7392 (toll-free)
Phone: 1-800-557-7395 (for TTY users)
Web site: loanconsolidation.ed.gov/ (no "www" prefix)

Department of Education Loan Guarantee Agency Site

If your parents can't find a lending institution for their FFEL PLUS Loan, each state has a *guaranty agency* that can provide a list of appropriate local lending institutions. You can find a directory of these agencies at www.ed.gov/Programs/bastmp/SGA.htm.

Direct Loan Servicing Center

If you need to find out about obtaining forbearance or cancellation of your Direct PLUS Loan, call the DLSC at 1-800-848-0979.

Kaploan

This portal site (www.kaploan.com) offers links to resources about student loans, student loan consolidations, scholarships and other financial aid, and general college matters.

National Student Loan Data System

Another great resource operated by the U.S. Department of Education, this site (www.nslds.ed.gov) is the department's central database for student loans. Information on all government-based loan programs and a glossary of loans terminology are available. In addition, this site allows students to track their own loans, update contact information if they move, and get ideas about different repayment options. This secure site requires you to register beforehand, and you can obtain personal information only after submitting your name and PIN.

Sallie Mae

This organization has tons of useful information for students and parents alike, including information on loans and consolidations. Here's how to reach Sallie Mae:

Phone: 1-888-2-SCHOOL (1-888-272-4665)
Web site: `www.salliemae.com/manage/consol.html`

Private lenders in the student loan business

There are far too many private lenders active in the student aid sector to mention them all here — but the following list includes a few that have particularly useful information on their Web sites.

Citibank

The banking giant offers step-by-step information on the student loan process, along with tips, counseling, and a ton of other useful resources.

Phone: 1-800-967-2400 or 605-331-0821
Web site: `www.studentloan.com`

Educaid

Operated by Wachovia Corporation (an organization that merged with First Union), this Web site offers information and online seminars for borrowers. Information targeted to college financial aid administrators and high school counselors is also available.

Phone: 1-800-EDUCAID (1-800-338-2243)
Web site: `www.educaid.com`

Independence Federal Savings Bank

Much of this organization's information is simplified, making it easy to understand. Its motto is "The nicest bank in the world," so we simply had to list it here!

Phone: 202-628-5500
Web site: `www.ifsb.com`

U.S. Bank

It's not obvious from the home page, but U.S. bank operates a separate area on its Web site devoted to student banking. You'll find information on scholarships and general college tips along with details about loans and other financial aid.

Phone: 1-800-444-1244, extension 5702
Web site: www.usbank.com (click on "Personal," then "Products & Services," and finally "Student Banking")

Resources for international students

An international student is an American student attending an institution in another country or a student from another country studying in the United States. The resources listed here are for both types of students.

The College Handbook Foreign Student Supplement

Produced by The College Board (www.collegeboard.com), this guidebook is available in selected major bookstores in countries such as Canada, Australia, and the European Union countries, or by writing to

College Board Publications
Box 886
New York, NY 10101-6992
USA

EduPASS

This site (www.edupass.org) provides information for international students interested in studying in the United States. Topics include financial aid, admissions, visas, and culture shock. One page lists the U.S. colleges that give financial aid to foreign undergraduate students, while another page offers links and resources about scholarships available to foreign students.

International Education Finance Corporation

Loans for foreign study are available through this organization, whether you are an American wishing to study abroad or an international student wishing to study in the United States. Contact the organization at

International Education Finance Corporation
222 Forbes Road, Suite 406
Braintree, MA 02184
Phone: 781-843-5334
Phone: 1-888-296-4332 (toll-free)
E-mail: contact@iefc.com

Institute of International Education

You'll find lots of information about scholarship programs here (including the Fulbright Scholarship that is administered by the IIE). It has offices around the country and around the world, but the main organizational headquarters are located in Washington, D.C.

Phone: 212-883-8200
Fax: 212-984-5452
Web site: www.iie.org

Overseas Educational Advising Centers

Operated by The College Board (www.collegeboard.com), these centers offer information, tips, and links for individuals who want to study abroad. The site is apps.collegeboard.com/cbsearch/center/searchOverseas AdvCenter.jsp. (Note there's no "www" prefix.)

Rotary International

Rotary International's Ambassadorial Scholarships provide millions of dollars in grant money for students to study abroad. Find additional information later in this chapter, in the section "Scholarship-granting organizations."

The Study Overseas Site

As the name suggests, this site (www.studyoverseas.com) is chock-full of information about studying overseas, including professional advice, personal anecdotes, and searches.

Test of English as a Foreign Language (TOEFL)

Foreign students for whom English is not their first language must submit the results of this test when applying for entry to American colleges. On the Web site (www.toefl.org), you can find the testing center nearest to you, test dates, fees, registration information, and more.

United States Information Agency, Office of Public Liaison

This agency provides information about Fulbright Scholarships and a bevy of other interesting resources. You can contact the agency at:

301 4th Street, SW, Room 602
Washington, DC 20547
Phone: 202-619-4355
Fax: 202-619-6988
E-mail: inquiry@usia.gov

U.S. Network for Education Information

This organization provides information to American students wishing to study at international schools and to international students wishing to study and live in the United States. Here's how to reach them:

Phone: 1-800-424-1616
Web site: www.ed.gov/NLE/USNEI/index.html
E-mail: USNEI@ed.gov

Standardized tests

Most standardized tests are administered by the College Board (www.college board.com) or Educational Testing Service (www.ets.org), so don't be surprised if the following telephone numbers and Web links lead to these organizations.

Advanced Placement Exams

Advanced Placement courses taken in high school lead to AP exams (and possibly to AP scholarships). These can be used as equivalencies for college courses, depending on the particular college. For more information, call or log on:

Phone: 609-921-9000
Web site: http://apcentral.collegeboard.com/ (no "www" prefix)

American College Test (ACT)

ACT is one of the standard academic aptitude tests that colleges require to assess prospective applicants for overall admission. Some schools and third-party scholarship organizations also use the ACT to award merit-based scholarships. ACT is also the independent not-for-profit organization that administers the test.

Phone: 319-337-1000
Web site: www.act.org

College-Level Examination Program (CLEP)

These examinations can be used for equivalencies for college courses, depending on the particular college. The Web site is www.collegeboard.com/clep.

PLAN

Like the PSAT is to the SAT, this test is taken prior to writing the ACT. Generally taken in the sophomore year of high school, it helps students gauge their likely results on the ACT. Depending on results, students may choose to do extensive study and even take courses to help them improve their results.

Phone: 319-337-1029
Web site: www.act.org/plan/index.html

Preliminary Scholastic Aptitude Test (PSAT)

The PSAT is like the SAT I (Scholastic Aptitude Test) but shorter and slightly easier. It is taken to prepare for the SAT I, usually in the junior year of high school. The PSAT is a qualifier for National Merit Scholarships.

Phone: 609-771-7070
Web site: www.psat.org

Scholastic Aptitude Test (SAT)

These tests are offered several times per year at testing centers around the country and around the world. The SAT is divided into the SAT I (testing general aptitude and reasoning skills) and several SAT II tests (focused on specific subjects).

Phone: 609-771-7600
Web site: www.sat.org

FairTest — The National Center for Fair & Open Testing

If you want to get information about fair testing (that is, testing that is standardized without obvious or hidden racial, gender, or sexist stereotyping), an organization called FairTest wants to hear from you. You can reach the organization at

FairTest
342 Broadway
Cambridge, MA 02139
Phone: 617-864-4810
Fax: 617-497-2224
Web site: www.fairtest.org

Private and Corporate Resources

If you thought government resources were never-ending, you're really going to get overwhelmed by all the private resources available. We list a few of them here, but *many* more are available. The scholarship-granting organizations listed represent only the tip of the proverbial iceberg. For complete lists of scholarships and the organizations that grant them, consult some of the directories we list later in this chapter in the section "Useful books for the college bound." Good luck!

General information sources

These are some of the best sources of college information. One of the reasons they're such great resources is that they include lots of links to *other* fantastic sites. Always check these sites for the resources they list.

Chronicle of Higher Education

This magazine and Web site (www.chronicle.com) are the places to go for information about issues, news, statistics, and resources relating to college and university administration. Some of the useful resources include lists of college endowments, grants awarded to colleges in a given year, and a wide assortment of categorized links. Premium searches require registration.

College Board

This national membership organization of post-secondary institutions provides extensive information for college bound students and their families. Do not miss this resource! Check it out at www.collegeboard.com.

College Scholarship Service

Administered by the College Board, this service assists in the administration and distribution of financial aid for colleges and universities, as well as state programs and private scholarship organizations. CSS administers the Financial Aid PROFILE.

Phone: 609-951-1025
Web site: profileonline.collegeboard.com (no "www" prefix)

CollegeNET

This site (www.collegenet.com) offers a college search, a scholarship search, financial aid information, lots of helpful links, and many other resources.

Colleges, College Scholarships, and Financial Aid Page

This site covers a range of topics and offers a free scholarship search, as well as links to information about colleges throughout the country, listed by state. You'll probably want to avoid the advertising smack dab in the middle of the site, but hey, the resources are free, so it's hard to complain too much about the ads. You can find this site at college-scholarships.com (no "www" prefix).

College Xpress

Search for colleges, scholarships, and student loans at this Web site (www. collegeXpress.com). The site also has information about planning, a college financial aid calculator, and good forms to download.

EStudentLoan

This site (www.eStudentLoan.com) features a helpful loan finder and tools to compare competing loans, along with other information to assist you in finding lenders in your particular state. The only drawback is that you need to register to use its services.

FastAID

This site (www.fastaid.com) is rather flashy, but it has a good free scholarship search and access to other information. You need to register to use the services, and you may get some pop-up ads, but it's worth a look.

Fast Web

Use this site (www.fastweb.com) to quickly find out which scholarships you qualify for based on an impressive search engine. You create a personal student profile that is then matched against a database of 600,000 scholarships worth over $1 billion from over 4,000 American colleges! It's a free service but includes lots of advertising to help finance it, so have patience — the results can be quite rewarding.

FinAid

The Financial Aid Information site (www.finaid.org) has lots of information for students looking for free money, including advice and resources.

Also check out the calculators that help you play "what if" by plugging in all sorts of different scenarios at www.finaid.org/finaid/calculators.

HispanicScholarship.com

This site (www.HispanicScholarship.com) lists scholarships specifically designated for Hispanic students and also offers support materials, including checklists, sample letters, resumes and other documents, and tips.

Mapping Your Future

The broad-based Web site helps students and their families plan for a career, select a school, and find out how to pay for their education. Resources include student loan counseling, standardized testing information, and scholarship resources. This is a not-for-profit initiative sponsored by certain guaranty agencies that participate in the Federal Family Education Loan (FFEL) program. It's free, accurate, and if you're considering a FFEL, definitely worth the effort. Check it out at mapping-your-future.org (no "www" prefix).

Sallie Mae Wired Scholar

This excellent site (salliemae.wiredscholar.com — no "www" prefix — or www.wiredscholar.com) has a scholarship search plus lots of information about selecting a college, applying for admissions and scholarships, and obtaining financial aid.

Scholarship Resource Network Express

This Web site (www.srnexpress.com) offers a free scholarship search in its database of 8,000 programs. This private company also has a commercial component.

ScholarStuff

This site (www.scholarstuff.com and www.scholarstuff.com/webring.htm) has a lot to offer. At ScholarStuff, you find a college directory, a graduate school directory, a terrific Net guide, and a popular chat network. The Net Guide lists links and relevant books on topics such as scholarships for specific minorities, student travel, and job searching. Another cool feature of the site is the Webring that links 53 active sites concerned with higher education.

Student Awards

This site (studentawards.com — no "www" prefix) is another free search engine that helps you find the scholarships for which you are eligible.

Texas Guaranteed Student Loan Corporation

This is a not-for-profit corporation (www.tgslc.org) that administers the Federal Family Education Loan (FFEL) program. Yes, it's focused on Texas — and offers a vast list of lenders and other state resources — but its "Adventures in Education" Web site (www.adventuresineducation.org) also has lots of general information about the college financial aid process.

U.S. News and World Report

The "Education" section of this excellent magazine and Web site is full of important information for students, parents, and educators alike. Each year, it publishes a special edition that ranks America's Best Colleges according to various criteria. You'll find competitiveness, matriculation numbers, and lots more to compare. The Web site (www.usnews.com) also offers a scholarship search and a guide to government programs.

Scholarship-granting organizations

There's simply no way we can list all scholarship-granting organizations — there are literally thousands of them! The ones we've chosen to list here are some of the larger organizations that give out some of the largest awards, along with a few of the more interesting or better-known foundations, even if they don't cumulatively give out the most money. For fuller lists of awards, consult any of the many scholarship directories published by the College Board, Princeton Review, Petersen's, and others.

American Indian Graduate Center (AIGC)

We talk about this organization in Chapter 22. Here's where to find it:

4520 Montgomery Boulevard, NE, Suite 1B
Albuquerque, NM 87109
Phone: 1-800-628-1920 or 505-881-4584
Web site: www.aigc.com

American Legion

The organization offers extensive need-based and merit-based awards, a search service (for a nominal charge), and a guidebook called *Get a Lift*. There are local chapters all over the United States and many other countries around the world. Both the American Legion and the American Legion Auxiliary (a women's patriotic service organization) administer scholarships and other student support.

American Legion
National Headquarters, Indianapolis Office
700 North Pennsylvania Street
P.O. Box 1055
Indianapolis, IN 46206
Phone: 317-630-1200
Fax: 317-630-1223
Web site: www.legion.org
E-mail: acy@legion.org

American Legion Auxiliary
777 North Meridian Street, Third Floor
Indianapolis, IN 46204
Phone: 317-955-3845
Fax: 317-955-3884
Web site: www.legion-aux.org
E-mail: alahq@legion-aux.org
Auxiliary scholarships:
Web site: www.legion-aux.org/scholarships/docs/scholarships.html

California Labor Federation, AFL-CIO

Several $1,000 scholarships are available to California AFL-CIO members or their dependents. The union has programs in other states, so check the main Web site for details, and ask your parents about their affiliation.

California Labor Federation, AFL-CIO
Scholarship Department
417 Montgomery Street, Suite 300
San Francisco, CA 94104
Web site: www.aflcio.org

Coca-Cola Scholars Foundation, Inc.

The soft drink company gives away 200 awards of $4,000 and 50 awards of $20,000 annually, based mostly on leadership, but other qualities, such as academic achievement, community involvement, and extracurricular activities, are also considered.

Coca-Cola Scholars Foundation, Inc.
P.O. Box 442
Atlanta, GA 30301-0442
Phone: 1-800-306-2653
E-mail: scholars@na.ko.com
Web site: www.thecoca-colacompany.com

Daughters of the American Revolution (DAR)

We talk about this organization in Chapter 22. Address requests for scholarship information to

Office of Committees, NSDAR
Scholarships
1776 D Street, NW
Washington, DC 20006-5303
Web site: www.dar.org

Elks National Foundation

This service organization has over a million members in over 2,000 chapters across the country. It gives out 1,000 awards a year for undergraduates studying inside the United States and in certain institutions in other countries. The amount of the Elks Most Valuable Student Scholarship ranges from $1,000 to $15,000. For more information, contact

The Benevolent and Protective Order of the Elks of the United States of America
2750 N. Lakeview Avenue
Chicago, IL 60614-1889
Phone: 773-755-4700
Fax: 773-755-4790
Web site: www.elks.org

Gates Millennium Scholars Program (GMSP)

We discuss this program in Chapter 22. Here's the contact information:

Gates Millennium Scholars
P.O. Box 10500
Fairfax, VA 22031-8044
Phone: 1-877-690-GMSP (1-877-690-4677)
Web site: www.gmsp.org

Hispanic Scholarship Fund (HSF)

We discuss this organization in Chapter 22.

Hispanic Scholarship Fund
55 Second Street, Suite 1500
San Francisco, CA 94105
Phone: 1-877-HSF-INFO (1-877-473-4636)
Web site: www.hsf.net

Miss America Organization

We discuss this organization in Chapter 22.

Miss America Organization
Two Miss America Way, Suite 1000
Atlantic City, NJ 08401
Phone: 609-345-7571 (general)
Phone: 609-345-7571, extension 27 (for scholarship information)
Fax: 609-347-6079
Web site: www.missamerica.org/scholarships/
E-mail: info@missamerica.org

National Association for the Advancement of Colored People (NAACP)

We discuss this organization in Chapter 22. You can obtain a Scholarship Package by contacting

NAACP Education Department Scholarships
4805 Mount Hope Drive
Baltimore, MD 21215
Web site: www.naacp.org/work/education/eduscholarship.shtml

National Merit Scholarship Corporation (NMSC)

This not-for-profit organization administers two prestigious privately financed annual scholarship competitions: the National Merit Scholarship Program and the National Achievement Scholarship Program. Special scholarships sponsored by various large corporations and other organizations are also administered through the National Merit Program.

National Merit Scholarship Corporation
1560 Sherman Avenue, Suite 200
Evanston, IL 60201-4897
Phone: 847-866-5100
Web site: www.nationalmerit.org

National Honor Society (NHS)

We discuss this organization in Chapter 22.

National Honor Society
1904 Association Drive
Reston, VA 20191-1537
Phone: 703-860-0200
Web site: www.nhs.us
E-mail: nhs@nhs.us

National Urban League (NUL)

We discuss this organization in Chapter 22.

The National Urban League, Inc.
120 Wall Street
New York, NY 10005
Phone: 212-558-5300
Fax: 212-344-5332
Web site: www.nul.org
E-mail: info@nul.org

You can also download the *NUL Scholarship Guidebook* at www.nul.org/caaa/scholarship/school_guidebook.html.

Organization of Chinese Americans (OCA)

We discuss this organization in Chapter 22.

Organization of Chinese Americans
Gates Millennium Scholars
1001 Connecticut Avenue, NW, Suite 601
Washington, DC 20036
Web site: www.ocanatl.org

Princess Grace Foundation

Scholarships from the foundation of the late former actress (and Princess of Monaco) are for artistic excellence, ranging from $2,500 to $25,000.

Princess Grace Foundation-USA
150 East 58th Street, 21st Floor
New York, NY 10155
Phone: 212-317-1470
Fax: 212-317-1473
Web site: www.pgfusa.com

Rotary International

This esteemed service organization betters the community in many ways. The best-known scholarships offered through Rotary International are the Ambassadorial Scholarships for students studying in another country. In the 2002/2003 academic year alone, more than 1,100 scholarships were granted to students from 69 countries. Rotary grants total about $26 million. This makes it one of the largest private scholarship organizations in the world.

Rotary International
One Rotary Center
1560 Sherman Avenue
Evanston, IL 60201
Phone: 847-866-3000
Fax: 847-328-8554 or 847-328-8281
Web site: www.rotary.org

Regulating organizations

Athletic and fine arts scholarships are regulated by independent not-for-profit organizations. If you want to know anything about the process of receiving such awards or getting recruited, these are the places to go.

National Collegiate Athletic Association

If you're at all interested in athletic scholarship options, you owe it to yourself to research this best-known and well-organized college athletic regulating organization.

National Collegiate Athletic Association
Membership Services
P.O. Box 6222
Indianapolis, IN 46206-6222
Phone: 317-917-6222
Fax: 317-917-6622
Web site: www.ncaa.org

Registration forms and a brochure are available at www.ncaaclearinghouse.net or by writing to

Initial-Eligibility Clearinghouse
2255 N. Dubuque Road
P.O. Box 4044
Iowa City, IA 52243-4044

You can also call the NCAA publications hotline at 1-800-638-3731 and ask for a free copy of the *Guide for the College-Bound Student-Athlete*. It's a great reference for any student heading to college and hoping for an athletic scholarship. The guide makes sense of the often-complex rules and regulations surrounding athletic scholarships.

If you get further involved in athletic scholarships, you'll need to know all about National Letters of Intent (NLI). You can find this information at www.national-letter.org or by calling 205-458-3013.

National Association for Intercollegiate Athletics (NAIA)

Though lesser known than the NCAA, the NAIA organization is also active in college athletic scholarships at its 309 member colleges. The Web site is www.naia.org.

Download its *Guide for the College Bound Athlete* at www.naia.org/local/collegebound.html.

National Office for Arts Accreditation

The National Office for Arts Accreditation (www.arts-accredit.org) offers information on the following:

- National Association of Schools of Music:
  www.arts-accredit.org/nasm/nasm.htm

- National Association of Schools of Art and Design:
  www.arts-accredit.org/nasad/default.htm

- National Association of Schools of Theater:
  www.arts-accredit.org/nast/default.htm

- National Association of Schools of Dance:
  www.arts-accredit.org/nasd/default.htm

Useful books for the college bound

The following are the most recent versions available at press time. However most of these books are published annually or revised periodically. Make sure you get the most up-to-date publication before you buy.

- *The ACT For Dummies* by Suzee Vlk (Wiley)

- *Athletic Scholarships* by Andy Clark and Amy Clark (Checkmark Books)

- *The Government Financial Aid Book: The Insider's Guide to State and Federal Government Grants and Loans* edited by Student Financial Services (Perpetual Press)

- *Peterson's Basic Guidance Set: 4 Year Colleges/Scholarships, Grants & Prizes/College Money Handbook/2 Year Colleges* edited by Peterson's Guides (Peterson's Guides)

- *SAT I For Dummies* by Suzee Vlk (Wiley)

- *SAT Vocabulary For Dummies* by Suzee Vlk (Wiley)

- *The Scholarship Advisor: Hundreds of Thousands of Scholarships Worth More Than $1 Billion* by Christopher Vuturo (Princeton Review)

- *The Scholarship Book: The Complete Guide to Private-Sector Scholarships, Fellowships, Grants and Loans for the Undergraduate* by National Scholarship Research Service (Prentice Hall Press)

- *Scholarship Handbook* edited by The College Board (College Entrance Examination Board)

Part VI
The Part of Tens

The 5th Wave   By Rich Tennant

"WE WERE LOOKING FOR A COLLEGE THAT OFFERED AN EXTENSIVE NIGHT SCHOOL CURRICULUM."

In this part . . .

The Part of Tens is our favorite part because we get to boil down all that you really need to know into handy bite-sized lists. You can find out what to do, what not to do, and where to look when prospecting for free money. After reading our lists, you may be inspired to go back to some of the previous chapters, and we encourage you to do so. The lists provide the basics, and the chapters hold the details. In short, you need both to accomplish your task of winning as much free money as possible for your college education.

Chapter 21

The Ten Best Ways to Get Free Money for College

*N*o matter when you start planning for college, you can spend only so much time trying to get your hands on free money. So you have to assess all your options and opportunities, and then prioritize your actions. So, what are the *most* important things to do?

Do Well in School

We have to admit that some people do obtain grants, need-based funding, and certain types of scholarships without a high GPA. However, here are two very good reasons why investing extra time in your schoolwork makes good financial sense:

✔ **If your grades aren't high enough, you won't qualify for college at all.** Remember, even *if* you can obtain scholarships for your leadership activities, athletic skills, or musical talent, you still need to get into college academically. And, in case you were wondering, if you're awarded a scholarship or grant but can't qualify for college, you don't get to keep the scholarship money. Sorry about that.

✔ **Most merit-based funding goes to students with high marks.** Sure, some awards are based mainly on community service and other qualities, but even these scholarships tend to have minimum GPA requirements. If it comes down to two students with the same qualities, the applicant with the higher marks typically gets the scholarship. Plus, most of the money that's offered automatically (meaning that you don't have to apply for it) is for high marks.

Besides, the whole point of going to college is to get an *education.* If you're not interested in (or not good at) studying while you're in high school, chances are you'll have a tough time in college. If students work hard only to get the money to pay for their schooling, they've missed the point entirely.

Take the Tests

Standardized test results may be required to apply for college, scholarships, and other awards, or they may be used to get you through college more quickly. Read on to find out how all this works.

ACTs, SATs, and PSATs — it's all in the acronyms

Pretty much every college in this fair land will want to see your scores from either the *Scholastic Aptitude Test* (SAT) or the *American College Test* (ACT) as part of your application for admission. Even if the college you want to attend doesn't require your test results, it's a good idea to take one (or both) of the tests. Many merit-based scholarships require students to take the tests and exceed a minimum score to qualify.

Before you take the SATs, you'll want to take the *Preliminary Scholastic Aptitude Test* (PSAT). Blowing off the PSAT can be a big mistake. Besides being used as a college scholarship indicator, the PSAT is a qualifier for the National Merit Scholarship Program. If you don't take the PSAT, you won't be eligible to win a National Merit Scholarship, no matter how smart you may be and no matter how high your GPA.

Just to show how important the PSAT is to qualifying for the National Merit Scholarship program, the test is often referred to as the PSAT/NMSQT, an acronym for *Preliminary Scholastic Aptitude Test/National Merit Scholarship Qualifying Test.* Other than its value as a qualifier, the PSAT can help you discover your strengths and weaknesses before you take the SAT. Plus, nobody else needs to see your PSAT mark if you prefer. In contrast, your current (and last six) SATs must be sent to your prospective colleges as part of your application package, regardless of how well you do.

Advanced Placement exams

You can experience the fascinating, challenging world of college courses while you're still in high school. Do you have to make a fake college student ID? No, just take an *Advanced Placement* (AP) course!

AP courses are valuable in preparing you for your college curriculum, but they also have a financial incentive as well. If you take the $80 AP exams (and do well), you can apply these courses toward your freshman year at college. Pass enough of the 23 available exams with high enough scores, and you'll start your first year as a *sophomore* at any of more than 1,400 participating colleges. Exactly how many courses are "enough" varies from college to college. Many require that you pass only four AP courses, getting a score of at least 4 (or, sometimes, even 3) out of 5, to qualify for sophomore standing. That means you'd pay $320 instead of the usual $4,500 for a year at UCLA, or $40,000 at Columbia!

AP exams are taken in May. Thus, if you take these courses in your senior year, your prospective colleges won't receive your results until the summer before you start college. Consequently, let them know well in advance if you plan to take the AP tests and want to be considered for advanced standing. Ask your high school counselor and college admissions officer for details.

The CLEP

The *College-Level Examination Program* (CLEP) is similar to the AP program. More than 2,900 colleges give advanced standing or credit for CLEP exams. The exams each cost $50, and they cover a wide range of subjects. Scores range from 20 to 80, and many colleges require students to get 50 to 60 in order to qualify for advanced standing. Find out more information at www.collegeboard.org/clep.

Take the Right Courses

The *types* of courses you take count a lot more than you may think. Many admissions officers and scholarship committee members look for how much you've *challenged* yourself during high school. They look for the core courses, and they also take notice how many math, science, foreign language, and other challenging courses are listed on your transcript.

Some of these core courses — including English, algebra, geometry, history, and geography — are required courses for many fields of study. Without the required courses, you simply won't get into the particular major, no matter how high your grades in other courses may be. The tougher courses also lead to Advanced Placement tests, as we discuss earlier in this chapter.

Students also need to know how to study well before they get to college. The independent atmosphere at most colleges demands dedication and excellent study habits that successful students pick up in high school through taking advanced courses. If you don't know how to study in high school, you still may be able to get good marks. If, however, you don't figure out how to study by the time you reach college, you're going to have a tough time ahead.

Arrange Your Finances Strategically

Make college preparation a team event, including your entire family — and your family financial planner, accountant, or banker. If you want to attend college, chances are your siblings will probably want to go to college someday, too. It's best for your parents to plan ahead as far as possible to ensure that they have what it takes, or at least ensure that they've arranged their finances so that you'll be able to obtain the most free money possible.

What should they do? First of all, your parents should talk to their accountant to get some ideas about minimizing their tax liability with respect to educational expenses over the years. Long-term planning requires professional insight and experience. And don't forget that tax laws change frequently, so fine-tune your educational investments regularly.

Next, start saving. Sure, if your family has too much income, you won't get any need-based money. But you have to make a fair amount not to qualify for anything. Besides, if your family earns less than $50,000 in the year you apply, savings aren't usually taken into account.

Your parents can use this fact to help them make future plans. If your mother was considering taking a few years off, or if your father was planning to retire early, there's no better time than the year before you apply for college.

What can your parents do with their savings to maximize your assessed need? In general, put more into home equity and retirement funds, and less into bank accounts and the stock market. When governments are considering your need, they don't typically include your primary residence and retirement funds in determining your *expected family contribution* (EFC).

Lots of scholarship committees use the same formulas as the U.S. Department of Education to determine need, so this practice will also help you when applying outside of government circles. Some colleges and scholarship committees, however, have their own way to determine need. They may include the entire net worth of the family, so financial strategizing may not necessarily help you in these circumstances.

Another thing about bank accounts: If your grandparents or other relatives want to set up an educational fund for you, thank them sweetly but ask that they not give any money to you — yet. Let them set aside the funds in a separate bank account, and then hand it over to you after you've received your need-based money.

A final note: If possible, have your parents file their taxes well before the April 15 deadline. Both your FAFSA and PROFILE applications will benefit from early submission, so it would be helpful if your parents' taxes can be done before the April 15 date.

Get Involved

We've said it before and we'll say it again: Get involved in community events and be a leader!

Realistically, you can't do a whole lot to change your situation in terms of receiving need-based money. For academic scholarships, you need to study, but you may not be able to break into the highest grade point levels no matter how hard you try. But *anyone* can get involved in his or her community.

Thousands of scholarships recognize community involvement. Lots of people, however, are members of service organizations and clubs. The way to set yourself apart from everyone else is by being a *community leader*. You organize that local soup kitchen! You throw a fundraiser for the local kids' crisis line! You arrange for your church group to read to folks at the convalescent home every week! Whatever you can do, do it!

Get to Know Important People

When the time comes for you to gather letters of recommendation, whom can you ask? Now is the time to start developing relationships that will lead to excellent recommendation letters. Get to know your school principal or a particular high school teacher. If he or she has a solid understanding of what makes you tick, your recommendation letter will read a lot better than just the standard "form letter reference" that other students may receive.

Find out which people in your community are the most important in the areas that interest you and approach them. The editor of your local newspaper, for example, may welcome a column by you on matters of interest to teens — and this kind of recommendation will certainly impress the scholarship committee for the journalists' organization where you might eventually apply.

Prepare

You've got a lot to do, but if you give yourself the time that you need, you can methodically bring together the necessary information to submit a fantastic (and winning) scholarship application package. This package includes the following elements:

✔ **The applications:** Make sure that you have the most up-to-date forms to fill out. And make several photocopies of these forms so that you can make your mistakes *before* you fill out the final version. Fill out one copy immediately (after you've made copies), and then use a yellow marker to indicate what information is missing . . . and then *find* the missing information. Don't wait until the night before you need to send the package to realize that you don't have key facts or addresses.

✔ **Financial information:** You need accurate information on yourself and your parents, including federal and local tax returns, bank statements, employment income, investment income, other income, the value of major assets (especially real estate), and business records.

✔ **Documents:** Ask for copies of your transcripts a few months before you need them. If there's a paperwork mix-up, you need to have that dealt with *pronto*. Then again, if you transferred from another school, you should get your transcripts before you move. You also want to keep copies of your awards, certificates, citizenship papers (if relevant), and any other significant documents in your life on hand and ready to go.

✔ **Your bio and resume:** Your bio and resume are important because they tell the scholarship committee who you are. Keep a diary or journal of your own history, focusing on significant events and accomplishments that will look impressive to a scholarship committee. Make note of all the details, such as full names and dates for employment and volunteering, awards that you've won, competitions in which you participated, and all the assorted activities that make up your life.

✔ **Essays:** The only times we've heard of essays being successfully pulled together at the last minute is from students who had already used the essays in several other applications. All that was needed was simple tweaking to make the essay relevant to the scholarship committee. Generally, finding the perfect topic is difficult. You then need to outline your thesis, structure your points, add humor and humanity, and then revise, revise, revise. All this work takes time and effort. You can't pull an "all-nighter" just before the application is due and expect to turn out a winning essay.

✔ **Cover letters:** We know that a cover letter seems like something you can do at the last minute, but as you've probably figured out by now, nothing is effective when done at the last minute. The cover letter is the first thing the scholarship committee sees (and uses to judge you), so make sure that it's neat, concise, and effective. If you or a friend is skilled at simple graphic arts, create an elegant and professional-looking letter-head. And get yourself an e-mail address that doesn't sound foolish. You may like being, for example, BabeMagnet@loveme.com, but that won't impress the selection committee.

- **Recommendation letters:** Talk to your potential references months in advance to ensure that they're willing to send a recommendation on your behalf, and to ensure that they know you well enough to say the right things. Prepare a "sample" letter to help make the process easier for them. If the recommendation letter must be sent directly to the committee, remind all references to send in their letters a few weeks before the due date.

- **Interview responses:** Many colleges and scholarship committees want to meet you before they accept you or give you money, so you need to know how to conduct an interview. This interview is your opportunity to wow them! You need to present yourself and your achievements in the best possible light, but resist being boastful or arrogant. Be interesting, but don't dominate the conversation. Prepare stories, but don't memo-rize to the point that you sound unnatural. Conduct practice interviews well in advance of having to appear before a scholarship committee. This way, when you find yourself in front of a scholarship committee, you'll already know how to respond to that once-terrifying request, "Tell us a little about yourself."

Apply for Winnable Scholarships

You have to be realistic in assessing your scholarship prospects. You don't have time to apply for every scholarship listed in those huge directories, nor is there any reason to do so even if you had the time.

First, find the scholarships that pertain to you by some connection — your family, friends, employment, organizations, or anything else. These awards are the ones that almost jump out at you because they look like they're writ-ten expressly for you. Make these scholarships the first ones on your list.

Next, go through those big scholarship directories and focus on the cate-gories that are most relevant to you. You may ask, for example, *why should I win an award just because I happen to be born to Armenian parents?* Simple: Because you can! Sometimes, fate just smiles on you: Apply and enjoy.

Then, Apply For The Rest

Okay, you don't have to be *that* realistic. If you have time after applying for your best prospects, keep sending out more applications. After all, you've already put together your information, transcripts, essays, and other materials. Why not use these materials to apply to scholarships that hundreds of thousands of other students apply to as well?

Hey, somebody has to win. How do you really know the quality of the other applicants? After all your preparation and revising, you've assembled a solid scholarship application package, right? Besides, we've found that the more applications you send out — good applications, mind you! — the more likely you are to win *something*. That said, don't bother applying to those scholarships for which you are obviously not eligible. If, for example, the particular award is for people over 25 and you're only 17, move on. You can still find plenty of other awards out there!

Follow Up

To make sure that your applications arrive well before the deadline, send them early and then e-mail or call to confirm. Send thank-you notes to your principal, teachers, counselors, or anyone else who helped with the application process. Be especially sure to send thank-you notes to anyone who wrote a recommendation letter for you.

You aren't doing this just to be polite. The committee may contact your references for more information about you. It would look pretty cool if the person recommending you can say, "I just happen to have a thank-you card from Marie here on my desk. She's such a conscientious student!"

Finally, after the awards have been announced, send thank-you notes to the scholarship committees. Send them whether you won or not. You may wish to apply again next year, and you want them to have good memories of you.

If you *did* win an award, go beyond a simple thank-you by also sending a letter later in the year telling the committee how its money has been put to good use. Let the folks there know how much you're learning and how you plan to make the world a better place with the education you received through the committee's generosity. Being humble and ingratiating never hurts.

Chapter 22

Ten Places You May Not Think to Look for Free Money

. . . .

In This Chapter

▶ Looking beyond the obvious

▶ Getting money from groups you want to join

. . . .

*I*n this chapter, we profile a few of the scholarships, funds, and other sources of free money that escape the attention of many students. This list is not complete — the list can *never* be complete because scholarship sources are forever changing. The purpose of this chapter is to help you think beyond the obvious when searching for scholarships that apply to you.

Your School Guidance Counselor

School counselors are trained people who want you to do well at high school and beyond. Some counselors are better at counseling than others, but *all* counselors are paid to help students just like you. Most students don't know, however, that local and state governments reward many school districts when student test scores go up, and school officials are promoted when their students' college admission statistics increase. Thus, asking questions may help your school as well as you!

Most counselors know huge amounts of information about colleges, financial aid packages, and scholarships. Your counselor will also likely know some of the scholarships you may qualify for based on your marks, extracurricular activities, and academic goals. Provided you start early enough in your education, your counselor can also help you figure out how to raise your marks to get the scholarships for which you don't yet qualify.

National Honor Society

You've probably already thought about the *National Honor Society* (NHS). After all, it's one of the better-known organizations in the scholarship business, offering free money administered through its national office along with thousands of local chapters. The National Honor Society is the kind of organization that parents point at to motivate their kids to study harder. Consequently, it's the kind of organization that some students avoid — and don't feel smart enough to get involved with during the nomination process. Guess what? Many students who would otherwise qualify for an NHS award don't bother to apply because they think that their grades are too low.

The thing is, the NHS has a whole host of scholarships and awards, even though most students only think about the obvious one: the National Honor Society Scholarship. Although you certainly can't sit in front of the TV set all year and expect to get anything from this organization, you don't need a perfect GPA to get some cash, either!

Miss America Pageant

As you probably already know, this award is almost exclusively for *female* students. Call it sexist or exploitative if you wish, but the Miss America Organization makes more than $40 million in scholarship funds available every year, making it one of the largest nongovernmental sources for free money for college. If you're interested in pageant life, check out the options.

Before you head down this path, however, recognize that competing in pageants takes a particular type of person. Competition can be both daunting and intimidating, and competitions of this sort require a *significant* time and emotional commitment. In other words, you can't enter the Miss America Pageant half-heartedly and expect to take anything away — either in terms of scholarship money or a worthwhile experience.

Perhaps surprisingly, you don't have to be crowned Miss America to be eligible for most of the financial awards. In fact, you don't even have to *compete* in the final round. On the other hand, as you go higher in the pageant system, more and more money becomes available to you. More than 12,000 young women who compete at the state and local levels are eligible for awards offered through the national organization as well as those offered through the state and local organizations. Each state and area has different awards available, so check out your particular options.

Even those young people who don't compete directly in the pageant can win scholarships with the Miss America Pageant! Money is available for those on the *hostess committee* and for those who are part of a high school marching band that participates in the Miss America Parade — and yes, these recipients can be either female or male. Usage of the funds is fairly open, as long as the money goes toward your college education. You can even apply your awards to student loans accumulated in previous years of college.

You can find the scholarships available through the Miss America organization at www.missamerica.org/scholarships/, or you can call the Miss America Scholarship Department at 1-609-345-7571, extension 27. To scope out your local state competition, go to the state area on the main site at www.missamerica.org/competition/stateinfo.asp. Then click on your state.

Daughters of the American Revolution

"No, this won't work," you're thinking. You're not a descendant of anyone who fought in the American Revolution. Perhaps you're a first- or second-generation American. How can an award that hearkens back to the days of George Washington possibly be available to you?

Well, it is. Eligibility for most Daughters of the American Revolution (DAR) scholarships is dependant only on American citizenship. You don't even have to be a *daughter* — sons are eligible, too. In fact, race, religion, gender, and national origin are irrelevant for these awards.

To apply, you must obtain a letter of sponsorship from your local DAR chapter. You must also send the appropriate application and supporting materials, including a financial need assessment. Winners are chosen based on academic merit, financial need, and commitment to a field of study. These fields of study range from American history to pre-med.

Other, less general, scholarships are also available through DAR. Some are for children of DAR members, while others are only for those who attend a particular college. Regardless of your status, perusing the Educational Outreach section of the Daughters of the American Revolution Web site (www.dar.org/natsociety/edout_scholar.html) is definitely worth your time.

Gates Millennium Scholars Program

Not only does Bill Gates make tons of money selling computer software every year, he and his wife, Melinda, also give tons of it away every year. Although Mr. Gates himself dropped out of Harvard, the multibillionaire has a strong commitment to education and health, and he lets his money do the talking.

The *Gates Millennium Scholars* (GMS) program is a newcomer to the philanthropic world of college free money, so many students haven't heard of it yet. Established in 1999, the program has already given out more than 6,000 awards, and it currently gives out 1,000 awards a year.

The GMS program aims to provide outstanding African-American, American Indian/Alaska Native, Asian- or Pacific Islander-American, and Hispanic-American students with an opportunity to complete an undergraduate college education in all discipline areas. Eligible students must be entering full-time accredited college or university study, have a minimum 3.3 GPA, have demonstrated their leadership skills in the school or community, and have significant financial need. The fund also supports graduate education for existing GMS students in select disciplines.

The United Negro College Fund (UNCF) administers the GMS program, and it works with other organizations such as the Hispanic Scholarship Fund, the Organization of Chinese Americans, and the American Indian Graduate Center (we discuss these organizations later in this chapter). Educators selected by the individual organizations weed through the applications and rank individuals based on their academic achievement, community service, and leadership potential.

To get more information about the Gates Millennium Scholars program, check out the organization at www.gmsp.org. If you have further questions, call 1-877-690-GMSP (1-877-690-4677) or send a letter to Gates Millennium Scholars, P.O. Box 10500, Fairfax, VA 22031-8044.

Hispanic Scholarship Fund

As you may guess by its name, the *Hispanic Scholarship Fund* (HSF) is an organization supporting college education for Hispanic-Americans. The HSF was founded in 1975 with the mission to double the rate of Hispanics earning college degrees. It has awarded more than 54,000 scholarships during its nearly 30-year history. These awards — given to students studying at more than 1,300 universities and colleges throughout the United States, Puerto Rico, and the U.S. Virgin Islands — total nearly $89 million. The annual amounts have grown from about $3 million to $25 million in the past five years.

According to the HSF, successful students are chosen on the basis of academic achievement, personal strengths, leadership, and financial need. Qualifications and applications are different for each award — you can download details from the HSF Web site. Applicants must be of Hispanic heritage, defined as having one parent full-blooded or both parents half-blooded Hispanic. If you're unsure about your eligibility, just ask.

Based in San Francisco, the HSF has branches in New York, Los Angeles, Dallas, Chicago, and other major cities — but the best place to get initial information about this organization's scholarships is its Web site (www.hsf.net). You can reach the head office of the HSF by telephone at 1-877-HSF-INFO (1-877-473-4636). You can also get information by mail by sending a letter to 55 Second Street, Suite 1500, San Francisco, CA 94105.

National Association for the Advancement of Colored People

Generally referred to simply as the NAACP, this well-known organization promotes equality in education through lobbying, activism, and court cases. Many Americans, however, don't know that the NAACP also offers scholarships to more than 100 deserving students every year. Some scholarships are renewable and most are at least partially need-based.

Perhaps surprisingly, race isn't a factor for eligibility. Membership in the NAACP is highly desirable (and is looked on very favorably by the scholarship committee); however, ethnicity is irrelevant. One of the NAACP's stated goals is to "remove all barriers of racial discrimination through democratic process," and it follows through on this lofty goal.

The United Negro College Fund helps the NAACP administer the scholarships. Together they comb through more than 15,000 requests for information annually. The applications are sent directly to the UNCF office in Fairfax, Virginia, but the ball gets rolling through the NAACP.

Check out www.naacp.org/work/education/eduscholarship.shtml and then send a letter requesting a scholarship package to NAACP Education Department Scholarships, 4805 Mount Hope Drive, Baltimore, MD 21215.

National Urban League

Devoted to "empowering African-Americans to enter the economic and social mainstream," the *National Urban League* (NUL) offers scholarships to almost 300 students annually. Most of these scholarships are renewed in subsequent years, so students aren't left out in the cold after their freshman year. And, similar to the NAACP, not all scholarships awarded by the NUL require the applicant to be African-American.

All the rules, qualifications, and regulations are contained in the *NUL Scholarship Guidebook* available from many guidance offices and downloadable from www.nul.org/caaa/scholarship/school_guidebook.html. Individual scholarships are listed on a different page on the National Urban League's Web site at www.nul.org/caaa/scholarship/index.html.

Organization of Chinese Americans

The *Organization of Chinese Americans* (OCA) is another little-known resource for free money. Founded in 1973, the OCA is a national nonprofit, nonpartisan advocacy organization dedicated to promoting the rights of Chinese American and Asian American citizens and permanent residents throughout the United States. The organization also runs a highly regarded internship program (www.ocanatl.org/programs/jobs4.html) in which college students are placed as interns for Congress, federal agencies, and at the OCA national headquarters.

For more information about the OCA, check out its Web site at www.ocanatl. org or send an inquiry letter to Organization of Chinese Americans, Gates Millennium Scholars, 1001 Connecticut Avenue, NW, Suite 601, Washington DC, 20036. If you have any questions about its programs, you can e-mail the OCA at oca@ocanatl.org. You can also reach the folks there by telephoning them at 1-866-274-4677 (toll free) or 202-530-8894.

American Indian Graduate Center

Native American students should check out the *American Indian Graduate Center* (AIGC). Established in 1969, this private nonprofit charitable organization was formed to help American Indian college graduates continue their education at the master's, doctorate, and professional degree levels.

You can download the necessary application from the organization's Web site at www.aigc.com, but you can also reach the AIGC by mail (4520 Montgomery Blvd. NE, Suite 1B, Albuquerque, NM 87109) or by telephone (toll free at 1-800-628-1920 or long distance at 505-881-4584).

Chapter 23

Ten College Payment Plans That Just Don't Work

In This Chapter

▶ Avoiding the big mistakes

▶ Understanding life's harsh realities

▶ Doing it right means not doing it wrong

*I*f you're thinking up ways to pay for college and any of the following ideas occurs to you, you'd better rethink your options and read this book carefully (read it again if you've already made your way through once). We know, they sound pretty good off the top of your head, but each plan has a lot of problems attached to it. Breeze through, accept that these methods won't work for you, and get back to writing those scholarship applications.

Assuming Your Parents Will Take Care of College for You

Do you think so, Miss Rockefeller? Sure, why not just go to the bank and withdraw a couple hundred thousand dollars from your immense trust fund. Well, unless Rockefeller really is your name, think again.

Most parents would love to be able to send their kids to the top schools and not have to worry about how much it costs. In reality, though, college expenses keep parents up nights wondering how they can possibly help out their kids.

Think about it from their perspective. *If* your parents went to college, the experience was very different in their day. College tuition has increased much more than the basic cost of living, making it a far more expensive proposition to go to college today than, say, back in the 1960s or 1970s. Meanwhile, a college education has become far more common (and many would argue, *more necessary*), with a higher percentage of the population going on to higher education after high school.

Over the years, while tuition has increased steadily, an extensive range of grant, scholarship, and loan programs have developed. Most of these programs weren't available when your parents were your age, and almost all that were around have changed the way that they're administered. So don't expect your parents to know what options are available to you. It's up to you to search them out.

Also admit the possibility that, when the time comes for you to go to college, one of three things might have happened:

- ✔ Your parents may have had a financial setback. All those families that invested in Enron and WorldCom suddenly lost their nest eggs. Your family may be in a similar (empty) nest.

- ✔ Even if your parents started saving money for your education when you were a baby, chances are good that they won't have saved enough. First, you may not be their only child, so the savings have to be split among your other siblings. Besides that, how were your parents supposed to know how much to put away eighteen years ago? Back then, about $5,000 might have covered all four years of college. Now, it might cover one *semester.* Your parents couldn't possibly have known that the cost of college would increase so dramatically, so they're probably unprepared for the full sticker price for the college of your choice.

- ✔ You may have a falling out with your family. It happens. Then, suddenly, you're on your own with no savings and only yourself to turn to for support.

Even if your parents are able to scrape together the money for your tuition, they'll probably have to sacrifice a lot to do so. They may have to take another mortgage on the house, work an extra job or a bunch of overtime, or simply do without the pleasures that make *their* lives comfortable and special. You're probably starting to feel guilty just from those two sentences. Think about what that guilt feels like stretched over three or four years of college and, possibly, for the rest of your life.

Planning to Take Out Student Loans and Then Declare Bankruptcy after You Graduate

Guess what? You're not the only student to think of doing this. Let us break it to you now — this plan is not an option!

First, there's the moral thing. We're sure that you've heard the arguments before: Everybody should pull his own weight. The money will have to be paid back somehow, so, in the end, others will have to pay your share. Your actions will just make it that much harder on others trying to get loans. Yadda, yadda, yadda.

The fact is, however, if you even thought of this as an option, you probably don't care too much about morality. Or maybe you think that banks or the government can afford it; you deserve an education and you'll be a productive member of society afterward, so what's the real harm? However you want to rationalize it, it's still obviously immoral.

Allow us to move on to more practical reasons why the loans-to-bankruptcy theory doesn't work:

- ✔ If you get a government-sponsored loan, bankruptcy rarely discharges your bad debt. The government will still get its money from your tax refunds (and maybe even your *paychecks* once you start working). And don't forget the interest! Until you repay, your debts will still be accruing interest — lots of it!

- ✔ Many loans require a guarantor, such as your parents, who guarantee to pay back the loan against their own collateral. This is the case for Federal PLUS Loans and for pretty much any loans you obtain from a source other than the government. If you declare bankruptcy, your guarantors become liable for the debt. The financial institution may just call in the loan once you've declared bankruptcy, reasonably fearing the loss of its original capital. If they do so, your guarantors stand to lose whatever collateral they pledged, such as the family house!

- ✔ A solid credit record is important, so starting off your adult life in bankruptcy is not a wise career move. A bad credit history stays with you for many years, and because databases are so widespread, one little bankruptcy may *never* be properly expunged from your record. For at least five years after college, you'll have trouble getting a major credit card, and if you do get one, your interest rate will likely be higher than average. You probably won't be able to secure a loan to buy a home or a car. Many apartment rental companies require a credit check, so you may find it difficult to find a place to live. More and more companies conduct credit checks on prospective employees before hiring them, so you may find yourself unable to get your dream job after working so hard in college, even if you have all the qualifications. If you want to start your own business, you'll find it extremely difficult to obtain financing. After all, would you invest *your* money in someone who'd just bilked someone else out of several thousand dollars? Probably not.

Enough said. You get the idea. If you take out loans, plan to pay them back. And then actually pay them back.

Some people don't pay back their student loans

In some cases, financial institutions working with the government will forgive student loans. Students who go on to work as teachers, especially in low-income regions, may have part or all of their government-authorized student loans forgiven. Those who volunteer with the Peace Corps, Americorps, or Volunteers in Service to America (VISTA) may have some or all of their loans forgiven as well. In some cases, the same is true for students who go on to study law, medicine, or physical therapy and use their new skills in the community's service.

Students who have suffered particular setbacks during college or just after college may also be able to have their loans forgiven. These students can apply for forgiveness of their loans in cases where bearing the loan would cause undue hardship.

We know what you're thinking: *Any loan would cause me undue hardship!* Sorry, but something a fair bit more substantial has to happen to you to get forgiveness. Wiping out the debt is very rare and only occurs under extreme circumstances, such as permanent physical disability, death of a supporting family member, or inability to obtain gainful employment for years. We discuss forgiveness options in Chapter 6.

Depending On Getting an Athletic Scholarship

You're the star quarterback on your high school team. Your coach has told you that all the top colleges will want you. What could possibly go wrong? Plenty! Check out the following list of possibilities:

✔ You're playing the final game of your senior year and just as you make a spectacular play, a player on the other team makes a spectacular play *on you*. He tackles you, and you feel a horrible shooting pain — your knee is broken in five places, and, suddenly, you can't play football anymore. No football means no football scholarship.

✔ Although your coach may think that you're terrific, college scouts compare you with the best players from around the country — and perhaps several *from around the world!* You have to consider that you might get only a partial scholarship, or you may not even make the team.

✔ Suppose that you do make the team and get a full scholarship, but you find that playing football takes all your time. You flunk out because you have no time to study. The whole point was to get a free education. If you don't have time for your schoolwork, all you're doing is playing football, which is fine if you're good enough for the NFL, but not great if you want to become a sports physician.

Figuring You're Soooooo Smart, Colleges Will Be Begging for You

Right. Uh-huh. Okay, time for a reality check. You're accustomed to the competition within your high school. In college, you're competing with the top students from all the high schools across the country. Maybe one percent of those students will get a full academic scholarship for their entire college career. Maybe.

This reality check doesn't mean that you can't get free money. It does, however, mean that you must at least *ask* for it. You have to fill out the forms, send in your grades, and do the essays and the interviews.

You also have to realize that you're probably not going to get *all* the free money you need from your college in recognition of how well you did in 12th grade algebra. If you want to get a free ride, you have to work for it. (Okay, we know that if you're working for it, it's no longer exactly free, but as you'll learn in Economics 101, there's no free lunch, either.)

Planning to Work for a Year before College to Save Up

This plan is a noble one, but four years at a private college will cost you at least $80,000. There aren't many jobs for someone with a high school diploma that will net them that much money. That's how much you have to save *after* taxes and *after* paying for your basic living expenses.

Frankly, most people can't find a job paying $80,000 *before* taxes and expenses, even *after* they graduate from college.

Besides, the problem with working for a while before you go to college is that many people never quit that job and get their college degree. They become accustomed to the regular paycheck, and they keep putting off their master plan. It takes a great effort of will to change your life, so you have to know that you have it in you to achieve your college dreams. On the other hand, sometimes a year in the workforce convinces people why they need to study hard in college to ensure that they get the career they truly want.

Working During College to Pay Your Expenses

Just like working for a year to save for college, you probably won't make enough money to pay all your expenses. However, this option raises another concern. College is a full-time job, requiring many hours of study and work for each hour in class. If you don't have the time to devote to your studies, you won't get all you might out of your college years. Because you are paying for this education and sacrificing three or four years of your life for it, missing any part of the experience would be a shame.

There is an exception to this rule: Part-time work in a related field may enrich your studies and help you get valuable hands-on experience. For example, assisting in a lab while studying chemistry or pharmacology will help you understand the practical applications of your schoolwork. One day a week spent filing at a law firm may help you decide if you want to be a lawyer.

However, these exceptions involve taking on related work to enhance your studies, not to pay for them. Often, the related work you can get doesn't pay very well. Certainly neither of the jobs we mentioned would pay enough to cover your college expenses.

Applying for Only the Scholarships You Need to Cover Expenses

You expect to win any scholarship you apply for, so why bother with more than you need? Well, aren't you a delight! Remind us to remove you from the list of any scholarships we ever choose to endow.

Seriously, confidence in your abilities is terrific. Arrogance, on the other hand, is not so great. Even if you are the cat's pajamas (we just wanted an excuse to use that phrase — what we mean is, even if you *are* brilliant, talented, *and* exceptional), so are lots of other applicants.

Why would someone else get favored over you? Well, scholarship committees are made up of human beings, and each individual has his or her own particular preferences. Perhaps one of the members of the scholarship committee became enthralled with another applicant because she could play the tuba, had a winning smile, or loved the same book that he loved.

Then again, some scholarships may suddenly cease to exist in just the year you happen to apply for them. No, we're not suggesting that you have any causal connection to the termination of scholarships. We're just saying that, sometimes, the money dries up. Scholarship endowments may be invested in blue chip stocks to produce the annual amount to be given away. If the stock goes down, no money may be available to give away. This money loss doesn't always happen. In fact, most scholarships are regular and dependable. However, you can't depend on any *specific* scholarship to pay your way.

Always apply for more than you need. Always assume that you won't win most of the scholarships for which you apply. Then, when you do win a few, you'll be pleasantly surprised.

Trying to Apply for Every Scholarship for Which You Qualify

Phew! We applaud your enthusiasm, but you need another reality check. Literally hundreds of thousands of scholarships are available. Let's say that 100,000 scholarships are available, and you qualify for 10,000 (there are, in fact, several hundred thousand scholarships and grants available, by the way). If you spend just *one* minute on each scholarship to find out if you qualify and another ten minutes on the applications for each of the 10,000, getting through them all will take you more than a year, working eight hours a day!

The lesson? You have a limited time to send in your applications, and if you try to send in too many, the quality of each application will suffer. You don't want to make silly mistakes, and you want to ensure that you make the best possible impression on the scholarship committee. After all, a bad application is worse than no application at all. All applications are generally kept on file. If you send in a sloppy application this year, it will diminish the effect of the stunning application you send in next year.

Paying Someone Else to Do Your Work

Hundreds of questionable people are waiting on the Internet and at the other end of the telephone to sell you scholarship services. When you hear them, you may be tempted to think that they can help you secure your college scholarship money. Many, in fact, *guarantee* that they'll win big bucks for you (although how one company can guarantee the actions of an independent scholarship committee is beyond our understanding).

A twist to the scholarship "services" is the folks who write scholarship essays on your behalf. Not only do many of them do a poor job (apparently their specialty is *sales* not essay writing), passing off someone else's work as you own is fraudulent, and it's a serious offense at the college level (in fact, it's grounds for being expelled in many schools).

Plus, many colleges buy essays from the same companies and compare them to what they receive from students. Imagine getting a phone call from your college admissions office asking you to explain the striking resemblance between your essay titled, *How Losing that Championship Game Taught Me a Valuable Life Lesson,* and one the college purchased over the Internet!

Plan? What Plan?

By far, the worst thing you can do is nothing at all. If you don't make a plan to pay for college, you probably won't be able to go. It's that simple.

College is a big investment, not only in terms of money — it's also an investment of your time. You'll spend two, three, or four (or more) years of your life in college. Before you go, you have a lot to consider. What do you want to do after you graduate? What kind of a person do you want to be? Much of what you have to consider has to do with your finances. How much will your education cost? How much can you afford to be in debt after you graduate? What will debt mean to your future?

Some students just figure that they'll take out student loans for the entire amount each year and then figure out later how to pay it off. If this is your plan, think about this: The average American student graduates with over $20,000 in debt, while the average salary for first-year college graduates is about $30,000. If the crushing debt load held by most college graduates alarms you (and it should!), you need to spend some extra time before college and during college planning your options and winning free money.

This may be the first time you've seriously considered money matters. It can be frightening, confusing, or just plain exasperating. Don't worry about it. You're in the same boat as thousands of other students your age, and you're way ahead of many other people.

Starting your adult life with sound financial-planning skills will benefit you in every stage of the years to come. The overall plan is simple. For now, you have to figure out how much college will cost you and then try to get the money you need. The execution (in other words, how you get this money) is only slightly trickier.

Chapter 24

Ten Things Colleges Don't Tell You

*W*ithout a doubt, college life is great. Many people will tell you that the best times of their lives were spent at college. And while you probably shouldn't expect your college years to resemble the plot line from National Lampoon's *Animal House,* you'll probably have a great time learning and living.

Now, before you think that we're painting the Ultimate Fairy Tale of College Life, realize that students learn several things about college life along the way. By the second or third year of college, most students already know these things, but — and it's a big *but* — the vast majority of high school students headed for college (and even freshman college students) do not.

Colleges Are Businesses

Colleges are increasingly pressured to make a profit while delivering their educational product. What does this fact mean to you, the student looking for a good deal and some free money for college? Rather than looking at every college-related situation from a purely educational point of view, put on your business hat and think about your college experiences from a financial angle.

Also keep in mind that colleges are there to help you — but you have to help yourself as well. Rather than waiting for colleges to offer you free money, ask them for it. Rather than taking the first financial aid offer a college sends you, think of it as the *start* of negotiations.

First-Year Discounts May Disappear

It's one of the dirty little secrets of college financing. Colleges pull you in with a great first-year incentive that can almost completely pay for your freshman year, but then you're left high and dry for the remaining three years. The college officials don't lie to you, but they don't emphasize that you may have to pay the full sticker price next year when the freshman-only award is no longer offered to you.

So what can you do? Remember that colleges are businesses. Unless they make a profit, they will go *out* of business. If you know about these tuition practices beforehand, you can (hopefully) take steps to avoid or at least mitigate them.

It's important to compare the *complete* financial aid package from each college. You may find that a small college that couldn't match a big city school's entrance awards does better over the four-year stretch. Until you look at *all four years* of tuition, however, you'll never know which college on your wish list is the best financial deal.

Remember to investigate whether your scholarships are *renewable,* and under what terms. Be honest with yourself. If you just squeaked into first year with an 80 percent average, how realistic is it to maintain this average considering the increased scholastic workload and all the other collegial distractions that can haunt students trying to learn and get high marks?

Tuition Fees Will Rise

The fact that tuition fees are rising is no secret. Over the past ten years, some schools have actually doubled their tuition fees. A few schools have raised tuition fees even more!

So what can you do? Besides the obvious priorities (such as working hard to get good marks and competing for all the relevant scholarships you can), investigate college tuition funds that let you pre-purchase future courses at today's prices. Rather than socking away *money,* some of these plans let you prepurchase actual college courses.

When prices rise (as we all know they will), the college will still honor the "old" price for the course. This way, you can *guarantee* that you can afford a college experience without having to worry about how much money the courses will cost after you get to college. We talk about the different kinds of state-based prepaid tuition plans in Chapter 10.

If you know that prices will rise over the long term, you'll also realize the importance of putting away money *now* for college. If you don't already have a Coverdell Education Savings Account, investigate how to set up at least one immediately (we talk about these savings plans in Chapter 8).

Scholarship Funding May Fall

Recent stock market losses have been catastrophic for many families, and the situation has also devastated many corporations (and colleges) that invested in these same now-defunct companies. In turn, the profits that were generated in the heyday of the so-called "Internet craze" have evaporated; so have many of the scholarships based upon the high prices that have now fallen so drastically. Predictably, students have been caught in the middle.

So what can you do? You probably can't do anything about the stock market, especially in the short term. What you can do, however, is make yourself more attractive to sponsoring organizations and concentrate on the organizations still offering the free money.

Rather than relying on last year's scholarship directory, use the new book. If you can't afford the often-hefty prices of these giant guides, check out your library to see if it has an up-to-date copy. Perhaps you can split the costs with a friend, spreading meager resources more efficiently.

Some Loan Interest Charges Start Accumulating Immediately

In Chapter 6, we discuss unsubsidized federal loans. If you haven't read that chapter or want to refresh your memory, go ahead. We'll wait on you. Ready?

The clock starts running on some federal loans and most private loans as soon as they're disbursed. Depending on your situation, your student loans may start accruing interest *immediately.*

So what can you do? You always have the option to accept or decline an unsubsidized Stafford Loan. Likewise, your parents can always decline a PLUS Loan offer, provided they can scratch together the necessary money from other sources. PLUS Loans are very similar to traditional bank loans where there's no grace period and very little chance of payment deferral or loan discharge.

Savvy students know, therefore, to watch out for colleges that expect you to ante up a sizable portion of your financial aid package with interest-bearing loans with little or no grace periods between disbursement and accrued interest. Remember to compare all the financial ramifications of each financial aid package offered by colleges.

You Have to Reapply for Scholarships Every Year

After all the aid forms are in and you've got your loans, grants, and scholarships, you can pretty much relax, right? Wrong. Every year, thousands of students fail to apply (or fail to apply *in time*) to renew their college-based grants and scholarships.

So what can you do? Keep a system to remind you when you have to reapply for all your financial aid. Enter the dates in as soon as you get an award, and make sure that the calendar lasts throughout your entire college career.

As well, never ignore anything from the Department of Education. Never. Knowing that audits are occasionally sent out may help you and your family keep an eye open for these types of letters. The Department of Education is simply trying to protect you (and the rest of America) from various frauds out there.

Read and act upon everything you receive from the colleges and the government. When in doubt, ask the appropriate agency. Your best bet is to be sure that you know what each form means, and if a reply is necessary, make sure that you get the form back before the deadline.

Missing Financial Aid Deadlines Can Be Expensive

All financial aid takes time to process. If you don't get your financial aid applications in early enough, you may not get your financing in time to pay for tuition, residence, and other fees. Instead, you may need bridge financing from your college (if available) or from your bank (likely very expensive) to start or continue at your school.

Bridge financing is typically used for short periods of time, usually to support you or *bridge you over* before a large sum of money comes in. The problem is that bridge financing is usually very expensive to compensate the lending institution for the short time of the loan.

So what can you do? Record and take action on all financial aid deadlines. Use your big wall calendar dedicated for this purpose and track important deadlines. Spend a few minutes every week or two to make sure that you're keeping up on all the deadlines. Don't pay the banks more money than absolutely necessary for your college education.

Some Scholarship Money Is Taxable

Get yourself a copy of *IRS Publication 520 - Scholarships and Fellowships*. This publication explains how you should organize your scholarship payments to minimize your tax exposure.

You can get a copy of *IRS Publication 520* by visiting www.irs.gov.

Savvy students use any scholarship money they receive to reduce the tax-free expenses (such as tuition, fees, and required equipment) before they apply their scholarship to taxable items, such as room and board.

If scholarship money is directly sent to your college, tell your college financial aid officer to apply all scholarship money toward tuition and tax-free expenses first. Only after all tax-free expenses are paid should any scholarship money be applied to taxable expenses. To be really sure, get written confirmation of how the college has used your scholarship money (and keep a written copy of your instructions) to file with your taxes.

If Your Sibling Leaves College, Your Aid Will Likely Drop

Your aid may be *removed* or *decreased* if an older sibling graduates or if a dependent grandparent dies. This is because the federal methodology underlying the calculation of your *expected family contribution* (EFC) takes note of how many people your parents are supporting. The more people supported by your parents, the more needy you appear. The fewer people your parents are supporting through college, the less needy you appear.

So what can you do? Understanding this situation is the first step. Knowing that you may have to lean on other sources of financial aid is the next. If your family's financial situation is about to change, be prepared. Speak with your financial aid office *before* you get the letter explaining that you have a larger aid gap than expected.

It Costs to Transfer Between Colleges

A common requirement for transferring students is that they must submit their transcripts as well as course descriptions to their new college. Although there is, sometimes, a small administrative fee for this service, it's usually charged only on a cost-recovery basis (meaning that students pay the college pretty much what it costs the school to generate the forms).

There is, however, another hidden charge of transferring, one that few colleges go out of their way to explain. Many schools disallow some credits from other schools, claiming that "no equivalent course" exists at the new school. The result is that the student has to take another course to make up for the disqualified course(s) on his or her own time and money.

A twist to this questionable practice occurs when the new school counts the old course as a "pass" rather than the original numerical mark. This change means that the student's cumulative GPA can suffer at the new school because really good marks aren't counted in the average. In-school scholarships at the new college may also suffer due to these lower marks, so the new school won't have to fork over any free additional money!

So what can you do? Savvy students do all the possible research on their college choices *long* before admission deadlines loom. Talk to existing students of all the colleges on your wish list, attend classes (when possible) in the subjects you plan to take, speak to your high school counselors about any transfer problems they've heard about, and perhaps even compare the course catalogs of the colleges (your first choice and the backup) to see which courses are exchangeable with each other.

Some schools publish lists of which courses they accept from other schools. If the colleges on your list are this helpful, check it out and consider taking courses from the "compatible" list. If you subsequently transfer to the backup college, you have a fair chance of making the switch painlessly.

Appendix

Glossary

• •

*B*ecause the world of student financial aid is filled with strange expressions and new terms, we assembled this handy glossary to help you decipher key phrases. Besides defining the term, we also include a chapter reference for certain key terms.

529 Plans: The technical name for IRS-recognized college savings plans under Internal Revenue Code Section 529 (26 U.S.C. 529).

acceptance form: The form accompanying an award letter. It must be signed and returned by the student to indicate acceptance, decline, or appeal of the award. Some types of acceptance forms are legally binding, meaning that after you sign the form, you must attend the particular college. Always read the fine print of any acceptance form, and if you have any questions, be sure to ask.

accrued interest: Interest that accumulates on the unpaid principal balance of a loan. Some loans have their interest *subsidized,* meaning that interest does not accrue for a certain period of time. Subsidized Stafford Loans are one example that we discuss in Chapter 6.

Advanced Placement Test (AP Test): Any of 23 tests offered by the Educational Testing Service (ETS) used to earn early credit for college courses studied while still in high school. Obtaining sufficient credits with sufficiently high marks allows a student to enter college as a sophomore. Depending on your situation, this can save a lot of money.

aid package: All the combined financial aid offered to a particular student by a particular college. Types of financial aid may include need-based grants, merit-based scholarships, loans, and work-study programs.

American College Test (ACT): Along with the SATs, the ACT is a major aptitude test required by some colleges as a criterion for admission. Also used to determine merit by scholarship committees. Most colleges require students to take the ACT or the SAT I for admission, so you must ask the school which test is applicable to your situation.

award: A generic term used to describe any financial aid offered to a student, usually in monetary form. College-based awards are typically given as tuition discounts, not actual cash.

award letter: The letter informing students that they're being offered financial aid awards, indicating the amount and any applicable stipulations. These stipulations might include exceeding a specified GPA or set mark in a standardized test or exam.

bachelor's degree: A degree granted for successful completion of undergraduate studies. Generally, this requires a four-year commitment, but a bachelor's degree can be awarded for three years of study. A bachelor's degree can be in any of a number of disciplines, but the most familiar are the BA (which stands for Bachelor of Arts) and the BS (contrary to what others may say, BS stands for Bachelor of Science).

base year: The calendar year that is used to determine how much financial aid you may be eligible to receive. Generally, this is the year *prior* to the next academic year when you hope to receive the reward. For the 2004/2005 academic year, for example, the base year is 2003. If your true financial situation is not reflected in your base year materials (for example, if your parents' previous tax return shows a large income but a parent has lost his or her job) make sure that you present supplementary information when applying for financial aid.

bursar: The college financial aid officer who is responsible for the collection and administration of all college tuition and other student fees.

cancellation: In the context of college financial aid, cancellation refers to canceling a loan, meaning that the borrower doesn't have to repay it. This happens under a few specific programs in which the borrower agrees to work under specific circumstances for a set period of time — for example, a teacher or nurse who works in a specified district. We discuss loan cancellations (and the circumstances under which cancellations are made) in Chapter 6.

citizen/eligible non-citizen: These two terms are used to describe people who can receive federal student aid. To be eligible for federal student aid, you must be a U.S. citizen, a U.S. national (and this includes natives of American Samoa or Swain's Island), or a U.S. permanent resident who possesses an I-151, I-551, or I-551C (an Alien Registration Receipt Card).

college: A post-secondary educational institution, which may grant two-year diplomas or four-year degrees. Some of the more prestigious colleges call themselves "universities," and many two-year colleges call themselves "community colleges."

College Board: A national nonprofit association comprised of more than 4,200 schools, colleges, universities, and other educational organizations. The organization provides excellent books and other resource materials for students heading to post-secondary institutions. The organization's Web site is www.collegeboard.com.

College Scholarship Service (CSS): Part of the College Board's College and University Enrollment Service (CUES), this service assists in the administration and distribution of financial aid for colleges and universities, as well as state programs and private scholarship organizations. CSS also administers the Financial Aid PROFILE.

consolidation loans: Consolidation loans help students (and parents) streamline college loans by combining several types of loans — sometimes even if they have different repayment schedules — into one, easy-to-understand, and (hopefully) easy-to-repay loan. We discuss loan consolidations in Chapter 6.

Consortium on Financing Higher Education (COFHE): An organization formed in the early 1970s by certain colleges to study the financing of selective private colleges. Today 31 private member colleges (including all Ivy League institutions) study and develop policies on funding of institutions and students.

contact period: College athletic recruiting terminology for the regulated time when coaches and other authorized members of a particular college's athletic department are permitted to contact you in person and off campus regarding your athletic scholarship. We discuss sports scholarships in Chapter 14.

cost of attendance (COA): The total cost for a year of college education, including tuition and college fees, room and board, books and materials, and all other necessary expenses. The total cost of attendance minus a student's expected family contribution equals that student's financial aid need.

Coverdell ESA (short for "Education Savings Account"): A trust or custodial account created solely for the purpose of paying the qualified education expenses of the designated beneficiary of the account. Coverdell ESAs were previously known as Education IRAs.

dead period: College athletic recruiting terminology for the regulated time when no contact is permitted by athletic staff whatsoever. Violations by college staff are punishable by the applicable athletic regulatory body and can be quite severe. We discuss athletic scholarships in Chapter 14.

default: A loan default is any situation where you fail to make your loan repayments on time. You can avoid default by submitting a request for a deferment (or full cancellation) by providing the required documentation *before* your next loan payment is due. Consequences of loan default are severe (including disastrous credit), so default should be avoided at all costs. We discuss loan defaults in Chapter 6.

departmental scholarship: An award by a specific department within a specific college for a student majoring in that department's field of study. Typically, the department itself determines who receives such scholarships, but the financial aid office of the college may handle some administration of the award.

dependent student: A student who is financially dependent on one or both parents or guardians, is not married, is under 24 years of age, has no legal dependents, is not an orphan or ward of the court, and is not a veteran of the U.S. Armed Forces. The parents or guardians of *dependent* students must provide their financial information to calculate expected family contribution — and the resulting calculation results in the student's eligibility for financial aid. The parents of *independent* students do not have to supply any financial information.

diploma: Awarded for successful completion of undergraduate studies at a two-year institution (usually called "community colleges"). In contrast, four-year colleges award *degrees*.

Direct Loan: A student loan issued under the William D. Ford Federal Direct Student Loan Program, including Direct Consolidation Loans, Direct PLUS Loans, Direct Stafford Loans, and Direct Unsubsidized Stafford Loans. We discuss various direct loans in Chapter 6.

Direct PLUS Loan: See *PLUS Loans.*

EAP: An education assistance program, this is generally set up by large organizations for employees and their dependants. EAPs are very useful for employees heading back to college to upgrade their skills or improve their qualifications. We discuss EAPs in Chapter 17.

early admission: As you might guess, this is an offer of college admission that is sent out earlier than most offer letters. Although many students seek out early admission (and thus know exactly where they're going to study the following year), early admission offers generally must be accepted (or rejected) before students receive notice of their financial aid packages. This can lead to unfortunate situations in which the student is legally obligated to attend an early-admission college, but the college doesn't pony up enough financial aid to allow the student to do so. The college knows that the student has little choice but to accept the low offer (or take a year off school), so it doesn't bother putting together a competitive aid package.

Education IRA: This (now-outdated) term describes tax-deferred savings and investment accounts for educational expenses. See Chapter 7 for more details.

Educational Testing Service (ETS): A company that develops and administers aptitude and achievement tests, such as the Scholastic Aptitude Tests (SATs).

eligibility: The determining factor in whether or not you meet the base criteria to apply for something, such as a scholarship or grant. Certain awards are targeted at minorities, mature students, individuals pursuing a particular field of study, and a host of other criteria. Those students who don't meet these criteria aren't eligible for the award.

entrance awards or scholarships: Also known as nonrecurring awards, these grants are given *only* to freshman students. These are generally offered to particular students as an inducement by colleges that want to entice better students without having to help support their studies for the full four years. The danger for students is assuming that these entrance awards will continue for subsequent years: In all but a few rare cases, entrance scholarships are for the first year only.

evaluation period: College athletic recruiting terminology for the regulated time when athletic staff can watch you participate in off-campus activities such as games, meets, or training camps. The evaluation period gives scouts and coaches time to evaluate your athletic talent and determine whether you're likely to be eligible to play for their team (and therefore qualify for athletic scholarships). During this evaluation period, however, college personnel can't contact you directly to negotiate. We discuss athletic scholarships in Chapter 14.

expected family contribution (EFC): The amount you and your family are expected to pay for your college fees and other expenses based on your need assessment. The government looks at what your family already has saved or can draw from (your family's assets) and what it earns (your family's income), taking into account your college's cost of attendance (COA).

FAFSA: The *Free Application for Federal Student Aid* — the government form key to obtaining financial student aid. There is no fee to submit this form, and it's widely available online, at high schools, and at colleges. Not only is the FAFSA a requirement for all federal aid, but it's also mandatory for most state and college aid programs. The information you provide on the FAFSA is used to calculate your expected family contribution. We discuss this form in Chapter 5.

Federal Family Education Loan (FFEL) Program: A variety of different loan programs that are insured by the federal government, although they are funded privately. These include Federal Consolidation Loans, Federal PLUS Loans, and Federal Stafford Loans. We discuss these loans in Chapter 6.

federal methodology: The methodology used by the federal government programs to determine your eligibility for financial aid and your expected family contribution.

Federal Pell Grants: Pell Grants are awarded to undergraduate students only and are based on a number of factors, including your expected family contribution (EFC), your cost of attendance (COA), whether you're a full- or part-time student, and whether you attend school for the full academic year. We discuss Pell Grants in Chapter 5.

Federal Perkins Loans: Another campus-based program, Federal Perkins Loans are low-interest loans that are available to both undergraduate and graduate students. Undergraduates can borrow up to $4,000 for each year of undergraduate study, while graduate students can borrow up to $6,000 per year. We discuss Federal Perkins Loans in Chapter 6.

Federal Supplemental Educational Opportunity Grant: See *FSEOG.*

Federal Work-Study Program: A program sponsored by the federal government and administered by colleges, designed to offer jobs to students with financial need as part of their financial aid package. Jobs pay at least minimum wage and are supposed to relate to the student's chosen field of study. We discuss Federal Work-Study in Chapter 12.

financial aid office (FAO): The college office that administers financial aid for students attending that college. The administrators in financial aid offices are generally fantastic resources for investigating all sorts of aid opportunities. Many financial aid officers are not in charge of athletic or departmental awards that the college may offer, so additional legwork is often necessary for students pursuing these other awards.

financial aid package: The aid package offered to you from any and all sources, including federal, state, and college need-based grants, scholarships for merit, work-study, and loans.

forbearance: A temporary delay in the repayment of a loan that is agreed to by the lender. Depending on the agreement, interest may be halted or may continue to accrue during forbearance.

Free Application for Federal Student Aid: See *FAFSA.*

free ride: A term used to describe a (rare) financial aid situation in which the student is given completely free education at a college for one year or more. Free rides are sometimes given to outstanding athletes or high-profile scholars and include tuition, room, board, and expense waivers.

FSEOG: If you have extreme need (for example, a particularly low expected family contribution), you may be eligible for Federal Supplemental Educational Opportunity Grant (FSEOG) money. Unlike Pell Grants, which are guaranteed to be available to all eligible students by the U.S. government, FSEOG is limited on a most-needed, first-come-first-served basis. Besides, not all colleges participate in the FSEOG program.

full grant-in-aid: The NCAA term for the maximum amount a student athlete can receive, comprising the full cost of attendance. This includes all tuition and college fees, room and board, required course-related books and supplies, transportation, and any sports-related expenses, such as uniforms, travel to games, and other regular expenses. We discuss this term in Chapter 14.

gap: The difference between your financial need and your financial aid (although it may also be the difference between your parents' expectations and your actual grade point average, or the store where you shop for all the cool clothes you'll wear to college).

GED: A General Education Development certificate is awarded after passing a GED test, usually considered the high school equivalency test.

grace period: A period of time after graduation (or cessation of full-time studies) before a student's loans become payable. We discuss grace periods in Chapter 6.

grade point average (GPA): A student's class marks as rated on a 4-point scale. GPA is one of the most important factors in determining college admissions and college scholarships.

grant: Financial aid that you do not have to repay, usually offered for financial need. The term is often used interchangeably with "scholarship."

HBCU: Historically black college or university.

Hope Scholarship Credits: Federal tax credits of up to $1,500 per year per dependent for the first two years of post-secondary education, intended to partially compensate parents (or other tuition payers, including independent students) for paying for college tuition.

independent student: A student who is financially independent of parents and guardians or meets any of the following criteria: is married, is 24 years of age or older, has legal dependents, is an orphan or ward of the court, or is a veteran of the U.S. Armed Forces. To calculate expected family contribution and the resulting eligibility for financial aid, only the financial information of the student (and possibly spouse) is required for independent students. Contrast with *dependent students*.

international student: Either an American student attending a college or university abroad or a non-American student attending a college or university in the United States. International students generally have fewer financial aid options from their new host countries but may still have some sources of financial aid available from their home country. We discuss options for international students in Chapter 15.

Lifetime Learning Credit Program: A tax credit program offered by Congress and administered by the IRS. Lifetime Learning Credits are designed for college students in their junior or senior years, as well as graduate students working on their advanced degrees. A taxpayer may claim a maximum tax credit of $1,000 per year. We discuss Lifetime Learning Credits in Chapters 7 and 8.

loan: Money that you receive under an obligation to repay the principal amount, (usually) with accrued interest. Repayment of student loans may be subsidized, in which case interest does not accrue and the principal and interest payments are not payable until after a particular date or occurrence, usually after a student has graduated or ceased enrollment in school.

MAGI: Modified adjusted gross income, a tax-related term. This amount is used to determine how much of a federal benefit (such as a Hope Scholarship Credit) you can receive. We discuss this term in Chapters 7 and 8.

merit-based funding: Financial aid provided based solely on merit, irrespective of need. Merit can be determined by any combination of grades, class standing, test scores, athletic or artistic ability, community service, leadership potential, and many other factors.

MGIB: Montgomery GI Bill. An extensive program to support and pay for many benefits due members of the U.S. Armed Forces during and after their service to their country. We discuss the Montgomery GI Bill in Chapter 18.

National Association for Intercollegiate Athletics (NAIA): An organization that regulates athletic scholarship programs at its 309 member colleges. Contrast with the *National Collegiate Athletic Association*. We discuss athletic scholarships in Chapter 14.

National College Athletic Association (NCAA): The best-known regulating organization for college athletic programs. Contrast with the *National Association for Intercollegiate Athletics*. We discuss athletic scholarships in Chapter 14.

National Letter of Intent (NLI): An offer letter from a participating NCAA college sent as part of athletic recruiting. If you sign and return the NLI, the document becomes a binding agreement between you and the college. In exchange for the college in question offering you financial aid for one academic year (provided you are admitted to the college academically *and* are eligible under NCAA guidelines), you agree to attend the college and participate in the athletic program. We discuss athletic scholarships in Chapter 14.

National Merit Scholarship Corporation: The not-for-profit organization that administers National Merit Scholarships and National Achievement Scholarships. These prestigious awards recognize scholastic achievement and other factors. We discuss these scholarships in Chapter 21.

National Merit Scholastic Qualifying Test (NMSQT): The PSAT (more formally called the "PSAT/NMSQT") is used as a qualifier for the National Merit Scholarship Program. We discuss these in Chapter 21.

need: The difference between your college COA (cost of attendance) and your EFC (expected family contribution). Many colleges attempt to meet the full need of students though a combination of financial aid sources.

need analysis: A process of analyzing a student's (and a student's family's) assets and income to determine the student's ability to pay for college. The determination also demonstrates the student's financial need.

need-based funding: Financial aid provided based solely on need, irrespective of merit.

nonrecurring awards: See *Entrance awards or scholarships.*

Pell Grants: See *Federal Pell Grants.*

Perkins Loans: See *Federal Perkins Loans.*

phaseout limit: The maximum MAGI (modified adjusted gross income) that will qualify for certain federal aid benefits (such as the Hope Scholarship Credit). Currently, the phaseout limit for the Hope Scholarship Credit is $51,000 for single parents of dependent students (the same for independent students) and $102,000 for two-parent families (or married independent students). We discuss phaseout limits in Chapters 7 and 8.

phaseout range: The dollar amount over which some federal benefits (such as the Hope Scholarship Credit) are decreased or *phased out.* For single payers, the phaseout range for the Hope Scholarship is currently $10,000 (because *full* credit is given to a single payer whose MAGI is $41,000 or less, and *no* credit is given to a single payer whose MAGI is $51,000 or more). Married payers have double the MAGI allowance and thus have double the phaseout range: $20,000. We discuss these limits in Chapters 7 and 8.

PLUS Loans: An acronym for *Parent Loans for Undergraduate Students*, PLUS Loans are given to students' parents and come in two varieties: Direct PLUS Loans and FFEL PLUS Loans. Plus Loans let parents who have a good credit history borrow enough money to pay some education expenses of their dependent children. We discuss these loans in Chapter 6.

post-secondary education: Any education program undertaken after completing high school or obtaining a GED. Post-secondary educational institutions may be two-year or four-year colleges or universities, trade schools, or certain other institutions.

prize: Generic term used to describe money given for a particular achievement, either in terms of high marks, community service, outstanding essay, or other competitive determination.

private college: An educational institution that receives little or no funding from state or federal sources. Due to this financial independence, private colleges tend to be much more expensive than state colleges.

PROFILE: Administered by the CSS, this is a financial aid form used by many colleges in addition to the FAFSA to determine financial aid. Students pay a fee to register for PROFILE.

PSAT/NMSQT: The Preliminary Scholastic Aptitude Test/National Merit Scholastic Qualifying Test is taken as a warm-up to the SAT. It is also a qualifier for the National Merit Scholarship Program. We discuss this test in Chapter 21.

quiet period: College athletic recruiting terminology for the regulated time when college athletic staff can discuss your scholarship prospects, but only on their own campus. During the quiet period, coaches and scouts can't contact you at home or in your high school. We discuss athletic scholarships in Chapter 14.

recruitment network: The term used for an unofficial group of individuals involved in athletic recruiting, made up of professional recruiters, college coaches, scouts, sports journalists and others. We discuss recruitment for athletic scholarships in Chapter 14.

recurring awards: Scholarship or grant money that can be renewed annually. The student may be required to achieve a particular grade point average in order to retain the award. Contrast with *entrance awards or scholarships.*

Reserve Officers' Training Corps (ROTC): U.S. military programs that support officers in training while they get a college education. Each of the ROTC programs — AFROTC (the Air Force's program), AROTC (the Army's program), and the NROTC (the program for students headed into the Navy and Marines) — is somewhat different, but each offers scholarships that pay at least part (but usually all) tuition in exchange for a future service commitment to the specific branch of the U.S. Armed Forces. We discuss military options for scholarships in Chapter 18.

scholarship: Generic financial aid term for an award that students do not have to repay. Scholarships are usually based on merit. Sometimes, however, the term is used interchangeably with need-based awards, such as grants.

Scholastic Aptitude Test (SAT): Divided into the SAT I and the SAT II, these tests are used to measure a student's potential to do college work overall (SAT I) or in particular subjects (various SAT II tests). We discuss the SATs in Chapter 21.

Selective Service Registration: By law, all male Americans who are at least 18 years of age must register with the Selective Service, a federal organization responsible for calling up conscripts in the event of a war or other national emergency. If you are in this category, you must register with Selective Service to receive any federal-based student financial aid. You can register at your local Selective Service office, by checking a box on the FAFSA or online at www.sss.gov.

state college: Colleges that receive extensive funding from the state (through state income taxes). State colleges tend to be much less expensive than private colleges for in-state residents. Out-of-state students are charged more than state residents because they don't contribute to the funding through their taxes — but state colleges are still a bargain relative to private schools.

Student Aid Report (SAR): A few weeks after you complete and submit your FAFSA (either the online or using the paper version), you'll receive a form called the Student Aid Report. This document also gives you a chance to correct, change, or fine-tune the answers you provided in your FAFSA. The SAR also notes your EFC. We discuss the Student Aid Report in Chapter 5.

Stafford Loans: Stafford Loans are a major source of financial aid for students attending college. Stafford Loans must be repaid, although sometimes repayment can be postponed, or in certain cases, the entire loan can be completely discharged or canceled. Stafford Loans can be either subsidized or unsubsidized. If you have a subsidized loan, you will *not* be charged interest while you're still going to school and for a small period afterward (typically called the *grace period*). If you have an unsubsidized loan, you will be charged interest from the time the loan is dispersed (that is, when you cash the check or the money is credited to your college account) until you repay the loan in full. We discuss Stafford Loans in Chapter 6.

subsidized loan: A loan that does not accrue interest until after a particular date or occurrence, usually after a student has graduated or left school. By contrast, an *unsubsidized loan* accrues interest as soon as it is assumed — and this interest must be paid during the entire life of the loan.

Survivors' and Dependents' Educational Assistance Program: This program offers up to 45 months of education benefits for survivors and dependents of military personnel who are permanently and totally disabled due to a military service-related condition, or who died while on active duty or as a result of a service-related condition. We discuss this in Chapter 18.

Test of English as a Foreign Language (TOEFL): This test must be taken by foreign students applying to an American college for whom English is not their first language. We discuss this test in Chapter 15.

tuition: The cost of taking courses at college. Savvy students know that tuition fees represent only a portion of the overall cost of attendance (COA) at a given school.

tuition discount: A reduction in tuition offered to a particular student. This discount may be offered because of simple eligibility (for example, you're the child of a college professor) or because the college wants to entice you to attend. Sometimes, entrance scholarships are called first-year tuition discounts.

tuition waiver: A complete reduction in tuition, meaning no tuition is payable by the student. Other costs, such as hefty residence fees, meals and transportation, may still be levied. Contrast with *free ride*.

undergraduate: A student working toward a bachelor's degree.

university: A post-secondary educational institution that grants four-year degrees. Often used interchangeably with *college, university* usually denotes a post-secondary school that also grants higher degrees, such as doctorates and professional degrees.

unsubsidized loan: A loan that accrues interest as soon as it is assumed — and this interest must be paid during the entire life of the loan. By contrast, *subsidized loans* do not accrue interest until after a particular date or occurrence, usually after a student has graduated or left school.

Index

• F •

• O •

• *V* •

• *W* •

• *X* • *Y* • *Z* •

FOR DUMMIES®

The easy way to get more done and have more fun

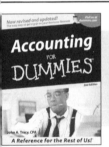

FOR DUMMIES®

A world of resources to help you grow

HOME, GARDEN & HOBBIES

0-7645-5295-3

0-7645-5130-2

0-7645-5106-X

Also available:

Auto Repair For Dummies
(0-7645-5089-6)

Chess For Dummies
(0-7645-5003-9)

Home Maintenance For Dummies
(0-7645-5215-5)

Organizing For Dummies
(0-7645-5300-3)

Piano For Dummies
(0-7645-5105-1)

Poker For Dummies
(0-7645-5232-5)

Quilting For Dummies
(0-7645-5118-3)

Rock Guitar For Dummies
(0-7645-5356-9)

Roses For Dummies
(0-7645-5202-3)

Sewing For Dummies
(0-7645-5137-X)

FOOD & WINE

0-7645-5250-3

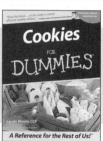

0-7645-5390-9

0-7645-5114-0

Also available:

Bartending For Dummies
(0-7645-5051-9)

Chinese Cooking For Dummies
(0-7645-5247-3)

Christmas Cooking For Dummies
(0-7645-5407-7)

Diabetes Cookbook For Dummies
(0-7645-5230-9)

Grilling For Dummies
(0-7645-5076-4)

Low-Fat Cooking For Dummies
(0-7645-5035-7)

Slow Cookers For Dummies
(0-7645-5240-6)

TRAVEL

0-7645-5453-0

0-7645-5438-7

0-7645-5448-4

Also available:

America's National Parks For Dummies
(0-7645-6204-5)

Caribbean For Dummies
(0-7645-5445-X)

Cruise Vacations For Dummies 2003
(0-7645-5459-X)

Europe For Dummies
(0-7645-5456-5)

Ireland For Dummies
(0-7645-6199-5)

France For Dummies
(0-7645-6292-4)

London For Dummies
(0-7645-5416-6)

Mexico's Beach Resorts For Dummies
(0-7645-6262-2)

Paris For Dummies
(0-7645-5494-8)

RV Vacations For Dummies
(0-7645-5443-3)

Walt Disney World & Orlando For Dummies
(0-7645-5444-1)

Available wherever books are sold. Go to www.dummies.com or call 1-877-762-2974 to order direct.

FOR DUMMIES®

Helping you expand your horizons and realize your potential

INTERNET

0-7645-0894-6

0-7645-1659-0

0-7645-1642-6

Also available:

America Online 7.0 For Dummies
(0-7645-1624-8)

Genealogy Online For Dummies
(0-7645-0807-5)

The Internet All-in-One Desk Reference For Dummies
(0-7645-1659-0)

Internet Explorer 6 For Dummies
(0-7645-1344-3)

The Internet For Dummies Quick Reference
(0-7645-1645-0)

Internet Privacy For Dummies
(0-7645-0846-6)

Researching Online For Dummies
(0-7645-0546-7)

Starting an Online Business For Dummies
(0-7645-1655-8)

DIGITAL MEDIA

0-7645-1664-7

0-7645-1675-2

0-7645-0806-7

Also available:

CD and DVD Recording For Dummies
(0-7645-1627-2)

Digital Photography All-in-One Desk Reference For Dummies
(0-7645-1800-3)

Digital Photography For Dummies Quick Reference
(0-7645-0750-8)

Home Recording for Musicians For Dummies
(0-7645-1634-5)

MP3 For Dummies
(0-7645-0858-X)

Paint Shop Pro "X" For Dummies
(0-7645-2440-2)

Photo Retouching & Restoration For Dummies
(0-7645-1662-0)

Scanners For Dummies
(0-7645-0783-4)

GRAPHICS

0-7645-0817-2

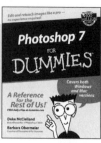

0-7645-1651-5

0-7645-0895-4

Also available:

Adobe Acrobat 5 PDF For Dummies
(0-7645-1652-3)

Fireworks 4 For Dummies
(0-7645-0804-0)

Illustrator 10 For Dummies
(0-7645-3636-2)

QuarkXPress 5 For Dummies
(0-7645-0643-9)

Visio 2000 For Dummies
(0-7645-0635-8)

Available wherever books are sold. Go to www.dummies.com or call 1-877-762-2974 to order direct.

FOR DUMMIES®

The advice and explanations you need to succeed

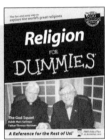
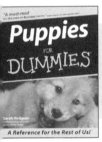